T0355797

Unforgivable

Unforgivable

AN ABUSIVE PRIEST AND THE CHURCH THAT SENT HIM ABROAD

Kevin Lewis O'Neill

UNIVERSITY OF CALIFORNIA PRESS

University of California Press
Oakland, California

© 2025 by Kevin Lewis O'Neill

Library of Congress Cataloging-in-Publication Data

Names: O'Neill, Kevin Lewis, 1977- author.
Title: Unforgivable : an abusive priest and the church that sent him
    abroad / Kevin Lewis O'Neill.
Description: Oakland, California : University of California Press, [2025] |
    Includes bibliographical references and index.
Identifiers: LCCN 2024026592 (print) | LCCN 2024026593 (ebook) |
    ISBN 9780520409118 (cloth) | ISBN 9780520409125 (ebook)
Subjects: LCSH: Roney, David, 1921–2003. | Catholic Church—Clergy—
    Sexual behavior. | Catholic Church—Moral and ethical aspects. | Sex
    offenders. | Sexual misconduct by clergy. | Child sexual abuse by clergy.
Classification: LCC BX1912.9 .O64 2025 (print) | LCC BX1912.9 (ebook) |
    DDC 282.092 [B]—dc23/eng/20240807
LC record available at https://lccn.loc.gov/2024026592
LC ebook record available at https://lccn.loc.gov/2024026593

Manufactured in the United States of America

33   32   31   30   29   28   27   26   25   24
10   9   8   7   6   5   4   3   2   1

For survivors, near and far

We are not only what we are, but what we might have been.

Ian Hacking, "Making Up People"

Contents

Preface

Minneapolis, Minnesota

March 17, 1994

Waves of businessmen ambled toward their respective gates at the Minneapolis–Saint Paul International Airport as Father David Roney waited patiently for his flight to Guatemala. He had a single suitcase at his side. It held his passport, a point-and-shoot camera, and five of everything that he was wearing: a pressed white shirt, dark pleated pants, and a pair of black socks. There were also cotton t-shirts and underwear that his mother had bleached months before her passing, as well as an extra pair of prescription glasses. He had a toothbrush but no toothpaste. He figured that he could buy a tube once he landed. He was traveling light.

A full month before his trip, once Roney had made the decision (*really* made the decision) to live out his days at a Catholic mission in the distant highlands of Guatemala, he began to shed as many of his belongings as he could.[1] His goal, however unreasonable it may have seemed at the time, was to fit his entire life into a single suitcase. No one needs three pairs of shoes, he reasoned, when one pair is enough. But then there were the books that he had lugged over the years from parish to parish, his many slides of Rome, and several boxes of memories that his mother had left for him. He placed these items with friends in Minnesota, promising to send for them at some point, but he never did. He even left behind a plaque that he had received just a day earlier, during a celebration of his fifty years of service as a diocesan priest in central Minnesota. There had been a nice meal and some nicer words, with glasses of wine raised to his priesthood. Though he commented that it was all very generous, he excused himself from the festivities a little earlier than expected, insisting that he needed to finish packing. But his suitcase was full. Nothing else would have fit.[2]

Roney's retirement to Guatemala might have provoked a twinge of nostalgia or melancholy. He was on the precipice of a momentous life transition, a self-conscious shedding of possessions and friendships. Yet he also had good reason to be excited for his future. His suitcase might not have fit his books and slides, but it also did not have room for a thick stack of psychological evaluations that he had accrued over the years: a medical archive that often fussed over how his "exhibitionism is clinically distinct from pedophilia."[3] None of that documentation would travel with him to Guatemala, and neither would his diagnosis. Roney would instead evade the archive and its effects by relocating to the Mission, which lacked not only telephone service and consistent electricity but also a diocesan Review Board for Sexual Misconduct. None of this board's confidential reports, clinical notes, and medical tests of sexual function would ever make it to Guatemala. Roney's move to the Mission would effectively set him free, and he knew it. So too did his bishop. As his plane lifted from the tarmac, the acceleration pressing his body back into his seat, Roney's future was suddenly as clear and open as the sky itself.

. . . . . .

Unforgivable tells the story of Father David Roney, a Roman Catholic priest and sexual predator, in five parts: from his prolifically abusive career in central Minnesota (part I); to his evaluation at a church-run sex therapy center in New Mexico (part II); to his semi-active retirement in the highlands of Guatemala, where he raised an Indigenous orphan as his own (part III). It also tells the story of the multimillion-dollar settlement that Roney's stateside survivors received from the Church (part IV); and the many attempts that the orphan (now a young woman) in Guatemala made to receive a settlement of her own (part V).

But this isn't a book just about Father David Roney.[4] It is a look at the Roman Catholic Church's longstanding practice of moving sexually abusive priests across international borders. The story of clerical sexual abuse has thus far been rather local. The first U.S. scandals surfaced in Louisiana and then Minnesota in the 1980s. There were others in New Orleans, Milwaukee, and Chicago in the early 1990s, and then a spate of cases in Boston in 2001. Many more followed, from Los Angeles, California, to Covington, Kentucky, to Anchorage, Alaska, with dioceses and religious orders paying nearly $4 billion in settlements to victims.[5] The coverage of these events has focused almost exclusively on how bishops across the United States transferred known perpetrators from parish to parish, often in a failed effort at shirking accountability for their clerics' crimes.[6] While this interest in interparish transfer has been important in demonstrating, to both juries and the general public, some of the Church's more pernicious maneuvers, it has sidelined a much bigger story: Church leaders routinely move sexual predators clear across the world to live, preach, and perpetrate crimes, often with total impunity.[7]

Unforgivable details the transfer of one such priest from Minnesota to Guatemala, but it could have told nearly the same story about hundreds of other sexually abusive priests. There was nothing extraordinary about David Roney, but by following his itinerary in granular detail, this book takes a first and important step not just in documenting the global movement of sexually abusive clerics, but also in rendering the conditions of clerical sexual abuse itself thinkable. It accomplishes this second task by showing how clerical sexual abuse can only exist in rather specific contexts: where there is, for example, the rule of law, a free press, psychological expertise, and a robust insurance industry. These are contexts where a diagnosis of sexual deviancy has practical consequences and where the identities of "abuser," "victim," and "survivor" mean something. The United States in the late twentieth and early twenty-first centuries was one such place, but the country of Guatemala, certainly at the time of Roney's first visit in 1973 and even at the time of his retirement in 1994, was not. It had neither the courts nor the journalists, therapists, or insurance companies necessary to sustain a framework for identifying and prosecuting clerical sexual abuse. Thus, in a very practical sense, clerical sexual abuse did not exist in Guatemala when Roney landed at the country's La Aurora

International Airport on March 17, 1994. The historical contingency of such abuse is this book's most important and least intuitive insight, but bishops have understood this point for decades, and that's why they sent Roney to Central America.

Roney's bishop also knew that no one would likely notice his arrival. Guatemala had been at war with itself for decades. In 1954, the United States' Central Intelligence Agency orchestrated a coup d'état against Guatemala's democratically elected government. The CIA's intention was to stop the spread of communism in Central America, but the results of the coup were disastrous. An increasingly militarized government, deploying scorched-earth tactics, riddled the nation with large-scale massacres, in the end murdering 200,000 civilians, disappearing 50,000 more, and displacing 1,000,000. Conveniently for Roney, the vast majority of those impacted by this genocidal violence lived in small Indigenous towns where the rule of law had all but been suspended.[8] Amid the fog of war, how could anyone question an American priest who cared so deeply for this country's orphans?[9]

In Guatemala, Roney lived not simply beyond the reach of therapists, law enforcement officials, prosecutors, and journalists but, more profoundly, beyond the conditions that make clerical sexual abuse possible.[10] A focus on the historical contingency of clerical sexual abuse, however, does not mean that the prurient touch of a priest can only affect a person once there are enough lawyers, psychologists, and journalists on the scene.[11] The experience of the orphan whom Roney raised in Guatemala is evidence enough to the contrary. "I slept in his home," she told me. "He bathed me. He had me bring my friends over to his house to play." Roney embedded himself in this young girl's life, shaping her trajectory in ways that were profound and indisputable. As this book shows, though, the process of taking such personal experiences and turning them into a set of public facts remains easier to do in the United States than in Guatemala. This is because the conceptual and administrative tools necessary to recognize clerical sexual abuse are not equally available everywhere in the world. Since at least the late twentieth century, U.S. bishops have leveraged a series of cultural disconnects between the United States and certain parts of Latin America to safeguard themselves and the Catholic Church from scandal and financial settlements. In the United States, but not in Guatemala, activists molded clerical sexual abuse into a focus for political action; in the United States, but not in Guatemala, psychologists empowered people to recognize themselves as victims of clerical sexual abuse and as survivors; and in the United States, but not in Guatemala, personal injury attorneys made clerical sexual abuse a vehicle for institutional accountability and constitutional reform. Experts made clerical sexual abuse recognizable in the United States, while an absence of expertise made the phenomenon unspeakable in Guatemala. This is why Roney so eagerly absconded to Central America with the support of his bishop. On the other side of a continent, this priest could do as he wished, while Guatemalans could do very little.

·   ·   ·   ·   ·

My research on Roney in Guatemala proved difficult—at times near impossible—and this too is why Roney's bishop sent him to Central America. In the United States, I had access to a wide range of materials that brought this reticent, arguably reclusive, priest into focus, including his school records, church sermons, and published writings. Credible accusations against Roney in 1987 also led to an avalanche of evidence: psychological evaluations, reports from his years of outpatient treatment, internal church memos, arrest records, confidential reports, survivor testimonies, insurance claims, depositions, affidavits, and then troves of even more documents that had been acquired through the legal process of discovery. I spoke with those whom Roney had abused in Minnesota, engaged archives from New Mexico to better understand the Church-run sex therapy center that first evaluated him, and spent months in Rome to try to understand the frequency with which bishops transferred priests from the United States to Latin America.[12]

Roney's archival record ends abruptly when he boards a one-way flight to Guatemala on March 17, 1994.[13] From that moment, until his death in Guatemala on January 27, 2003, the trail goes cold. There would be hardly any reports, claims, or memos about this man, and this is why I traveled to Central America. I visited the Mission and spoke to its staff, slowly extending my investigation into the broader community in search of additional lines of evidence. I met with Roney's former housekeeper and his many godchildren (*ahijados*). Roney, it turned out, was an avid photographer, and I analyzed hundreds of his photographs, studying the images for a sense of how he saw the world.[14] At the heart of my research was the orphan Roney raised, a young woman whom I call Justina.[15] We collaborated for years—on the research for this book but also in her pursuit of justice.

The narrative style of *Unforgivable* reflects a mix of methodologies, with the first four parts of the book historical in approach and the fifth part investigative. Together, they tell a largely chronological story, spanning from the spring of 1945 to the winter of 2024. The book draws on the aesthetics of biography, historical nonfiction, true crime, ethnographic inquiry, and philosophical criticism to make sense of the seven individuals who anchor this story. The first is Father David Roney (1921–2003), a lonesome parish priest whose illicit appetites drew him—with pockets full of candy—to schoolyards and playgrounds. The second is a woman from Minnesota whom I call Carol (b. 1954). Roney sexually abused her when she was just eleven years old, and as an adult, she played a key role in the civil suit that led to a major settlement by the Diocese of New Ulm. A third person is Jeff Anderson (b. 1947), the pioneering personal injury attorney from Saint Paul, Minnesota, who led that lawsuit and so many others. The fourth is Father Raymond Lucker (1927–2001), the bishop of the Diocese of New Ulm from 1976 to 2000 and the man most directly responsible for the career of David Roney. Lucker, it will become clear, was known as a kind man and a thoughtful priest, but he was a complete failure as a bishop, ultimately refusing to protect his parishioners in Minnesota and actively endangering those in Guatemala.[16] The fifth is Father Gregory Schaffer (1934–2012). Another priest from Minnesota under Lucker's charge, Schaffer directed the Mission in Guatemala for most of his career, in the end providing Roney with safe harbor in Central America. He too was a failure.[17] The sixth person is Justina (b. 1992), an Indigenous woman from rural Guatemala who suffered immeasurably at the hands of the Roman Catholic Church, and who did her best, once empowered by the expertise of a stateside lawyer, a therapist, and an anthropologist, to hold Roney's diocese in Minnesota accountable for his crimes.

I am this book's seventh character, an anthropologist from North America (b. 1977), appearing only in part 5, where the narrative perspective shifts from third to first person. There was no other way to write this story. My research in Guatemala and subsequent work with Justina transformed my role from observer to participant in ways that fundamentally altered not simply this book's narrative style but also me. I will never be the same. I first heard rumors about Roney back in 2016 while I was in Guatemala for a different research project. I thought that if these stories about an American priest and a Guatemalan orphan turned out to be true, they could change how the world thinks about clerical sexual abuse: that the phenomenon is (and always has been) as global as the Roman Catholic Church. I also thought that I might be up to the challenge. "Who else could do this research?" I remember asking myself. A cultural anthropologist with theological training, in Catholic social thought no less, I had grown up in the very kinds of Midwestern parishes that Roney had pastored; then, not unlike Roney himself, I spent decades in Guatemala. Relatively fluent in the history and culture of both milieus, with a wealth of contacts in each, I thought that I could handle the research. But I was wrong. I was unprepared for the scale of the abuse that I ended up documenting, the sophistication of the Church's maneuverings, and its callous indifference once caught red-handed. It was also heartbreaking to witness the toll that it all had on Justina, which is why I promised her, and then myself—and now you, reader—that this book is just the beginning. There is so much more work to be done to expose the global scale of clerical sexual abuse.

For the moment, though, this book begins small: in rural Minnesota with Father David Roney—at a lake, on a summer day, and with a young girl.

I   A Priest Forever, 1945–1987

Indescribably Lonesome

Willmar, Minnesota

Summer 1968

Wheat and corn and dairies and the occasional patch of woodland.

A man and a young girl were lying on a blanket, at a lake, while a rough-legged hawk circled overhead. A jumble of ferns, lindens, and birches crowded the shore. "God has a special job for you," Father David Roney told the six-year-old. "You're his chosen one."[1]

Wet swimsuits. A prairie breeze.

Sand in their shoes.

The town of Willmar was nowhere in sight. Once the center of the Great Northern Railroad and then hitched to the rise and inevitable restructuring of a poultry processing plant, this working-class town with a population of just over 12,000 was a rambling expanse of family farms held together by one daily newspaper, two stoplights, and twenty-nine churches. One of those steeples belonged to the Church of Saint Mary, a Roman Catholic congregation that did its best to serve one of the most rural dioceses in the United States. To its credit, it had done as well as any church could, running an elementary school and a mix of outreach programs, but its priest bristled at the isolation.

David Roney had grown up amid the skyscrapers of Minneapolis and Saint Paul with a wanderlust that dragged him around the world: from

Southeast Asia to Central America to the cobbled streets of Vatican City. But his bishop decided that he belonged elsewhere, assigning Roney to serve a series of country parishes that the slender and somewhat handsome priest came to experience, in his own words, as "indescribably lonesome." It was a mismatch from the get-go. "All the parishioners were farmers and I was a city boy," he would later write. "I felt betrayed and put upon at first." Maybe it was the fact that there were more cows than Catholics in central Minnesota, but Roney would come to describe these assignments as "the great tragedy" of his life. He felt adrift. "I used to sit, in good weather, on the front steps of the house just to see people."[2] He had other strategies to connect. In his spare moments, he would walk these towns, hang about their elementary schools, and drop in on parishioners for a cup of coffee. On the weekends, he took children to nearby lakes.

Parents appreciated Roney's interest in their children. With their kids in the care of their parish priest, these men and women could finally get some real work done. Often toiling day and night on their farms and sometimes holding down side jobs to make ends meet, most of these parents were short on time. Their children would often labor next to them to plant and harvest crops, feed and care for animals, maintain stalls and fences, and collect eggs and milk. Everyone woke up before dawn, and most of the kids milked cows every evening. All this hard work made the prospect of spending a morning or an afternoon at a lake nothing short of a miracle, a complete break from the ordinary.

Roney also had things to do. He managed the parish and balanced its books. He heard confessions and delivered last rites. He prepared couples for marriage, baptized newborns, led funerals, wrote sermons, and ministered to the sick while training deacons and altar boys on the intricacies of sacramental labor. He tended to all the details of parish life, from morning until night, while also spending an inordinate amount of time at the parish's school. It was a labor of love for him. "I enjoyed the elementary school," he once wrote. "In fact, I enjoyed it so much that I felt guilty, as if the only reason for keeping the school open was for the benefit of the pastor."[3] His priestly duties kept him occupied, at times even exhausted, but for all the masses and meetings, confessions and house calls, Roney always found time for the lake. He hardly ever missed a Saturday.

"Don't tell anyone," Roney whispered as he inched across the blanket. "This is our secret."[4] His hand reached toward the young girl's shoulder. Yet what happened next was not a complete secret, if only because the two of them were not entirely alone. The girl's brothers (one younger, one older) swam in the lake, a short distance away. They laughed and splashed within earshot until Roney sent them on some half-baked adventure to explore a nearby cove. They could have wandered back, and maybe they did; Roney probably wouldn't have minded if they saw. He only cared that these children kept quiet about the games that he played with them at the lake.

The people of central Minnesota tended to keep quiet. Some credit the stoic culture of the German and Irish immigrants who settled the area in the mid-nineteenth century. Others insist that the region's harsh winters foster a dogged culture of privacy, with Alberta clippers and two-story snow drifts effectively isolating families from one another. A renowned documentarian once reported from Willmar about a labor dispute. Unnerved by the townspeople's reluctance to discuss anything at all, let alone their feelings on workers' rights, he eventually got a local minister to explain the town's reticence: "People kind of feel that if they ignore things that are distasteful and out of the ordinary, they'll go away. It doesn't make any difference whether it is a teenager on drugs or equal rights for women, you ignore it. You bury it. When I say bury it, I mean bury. You don't talk."[5]

Roney leveraged this culture of silence to keep the girl from the lake quiet. "Do not make God mad," he told her. "Bad things could happen when God gets mad."[6] Roney invoked the wrath of God when he first touched her shoulder ("You're fighting what God wants"); whenever she flinched or turned away; and whenever she cried or refused to go to the lake.[7] "I don't know why she's being so shy," her parents once wondered aloud while they all stood in the kitchen. It was Saturday morning, and the young girl was hiding in her bedroom until Roney announced, just loudly enough for her to hear, that he would gladly take the two boys to the lake without her. To protect her brothers, to put her body in between this priest and her siblings, the young girl pulled on her swimsuit, climbed into Roney's car, and spent another afternoon on his blanket.[8]

Roney abused this girl for seven years. Relentless and brazen, he assaulted her at the lake but also in church vestibules, empty classrooms, crowded cafeterias, school playgrounds, church nurseries, public libraries, unoccupied bathrooms, bus stops, parking lots, parish offices, stairways, a room behind the altar, and his bedroom in the rectory. He even cut a hole in his pants pocket to take advantage of a small hand rooting around for candy or a quarter in plain sight of other parishioners.

And then there was the cape. Decades later, lawyers spent a considerable amount of time asking Father John Berger, a priest who had lived with Roney at the rectory, about his colleague's cloak. "You know, in the old days, priests would often wear those kinds of things, at least, going to the cemetery," Berger remembered. "It was common clerical garb in that era that's gone." Prosecutors then pressed Berger about whether Roney ever used the garment to abuse children in public places. "Not that I'm aware of," he answered. "I would say that we aren't huggy, touchy-feely kind of people."[9] In contrast to Berger, who was far more comfortable in a worn pair of trousers and a flannel shirt, it would eventually become clear that Roney preferred a cape not just to stay warm when he attended funerals and as he shuttled between buildings in the dead of winter, but for other, more sinister, purposes.

Roney had always been nostalgic for a bygone era of clericalism. He had been struck by the young priests he had once seen pacing the halls of the Vatican. They seemed bookish and purposeful, boyish and pious, with their close-cropped haircuts and layers of cassocks and capes that seemed to accentuate their every movement. His trips to Europe had planted in his urbane but inescapably Midwestern imagination an almost cinematic vision of the priesthood, which he tried to emulate in small towns such as Willmar by contrasting his own blond hair and blue eyes with an inky black biretta: a square cap with three peaks and a tuft on top. The hat went well with the cape, Roney thought.

People in central Minnesota were not impressed. Roney would often volunteer his time at his parish's elementary school, arriving with slide decks of his trips to the Vatican under his arm. In some effort at evangelization, by showing these children the center of the Roman Catholic Church, he would try to walk the class through the streets of Rome just as he had walked. There were images of the Colosseum, the Pantheon, and Saint Peter's Basilica. Some of them even featured Roney posing for the camera, looking quite serious in his biretta and cape. The kids, though, never seemed to care. Most stared out the window rather than at the screen. They seemed bored, and likely were. Most of them spent their mornings milking cows and clearing barns of manure; almost none had expectations of international travel. These sepia-tinted images made Rome appear as distant to these kids as the moon. All this left Roney feeling rather alone, talking to himself in a darkened classroom about a life once lived while sitting at a desk made for a child.

Decades later, Roney would admit that he "always felt kind of on the outside." Rightly or wrongly, he blamed his childhood. His father, a middling bookkeeper with little more than an eighth-grade education, was emotionally distant, without much of a vocabulary to express his feelings. He rarely spoke to his son. "I know he loved me," Roney later commented, "but was never sure he approved of me." His father was also quick to anger: "He could be hot-tempered over little things." Maybe his son's bookishness provoked him? Roney was a voracious reader. He spent hours indoors with stacks of detective novels rather than playing in the streets of downtown Minneapolis. This made him a precocious student, skipping the second grade entirely. "I was proud of this at the time," Roney later wrote, "but in retrospect, it probably wasn't good." It just threw him further out of sync with his peers. "I was always the youngest in my class," Roney lamented, "and, because my physical development was slow, usually the smallest." As a result, Roney's childhood memories could often evoke the clichés of schoolyard humiliation: "[I] was usually the last one chosen in ball games." Ultimately, it was being excused from military service in World War II (because of a limp) that seemed to set him permanently askew with the world: "I missed the experience of almost all my contemporaries."[10]

Roney's mother did not care about any of this. Lulu, as she was known, adored her son, supporting him at every stage of his life. Eventually, she even moved in with him to serve as the rectory's housekeeper after her husband passed away in 1960. "It was a prospect I greatly dreaded," Roney later admitted. "I was afraid she would continue acting as a mother, trying to run my life and the parish."[11] Their relationship was tense. Father Berger described Lulu as "a doting, sometimes overbearing mother," but the parishioners quietly adored her and so did Berger. "Oh, she was a lovely old lady who loved company," Berger would later recall. "There was nothing she liked more than at the last minute to be told there would be a couple more for dinner or lunch."[12] Lulu was not effusive or especially charismatic, but she made friends easily. Her popularity among parishioners only made it harder for all of them that her son spent most of his evenings alone in the rectory, flipping through his slide decks with a glass of scotch. Lulu would quietly retreat to her bedroom, padding down the carpeted hallway, after clearing the dinner table and washing the dishes.[13]

All this isolation might have played some part in the repurposing of the cape. On Sunday mornings, as his parishioners filed out of church, Roney often greeted the young girl from the lake with a smile. With the organist still filling the nave with music and the altar boys diligently snuffing candles near the altar, Roney would wrap her in his cloak as her parents and other parishioners stood only a few feet away. Its billowing folds created just enough cover for him to guide her hand along his erection.

Each encounter with Roney made this little girl's already small world even smaller. Roney manipulated her parents, brothers, and teachers, and even her fear of God, to make sure that these unspeakable acts of abuse remained unspoken. Once, at the lake, when she again flinched at Roney's advances, the priest made a threatening aside, mentioning that her younger brother "did not swim well."[14] She wondered: would Father Roney save him if he struggled? The priest's threats and transgressions—and the secrecy that enveloped them—help explain why this little girl never realized that she was not Roney's only target. There were many more children. Roney was not only relentless and brazen but also prolific in his abuse.[15]

Roney preyed upon dozens of children in central Minnesota with calculating precision, spending much of his free time at the elementary school, in its cafeteria and on its playground. Roney also had a knack for identifying kids who felt, as he did, like outsiders. One ten-year-old girl named Carol was the oldest of five children. She attended the elementary school on scholarship, wore secondhand clothes, and could never really connect with her classmates because she was always caring for her four siblings, the youngest of whom was a toddler who slept in her bed. Her father also worked three jobs, and her mother suffered from severe depression. Only a few days after this girl's mother very nearly died by suicide, Roney invited Carol to the rectory and then assaulted her.

Given the scope and scale of all this abuse—and Roney's particular interest in abusing children in broad daylight—it is difficult to believe that Roney could have kept word from traveling across central Minnesota. How had no one ever spotted any of these violations at a bus stop or in a church or at a lake? Roney touched children in front of adults—in front of their parents and even in front of his own mother—yet no one seemed to have said a word. Roney's cape allowed him some cover for his crimes, but it could not have completely erased suspicion.

It is this tension between concealment and revelation that made Roney's appetites into what anthropologists call a public secret: something that almost everyone knew but no one either admitted or completely articulated. These kinds of secrets must be known to be hidden. They need to be performed (in public, in front of people) so that they can be actively overlooked, with tricksters such as Roney using cloaks to disguise the fact that a secret has just been disclosed. Roney's cape clearly served an ecclesiastical purpose by identifying him as a priest, but it also transformed him into something of a magician, allowing him to conceal and reveal the truth of himself—for all to see and yet never completely understand.[16]

Secrecy is a delicate act, especially when performed in front of an unwitting audience, and Roney couldn't always sustain it. He had been caught—not just once but twice. On one occasion, a housekeeper at the rectory walked in on him and a young girl in his bed. The girl lay on her back; Roney was on top of her. They were both naked. From where the girl lay, she could see the housekeeper standing silently in the doorway. The housekeeper stood there until Roney acknowledged her presence and rolled off the bed. Roney was then caught a second time under similar circumstances: a different housekeeper walked in on Roney with a different young girl. On both occasions, the housekeepers did not say a word—not to Roney, or the girl, or Lulu, or the bishop, or the police.[17]

Not a Word

Willmar, Minnesota

Spring 1970

The Church of Saint Mary battled against the prairie's fundamental stillness—the limitless backdrop of open country—with incense, organ music, and wooden kneelers. *Pilgrimage* is probably too strong a word to describe the rhythm of Sunday mornings in central Minnesota, but most of the faithful traveled relatively long distances to attend mass, with even the most reluctant agnostics ironing their shirts and washing their faces as if quietly conceding that Sundays did indeed belong to God. It was a seemingly unshakable fact of country life that the men, women, and children of this Roman Catholic community found themselves once a week in their church's varnished pews and under its stained-glass windows—if for no other reason than to hear what their parish priest had to say.

Father David Roney was a practiced preacher. His manner was steady, cerebral, and slightly arrogant. He was never folksy. Not once did he try to win over his congregation with a joke or a self-deprecating story. Instead, he reasoned with his parishioners—not as equals, but from on high—leaning heavily on the philosophy and theology that he had studied during his time at seminary. In later years, when he had trouble falling asleep, he would peruse those same books, which he kept at his bedside. Although his thoughts on Thomas Aquinas and William of Ockham could bore even the most enthusiastic of churchgoers, the esotericism of it all carried the weight of truth in this farming community. It made him sound like God. So too did his sonorous voice, which caused his sermons to vibrate across the church's cavernous hollow. And sometimes, when the midmorning sun would backlight him in just the right way, Roney could appear to be floating at the pulpit.

Every Sunday morning, while preaching to his congregation, Roney enjoyed a clear line of sight to the children he abused. They sat with their parents, shared hymnals with their siblings, and invariably blushed when Roney made eye contact with them. He sometimes cracked an almost imperceptible smile that could be read as a smirk or maybe even a grimace. These quiet moments of recognition delivered a punch of adrenaline to these children as well as a not-so-subtle reminder that Roney alone had the authority to speak. He alone could be heard.[18]

The girl from the lake usually sat with her parents and two brothers near the back of the church. They could have flaunted their familiarity with their parish priest by sitting much closer to the front. Roney visited their home nearly every weekend, sometimes stayed for dinner, and even once celebrated a private mass in their living room. But they were a modest family. The young girl's parents quietly appreciated the interest that Roney had taken in their children, especially their daughter, but they never wanted to stand out or be set apart. To them, self-importance seemed like a sin. They slipped in and then slipped out of Sunday service as silently as possible, quietly shaking hands with family and friends; the young girl's father shushed his children every time one of them made a noise. Not a word, her mother would remind them as they entered the church.[19]

This hushing and tiptoeing puts into context just how much courage this young girl must have marshalled to speak out about her abuse. After years of increasingly violent encounters, of being told that "it hurts because you are fighting what God wants," she summoned the almost unbelievable strength to tell an older woman from Sunday service about the lake and the blanket and the wrath of God.[20]

This young girl attended the Church of Saint Mary's elementary school. The building was new construction, and it had an almost industrial appearance: linoleum floors, dropped ceilings, and plastered walls. The new chalkboards bounced back to their original state with the simple wipe of a wet rag. When the children poured into the building from recess or made their escape at the end of the day, all these right angles and hard surfaces turned the place into an echo chamber: one extended wave of jokes and laughter and taunts. In between bells, during class time, the school fell perfectly silent as children sat at their desks and minded their teachers. Even the sound of clacking heels in the hallway could distract from a lesson.

Thus, the knock at this young girl's classroom door came as a surprise to everyone and most viscerally to her. The day after she had confided in that older woman from Sunday service, Roney interrupted her class to ask the teacher whether he might have a word with this girl. It was all a blur, but in the hall, within earshot of her teacher and classmates, Roney delivered another reminder that he alone had the authority to speak. To impress this message upon the child, Roney instructed her to say prayers before, during, and after school for two weeks, which she did—alone at her desk.

She arrived at school early in the morning to pray for forgiveness in front of a crucifix. A bloody knot of muscle with a long, sad face, the cross hung above the chalkboard. She did the same during recess, while her friends played four square and tetherball, and then again at the end of the day once everyone had left. All the while, no one ever asked her why Father Roney had given her this penance: not her classmates, not her family, and not her teacher.

Over the years, other children tried to speak out about their abuse, but they could not be heard either. No one seemed to have the right words. Carol always sat with her family at Sunday service on the outer edge of the church, near the confessionals. Her mother was the one who never really recovered from a failed suicide attempt. At church, Carol wrangled her four younger siblings into the pew, often holding the toddler in her arms, as Roney read the Gospel, consecrated the Eucharist, and sang the hymns. He had a beautiful singing voice, she would mention years later, but whenever he preached, all she could do was scream—in her head, not out loud— "Liar! Cheater! Faker!"

Carol's abuse seemed surreal to her, so much so that she would later question whether it had happened at all. She knew that on at least one occasion Roney had invited her to the rectory. She was certain that he had brought her to his office. Carol remembers the room very well: there was a desk and a sitting chair; there were books on shelves; a window opening onto the world. Roney offered her some chocolates from a brandy snifter, pouring the candies unevenly into her small hands. But then what happened next? Carol heard glass breaking—in her head, not out loud—and then she experienced an event that did not make sense to her, one that she probably couldn't have described to an adult even if she had tried.

Given all her responsibilities, Carol had very little time for play, which should have been the first clue to understanding what happened a few weeks later. During a rare moment of free time, when there were no clothes to clean, no siblings to bathe, and no food to cook, Carol borrowed one of her sister's dolls. It was plastic and hollow. Its blonde hair looked soft but was in fact quite coarse. She then took a statue of Christ down from the mantel. It was solid, made of plaster, and depicted the son of God with long brown hair and feminine lips. This young girl, as her family went about their evening, stripped her sister's doll of its clothes and then pressed the two figurines together, the plaster statue dominating the plastic doll. A sibling caught sight of the scene and quickly tattled on Carol, but the mother did not know how to react. She didn't say anything at all. Instead, she quietly placed the statue back on its pedestal.[21]

There are many moments of silence like this. Here is one more: A young girl named April spent her free time praying at the church, lighting votive candles, and straightening missalettes. She and her friend would also write letters to missionary sisters in Africa, often daydreaming aloud about one day joining these nuns for an adventure with God. All of this stopped once Roney groped them near the church organ, where April sat with her family at Sunday mass. It was the terror of having to return to the site of this betrayal every Sunday that eventually prompted this courageous young girl to write a letter to her bishop.[22]

April wrote on lined paper with a sharpened pencil. Attending carefully to penmanship, her description of her encounter with Roney was almost forensic in tone, and it filled the front and the back side of the loose leaf. She wrote the letter in her backyard, near the hedges, where her family kept a shrine to the Blessed Virgin. There, she would usually say the rosary, but on that day, April read the letter out loud to check for grammar and syntax. The thought of writing her bishop intimidated her, and she wanted to get it right. As April read aloud to the Blessed Virgin what she had written, she began to imagine her bishop reading this note, line by line, in his office at the cathedral. The thought brought on something like vertigo: weak knees and a knot in her stomach. April began to tremble at the prospect that she, rather than Roney, might get into trouble, and at what this scandal would do to her and her family. Suddenly struck by the stakes of it all, April ran inside her house, rifled through the kitchen for a book of matches, and then scurried back to the hedges—to light the letter as she would a votive candle. She was stunned by how quickly the piece of paper went up in flames, as if it had never existed in the first place.

These children all sat with their families at the same Sunday service. They sang together, knelt together, and even drank from the same chalice. They were scattered about the church, but never far from each other. None of them knew about the others. Each one thought they were alone in their experience. The only moment when the voice of a child seemed to have any consequence at all was in the spring of 1970. A teacher at the elementary school reported that his six-year-old daughter had been sitting on his lap one day when she announced with the innocence that only six-year-olds can muster: "Daddy, your thing doesn't get big like Father Roney's!"[23] The young girl's father, at first frozen with fear, spoke with other parents, cautiously at first but then with a mounting sense of urgency. His concerns seemed to align with the suspicions of others. Why did Father Roney spend so much time at the elementary school? Was it necessary for him to hug the children so often? And why the cape? A cohort of disturbed parents formed, seeking answers, or at the very least a conversation. The father of the six-year-old girl approached a trusted priest for counsel.

In his sixties, with a plainspoken approach to the world, Father Francis Garvey had served as a chaplain at a nearby mental health facility for forty years before becoming the Director of Priest Personnel for the Diocese of New Ulm. He gave the impression of being wise and influential yet also discreet and humble, which seems to have been the exact wrong combination of virtues for the task at hand. Garvey quickly assured the father of this young girl that he would take care of the situation; indeed, he said, plans had already been put into motion. Despite the assurances, the fact is that Garvey's intervention amounted to very little. Decades later, lawyers pressed Garvey on the details of his one and only conversation with Roney. "I called and made an appointment to see Father Roney," Garvey explained, "and I went to see him. I had reported to him that this parent had come—he didn't want his name revealed—had come to me." The parents of this child, he explained to the lawyers, "were concerned about his inappropriate—what they considered inappropriate sexual contact on the playground."[24] The lawyers pressed Garvey on Roney's reaction:

LAWYER: What did Father Roney say?

GARVEY: Nothing.

LAWYER: Nothing?

GARVEY: Nothing verbally. His emotional expression was very bland. Not expressive. The encounter was very short. He didn't respond to my report, so I left.

LAWYER: He didn't admit or deny it?

GARVEY: Right. Neither one.[25]

The principal of the Church of Saint Mary's elementary school—a nun named Sister Virginia McCall—had a similar experience with Roney, after the same parent approached her with the same concern. Then in her mid-thirties, Sister McCall seemed to be all too aware of her limited power as a nun within the Church. Though she worried openly about what Garvey would describe decades later as "inappropriate hugging behavior," she also knew that questioning the actions of a priest would put her in a delicate position.[26] "Father Roney was always around the little children," she admitted. "I had never liked the way he put the children under his cape, but I would say to myself, 'Oh, don't be such a prude!'" She then added, "Because back then you would never suspect a priest of that kind of conduct."[27]

McCall was hesitant to do anything. "At no time did [anyone] ever suggest to me that I should arrange for psychological treatment for Father Roney," she later argued in her own defense. "I would have had no authority to do so in any event."[28] She did approach Roney, confronting her superior about her suspicions and creating some bright lines for him to obey. But Roney, again, proved eerily quiet on the matter. When McCall instructed him never again to go to the playground, "he said nothing, but complied." When McCall told him never again to attend the school's lunch hour, "he said nothing, and he complied." And when McCall insisted that Roney never again wrestle with the little girls, "he said nothing."[29]

At some point, Father Garvey and Sister McCall discussed the problem of David Roney, but the conversation, though grounded in the concerns of a few parents and bolstered by the nun's growing suspicions, did not go anywhere:

LAWYER: Did you [Garvey] ever follow up with [McCall] after that to see what she had observed?

GARVEY: No. I did not. I guess, I was—or I was waiting for her to report to me if there was—she observed any misbehavior.

LAWYER: And did she ever report to you?

GARVEY: No.

LAWYER: Did you report the information to the bishop?

GARVEY: No, I didn't.

LAWYER: And why didn't you?

GARVEY: I don't know. Outside the fact that—I don't know. It didn't seem to be the thing that we did in those days. I confronted the priest and I figured I did what I had to do.[30]

In Garvey's defense, and McCall's as well, both clerics did what they thought they had to do. Sister McCall overcame the hurdles of Church hierarchy to at least try to address the sexual appetites of her parish priest, and Garvey confronted a colleague at the behest of a parishioner. Arguably, this was all that either of them could have done at the time, given the information that they had. The only available evidence was a six-year-old girl's passing comment about a possible erection. No one had much reason to connect this young girl's comment to the trips to the lake, the visits to the elementary school, and the long hugs. No one could appreciate the full scope of the problem. This wasn't just true in central Minnesota but throughout the United States, and ultimately around the world. It was not until the mid-1980s, more than a decade later, that someone of any stature within the Roman Catholic Church would begin to put it all together, to sense the sheer magnitude of clerical sexual abuse, and even he was met with a brutal silence.

A Real, Present Danger

Washington, DC

February 1985

The Apostolic Nunciature of the Holy See occupies a three-story limestone building with a modest front yard and a garden out back. It is the Vatican's embassy to the United States as well as the administrative center of the Roman Catholic Church in America. The nunciature appoints bishops, tracks developments between the Holy See and the United States, and maintains an open channel of communication between the pope and the president. Staffed with lawyers, theologians, and diplomats with graduate degrees in moral theology and canon law, it tends to attract minds as square as the building.

Morally upright, with a broad-shouldered approach to truth, Father Thomas Doyle joined the nunciature in 1984 at forty-three years old. He arrived as a secretary-canonist after acting as a judge for the Metropolitan Tribunal of the Archdiocese of Chicago. Young and clean-shaven, with a full head of hair, he also served as a reserve officer in the United States Air Force, priding himself on seeing the world in righteous contrast: true or false; right or wrong; good or bad. His thesis for his pontifical doctorate in canon law tackled the topic of marital fidelity, leaving little room for interpretation when it came to the sanctity of marriage.[31] He was meticulous about facts.

At his desk in the District of Columbia, amid the humdrum of Church paperwork, Doyle received news from Lafayette, Louisiana, that shocked him to attention. Lafayette, he quickly learned, was a small, Roman Catholic town deeply committed to its priests, a devotion that made it difficult (at times almost impossible) for the community to come to terms with the fact that Father Gilbert Gauthe had sexually assaulted dozens of children across a variety of clerical assignments since his arrival there in 1972. These placements included small country parishes in and around Lafayette as well as the chaplaincy of the diocesan Boy Scouts.

The details that surfaced haunted Doyle. Gauthe took boys on camping trips and had them sleep over at the rectory. He barred his windows, kept a pistol at his bedside, and took photographs of the kids with a Polaroid camera. At one point, Gauthe's superior caught wind of it all, and promptly moved Gauthe to a second-floor bedroom so that the priest could no longer smuggle children in through his first-floor window. The attacks continued until Gauthe's sexual assaults sent one boy to the hospital. The parents promptly sued the diocese for failing to protect their ten-year-old son. The diocese countered with confidential settlements in the millions of dollars, and the office of the bishop processed the payouts and nondisclosure agreements so quickly that it seemed to some as if this were not the first time that the Diocese of Lafayette had dealt with clerical sexual abuse. As Doyle and others would later learn, it was not: the bishop of this diocese had been trying to manage multiple cases connected to more than a dozen priests.[32]

The trial of Gilbert Gauthe became the Roman Catholic Church's first national sex abuse scandal in the United States, and journalists were soon banging on the bishop's front door for comment. Major networks such as ABC, NBC, and CBS, as well as various newsmagazine shows such as *20/20* and *60 Minutes*, sent reporters to Louisiana. National print publications covered the story: the *New York Times, Washington Post, National Catholic Reporter, Vanity Fair, Mother Jones,* and *Rolling Stone.* Pulitzer Prize–winning authors scrambled for book advances while the American Bar Association conducted studies and scheduled panel conferences on what appeared to be a newly developing area of law: clerical sexual abuse. All the while, Church leadership flatly lied to the press. A priest named Alexandre Larroque had been charged with overseeing Gauthe, and he eventually spoke to a news correspondent. The correspondent asked Larroque how the Church could have allowed this abuse to go on for so long.

LARROQUE: We didn't know it was going on, and that's the simple answer.

CORRESPONDENT: But you did. You'd known as far as ten years back, the bishop had. You knew sometime in the 1970s.

LARROQUE: I don't know what was known in the past. . . . Knowing what we know now . . . there would have been a completely different chain of events.

CORRESPONDENT: You'd never had to deal with someone like this before?

LARROQUE: No.[33]

The United States Conference of Catholic Bishops, a governing body comprised of active and retired Church leaders in America, proposed a committee to study the scope and scale of clerical sexual abuse, but neither the committee nor its study ever materialized. Instead, Doyle collaborated with an attorney and a psychologist to write a confidential report titled "The Problem of Sexual Molestation by Roman Catholic Clergy."[34] Its intended audience was the United States Conference of Catholic Bishops, as well as the Vatican. Both a priest and a soldier, Doyle was well versed in the virtues of obedience—of protecting the Church at all costs. At the same time, he had always shown an interest in the pivot points of history, moments that forced even the most storied of institutions to recalibrate. Before he wrote his doctoral thesis in canonical law, Doyle completed three graduate degrees in the fields of philosophy, political science, and theology with theses titled "Organized Religion in Marxist-Leninist Philosophy," "Vladimir Lenin's Theory of Social Revolution," and "Liberation Theology in the Context of Social Needs in South America."[35] Morally committed to the coordinates of right and wrong, Doyle found himself at a historical crossroads for the Roman Catholic Church.

Doyle's report begins with alarm: "A real, present danger exists." Doyle saw the entire institution at risk. The abuse not only destroyed lives but also the integrity of the Church and its priests. In addressing the problem, Doyle insisted that "time is of the essence" if the Church wished to avoid "consequences never before experienced." He then tried to quantify the gravity of the situation in dollar amounts, written out in all caps. One lawsuit was projected to cost a diocese in the United States "TEN MILLION DOLLARS." If there were a hundred cases like this, Doyle extrapolated, the Church could end up paying "ONE BILLION DOLLARS"—a figure he underlined for effect. And with a class action lawsuit already threatening the Church with a "TEN BILLION DOLLAR" settlement, this could be "a conservative cost projection."[36] The future of the Roman Catholic Church in the United States was in peril.

Doyle's report is also shrouded in secrecy. There is mention of "sanitizing or purging files of potentially damaging material," moving other items into juridically "immune territory," and taking advantage of the Vatican's "secret archives." There is also an anxious undercurrent of concern about how reading the report might open its reader up to legal scrutiny. Doyle emphasizes in the opening pages of the document that "security for the entire Project is extremely important" and that the report must not end up in the hands of journalists or prosecutors. Doyle worried about further scandal, and therefore he insists that "each reader return the document to the person from whom they received same, without copying." He clearly had the institution's well-being in mind, but Doyle's commitment to confidentiality contributed to the Church's ability to evade accountability for its crimes. He stripped the report of "any fact in litigation which has not been publicly reported in the press" and retained legal counsel to review the document before its limited release. He also warned his reader that anyone in possession of his report could "become the target of a subpoena or other discovery device." The manuscript positively vibrates with a fear of litigation: "No copy [should] be retained by the reader."[37] Doyle insisted on what was at the time an increasingly familiar strategy: Church leaders should pass off the issue of clerical sexual abuse (just as they should pass off his report) to anyone else as quickly as possible.

The report is unsettling. It depicts a Church on the verge of financial and moral ruin, and Doyle offers a handful of concrete suggestions; but his document is really an exercise in issue-spotting that he hoped would drive the Church's future decision-making. Crucially, it poses over one hundred questions divided into four categories—civil, criminal, canonical, and medical—to help Church leadership with further research. The sheer range of these questions, along with their naïveté, indicates just how new these issues appeared to be and how little language there was to describe them. The questions also reflect a kind of flat-footedness. One gets the sense that no one saw any of this coming, or if they did, they must have looked the other way.[38] Here is a selection of questions from Doyle's report:

> What constitutes sexual abuse?
>
> Does sexual contact with minor children constitute a criminal offense?
>
> Does touching the buttocks of a fully clothed nine-year-old child constitute sexual abuse either in the law or from a psychiatrist's viewpoint?
>
> Does touching the covered genitalia of a fully clothed youngster constitute sexual abuse?
>
> Does masturbation of the child by the Priest or of the Priest by the child constitute sexual abuse?
>
> If the juvenile were a sixteen-year-old boy, would this imply that the abuse would have a lesser impact in the adult life of this victim?
>
> If the teenager appeared to initiate the sexual contact and seemed to continue to enjoy it over a period of time, would this change the offense in the eyes of the law or in the eyes of a psychiatrist?
>
> Should a record be kept of these allegations and investigations?
>
> Where should such a record be kept?
>
> Does the Bishop have any canonical/moral/pastoral obligations toward the victims and their families?[39]

Of all these questions, perhaps the most consequential was one that appeared slightly later in the report, where Doyle asks, "Is there a canonical entity known as the Roman Catholic Church in the United States?" Odd though it may initially seem, this line of inquiry would go on to shape the Church's attempts to defend its assets from the looming threat of civil litigation.[40] In essence, what Doyle was trying to figure out was whether there is a single Roman Catholic *Church* in the United States, or whether there are instead many different Roman Catholic *churches*. For the purposes of evading liability, teams of lawyers hired by the Catholic Church would eventually assemble behind the second option, arguing that the

United States has churches rather than a single Church. Leadership was far more comfortable with dioceses filing for bankruptcy than prosecutors setting their sights on the deep pockets of the Vatican. Doyle warns: "[There is a] trend to expand the circle of responsibility beyond the diocese of the priests in question to the National Conference of Catholic Bishops, the Apostolic Pro-Nuncio and the Holy Father himself."[41] Church leadership subsequently decided to read each instance of clerical sexual abuse as a single incident to be managed rather than a sweeping pattern to be interrupted. This meant dismissing Doyle's nearly one-hundred-page report as alarmist and hyperbolic. It also meant sidelining the one-time rising star to the extent that Doyle eventually decided to leave the priesthood.

Church leadership's decision to atomize the institution into singular entities and to treat clerical sexual abuse as a series of unique incidents set an important precedent. In 1985, Gauthe was the focus, but there were at least a dozen other priests in the Diocese of Lafayette who would be credibly accused.[42] As the public would eventually learn through court filings, this cluster of sexually abusive priests in Louisiana was not an outlier. In a diocese as thinly staffed as that of New Ulm, for example, Roney prowled about the prairie alongside dozens of other sexually abusive priests. Among them were Father James Fitzgerald (1919–2009), who abused children on the Tekakwitha Indian Mission in South Dakota and on White Earth Indian Reservation in Minnesota, at times bringing young children back to his parishes to serve as altar boys. Father John Gleason (1921–1998) abused at least one nine- to ten-year-old girl, with the assaults occurring, in the words of the young girl, "in the parish rectory after bedtime." Father Edward Graff (1929–) watched pornography with young boys "to prepare [them] for adult relationships" and then had them perform oral sex on him. Father Joseph Heitzer (1914–1969) was said to have targeted a boy after his father died in a car accident. Father William Marks (1908–1979) initiated his abuse with "whiskers and hugs" and then expanded his abuse "through kissing, fondling, and finally, simulated intercourse."

The facts associated with each case are painful to read, and the list of credibly accused priests in the Diocese of New Ulm can feel interminable—all the more so because complaints went unaddressed for years. A priest approached his bishop about Father John Murphy (1927–2001) but was told to mind his own business. Similar imperatives protected Father Michael Skoblik (1910–1989), Father Robert Clark (1958), Father Douglas Schleisman (1949–), Father Harry Majerus (1917–1995), Father Cletus Altermatt (1907–1978), Father Dennis Becker (1935–2021), Father Gordon Buckley (1924–1985), Father Arnold Berg (1908–2003), Father Rudolph Henrich (1906–1992), Father Francis Markey (1928–2012), Father Charles Stark (1915–1991), Father Edward Ardolf (1937–2016), Father Joseph Balent (1919–1986), Father John Cooney (1922–1988), Father John Hennessy (1934–), Father Anthony Plathe (1937–), Father William Sprigler (1946–), Father James Devorak (1945–), Father Richard Gross (1931–2022), Father Michael Guetter (1924–1988), Father Germain Kunz (1931–2016), and Father Sam Wagner (1977–).[43]

Hundreds of priests in Minnesota would eventually be accused of sexual abuse. These priests worked alongside each other, sometimes lived in the same rectory, and often traveled the world together. Their tacit agreements and quiet concessions put them in alignment with thousands of other priests who would be credibly accused of sexual abuse in the United States over roughly the same period. Events in Louisiana would soon give way to other scandals in Minnesota, New Orleans, Milwaukee, and Chicago in the early 1990s, and then several cases in Massachusetts in 2001. Others appeared across the United States and then around the world: in Latin America, Africa, parts of Asia, and much of Europe.[44] In 1985, it was Doyle alone who was willing to see clerical sex abuse as systemic—as a problem that exceeded individual cases and operated on a national scale—and even he seemed to understand that his warnings would not accomplish anything. It was too tempting for bishops and priests to interpret clerical sexual abuse as the unfortunate result of an occasional bad apple.

This temptation was all the stronger because the alternative—facing squarely up to the systemic nature of the problem—meant dealing with an intractable theological obstacle within the Roman Catholic Church: the permanence of ordination as a transfigurative rite. In his report, Doyle argued that abusive clergymen were given cover by the fact that ordination irreversibly transforms a seminarian into a priest. No matter how much they sin, the Church states clearly that it is impossible to un-priest a priest. This is why Doyle called for a newfound vigilance in the formation and ordination of priests in seminaries.[45] But this call for action ultimately came too late: a great many men of suspicious appetites had already been ordained, and many more were in training. It was also a proposal that overlooked something fundamental about seminary life, which, with its compulsive piety and unrelenting activities, muted—albeit temporarily—even the most wandering or predatory of desires. In every seminary, there were timetables and confessions, self-examinations and spiritual directors that kept cohorts of young men so busy that they did not have time to sin.[46] Yet neither did these young men have a chance to gain any practical skills that might have helped them avoid sin once ordained and sent out into the prairies, where open stretches of time would often expand outward toward the horizon. Instead, seminaries ran their students ragged in ways that buried almost any possible evidence of deviance. The Saint Paul Seminary, for instance, never gave Roney so much as a moment to understand himself. "I never knew if I was normal or abnormal," Roney would later write about his days as a student. "From occasional remarks and jokes, I knew that [my fellow seminarians] were sexual beings, but I never thought of anyone as bad as I."[47] Seminarians instead learned that as priests they would become permanent vessels of the living and breathing Jesus Christ. As priests, they would act in the person of Christ (*in persona Christi*), irrespective of their sins.

In Persona Christi

Saint Paul, Minnesota

April 18, 1945

A young David Roney stood nervously at a lectern. He had been tasked with delivering a student sermon to his fellow classmates at the Saint Paul Seminary. These were formal assignments set by professors as well as exercises in professional development: the rare chance for a seminarian to project himself in priestly terms. As such, the delivery of a student sermon tended to be a solemn affair. There was no music in the chapel, unlike on Sundays and Holy Days, and there was no incense. Candles in red glass jars lit the altar.

Roney preached that day about the "occasions of sin." He began with the story of Adam and Eve and a reminder that the two ate from the tree of knowledge and thus committed the first sin. His insight was that they not only bit into the fruit but also gazed upon the tree from afar. They then approached the tree, plucked its fruit, and held it in their hands. Thus, Adam and Eve made a series of willful decisions to be proximate to an environment of temptation—to the occasions of sin—and this proximity allowed for a wicked curiosity to well up inside of them: for their souls to become swollen with desire, positively engorged with disordered thoughts. Adam and Eve's original sin, he preached, was not just about biting into the fruit. The sin did not simply occur at the exact moment when their teeth entered the apple. The far subtler but no less substantive sin occurred when the two allowed themselves to drift ever closer to a tree from which they knew they must never eat. The pious priest, Roney insisted to his peers, must follow suit, prohibiting himself from entering spaces and places that might tempt him.

Roney, to be clear, was not the only seminarian interested in sin at the time. Nearly all the student sermons of this period address the topic in one way or another: to scan their titles is to become keenly aware of how sin preoccupied the minds of these young men. These were sermons whose titles foregrounded questions of "original sin" and "actual sin" as well as "temptation" and "pride." They offered reflections on "mortal sin," "venial sin," and "the force of evil habit," and these overlapped with treatises on avarice, lust, envy, gluttony, and superstition. Some of these sermons offered close investigations of a single topic, as when one seminarian delivered an address titled "Christ and the Sinful Woman." Others congealed into something like short lecture series, including one string of sermons that brought together titles such as "The Act of Contrition," "Why Go to Confession," "Frequent Confession," and "The Qualities of a Good Confession." Through their names—and, to an infinitely greater extent, through their contents—these sermons seem to express more than just an anxiety about the human condition in general. Taken together, they provide a portrait of young men who are worried, and maybe even frightened, by the future work that lies before them as pastors, as well as by the unwanted impulses that twitch inside them all.[48]

Oddly, for all this talk of moral failure—how to spot it, combat it, and repair its effects—these young men also learned in seminary that sin, from the perspective of their priesthood, was somewhat beside the point. A priest is always a priest no matter how often or how gravely he sins. In a survey course Roney took on Church history, a professor treated the permanence of the priesthood as a consequence of world events, a kind of work-around for a budding religious community trying to define itself. In other courses, like the one on sacramental theology or another on metaphysics, it was considered something of a philosophical fact, a condition of existence that was always already true. While Roney's fellow seminarians quickly learned that there was not much to gain from trying to settle on whether this permanence was premised upon historical developments or philosophical insight, the history did help them to understand the phi-losophy.[49] Here is what they learned:

Christianity in 64 AD became an illegal religion, with followers throughout the Roman Empire forced under pain of death to renounce their faith. Some Christians chose to martyr themselves, but others sub-mitted to authorities or fled for their lives. Those who betrayed their faith came to be known as *traditores*: a Latin word that literally means "those who handed over" scripture and sacred relics. This is the genesis of the English word *traitor*. The traitor raised deep ecclesiastical questions for the Church once the Roman Empire allowed Christians to practice their faith following the Edict of Milan in 313 AD. The status of these traitors was unclear: If a priest or bishop had handed over sacred docu-ments or if he had fled to evade persecution, could he still serve as a priest or a bishop? Having ostensibly lost his credibility as a Church leader by publicly renouncing or betraying his faith, should he be removed from office? And, most pressingly: if he continued in his role as a priest or a bishop, as many did, would his sacramental acts be considered valid? If a traitor baptized a convert, for example, would the newly baptized person be considered baptized? All this debate pivoted atop a fundamen-tal theological question about the relationship between the moral and spiritual status of a priest and the efficacy of his sacramental acts: did the former have any effect on the latter? Or to put a slightly finer point on the matter, could the sins of a priest compromise the status of his priesthood?

Two camps formed. Both agreed that the primary function of a priest is sacramental. Only ordained priests can facilitate the necessary rites of the Roman Catholic Church. These include the baptism of converts, the con-secration of the Eucharist, and the ordination of priests. But there was vigorous and at times violent disagreement about the moral qualifications required to confer these sacraments. One camp, known as the Donatists, argued that priests must be without fault, or at least without serious sin. Otherwise, any sacraments they delivered would be invalid. Petilian of Constantine, an eminent Donatist, made this abundantly clear in an address to priests in the fifth century: "Your blood-stained conscience makes your feeble prayers of no effect."[50] Donatism advanced a pious argument with grand expectations of self-discipline.

Augustine of Hippo offered a competing school of thought, arguing that the moral and spiritual state of a priest has no effect on the status of his priesthood, let alone on his ability to perform the sacraments. Sinners and saints can coexist in the same church, he claimed, because priests are no more or less pious than anyone else. This is a point Augustine would later emphasize in *Confessions*, an autobiographical portrait of his own sinful youth and conversion to Christianity, which evidences in no uncertain terms just how imperfect the most holy of Christians can be. "Grant me chastity and continence," Augustine famously prayed, "but not yet."[51] In the end, it is no surprise that Augustine argued that the sacraments depend on the power of God rather than on the purity of the priest. It is God's holiness, not the priest's purity, that facilitates baptisms and ordinations.[52]

It is possible that Augustine insisted on the moral imperfection of priests for very practical reasons. One does not need to sit with Donatism for too long to begin to imagine a community wracked by infighting over whether a given priest is or is not morally capable of delivering the sacraments—a church completely incapable of reproducing itself. The sins of a single bishop could undo cohorts of priests and generations of baptized Christians. Conversely, Donatism also ran the risk of placing priests on such a high pedestal that their perceived piety would distract from the Christian principle that Jesus was the only person to have ever lived a life free of sin.

Augustine, by contrast, understood the priest not as a reflection of God but rather as a channel of God's grace. This is an eminently functional argument, one that not only imagines priests as making up a kind of sacramental infrastructure that facilitates a connection between the human and the divine, but also disassociates the priest's ontic capacity to confer the sacraments from his moral standing as a Christian. In this sense, priests within the Church function something like pipes or tubes: they convey a force (here, the grace of God) from one source to another, operating as conduits irrespective of their own moral qualities or capacities for sin. Thus, it makes as much sense to ask about the moral and spiritual status of a priest as it does to evaluate the moral and spiritual standing of a pipe or a tube. Instead, the question is whether the pipes work—and the sacrament of ordination permanently empowers priests to "work."[53]

Important here is that once ordination takes place, it can never be undone. This is another legacy of Augustine's debate with the Donatists: neither the sins of a priest nor any other human action can reverse a priest's ability to deliver the sacraments. If a priest should fall from grace and become some modern-day manifestation of a *traditore*, he can be forbidden by leadership to exercise the sacraments in public, and he can be prohibited from representing himself publicly as a priest. He can also be barred from vesting himself in stoles and chasubles, and even from wearing the Roman collar in public. This is largely what it means when a priest has been defrocked or laicized. Their priestly clothing has been confiscated, and they have been ordered to live as a layperson. Crucially, though, being defrocked does not stop a priest from being able to perform the sacraments. As a conveyor of God's grace, a priest is a priest forever.[54]

The curriculum at the Saint Paul Seminary, like the Roman Catholic Church at large, emphasized the permanence of the priesthood, adding that the priest's capacity to exercise the sacraments constitutes a hierarchical distinction between clergy and laity. The priest, as theologians have long observed, is "inferior to Christ but superior to the people."[55] Lest there be any misunderstanding, it is a superiority of essence and not only of degree. The priest is what theologians refer to as *ontologically set apart from* (and thus fundamentally superior to) laypeople and even nuns because priests neither imitate nor mimic the image of Christ; rather, they serve as voluntary instruments for the presentation of Christ Himself, offering their own bodies to Him so that He can work through them. At the end of a church service, for example, the priest does not say "Let *us* go in peace." He instead speaks in the person of Christ (*in persona Christi*), proclaiming with what the Church understands to be the literal voice of Christ "May God bless you" and "Go in peace."[56] The Church holds that the living Jesus Christ speaks through the priest.

The only clarification that professors at the Saint Paul Seminary stressed is that the priest only speaks in the person of Christ while enacting the sacraments. When the priest is not consecrating the Eucharist— for example, when he is representing Christ as a teacher, mentor, or counselor—the priest is no different than any of the lay faithful. A priest is a man like any other man, but it would have been easy to miss this last point on the day of David Roney's ordination.

On April 18, 1945, the Cathedral of Saint Paul put forward candidates for the sacrament of Holy Orders. They were young and clean shaven, with plastered hair and freshly starched cassocks. Most drove from the seminary to the cathedral with their parents. Others took a streetcar marked "Grand Avenue." It ran directly from the doors of the Saint Paul Seminary to Union Station. From there, they climbed a long, steep hill to the cathedral. Given the significance of the day, at least for these men, the walk must have felt like a journey home.

The archbishop presided over the ceremony, progressing steadily through the ritual. Almost every word was in Latin and the service moved at such a clip that virtually no one in the pews understood anything. There were prayers and promises as well as the occasional reading of scripture, but no one stopped to give anyone in attendance any guidance. Then came the moment the faithful had been waiting for, the one ceremonial gesture that these candidates for ordination had told their family and friends to spot: the imposition of hands. This is the permanent conferral of the priestly office, and it happens when the archbishop lays his hands over the head of each candidate. The young men are then vested in stoles and chasubles, and their hands anointed with oil. They kneel before the archbishop as he reads from the Book of Psalms, also in Latin, translated here: "You are a priest forever according to the order of Melchisedech. May the Lord bless you from Zion, he that made heaven and earth. The Lord has sworn, and he will not repent: You are a priest forever according to the order of Melchisedech."[57]

You are a priest forever.

These young men would have demurred, of course, assessing with as much wisdom as possible the weight of their sudden transformation and the seriousness of their life's work. But modesty would have made little sense—on that day, at that moment—as the cathedral's organs roared to life and as the family and friends of these newly ordained priests, amid plumes of incense, rose from their seats to applaud the young men's vision and courage.[58] The newly minted priests could have been forgiven for having felt a jolt of optimism and excitement for what lay ahead. Having been run ragged by the strictures of the seminary, with the early mornings and late nights, and educated to a rigorous level of sophistication, they must have felt anticipation for the greatest of assignments. In the photograph that commemorates the Saint Paul Seminary's graduating class of 1945, the candidates for ordination stand shoulder to shoulder. Roney hunches near the middle of the scrum, with his brow slightly furrowed and his shoulders slumped. Each of these men has a bright, almost iridescent anticipation in his eyes, a youthful, somewhat brash confidence that seems to call to anyone who might listen: *challenge me.*[59]

Occasions of Sin

Lake Saint Croix Beach, Minnesota

February 1955

Population 513.

Sometimes less.

The adobe church, evoking monastic simplicity, sat atop a high bank overlooking a valley. It offered picturesque views in the summers and the feeling of complete isolation in the winters: gray skies, monstrous snow drifts, and a biting cold. The rectory, where Father David Roney lived, was connected to the Church of Saint Francis of Assisi. The entire set-up was as simple as could be. There was a small kitchen with a stove, and a modest living space with a table and some straight-back chairs. The bedroom was completely stripped of color, with a blanket the shade and texture of steel wool draped across the bed. The only signs of life were Roney's books from seminary, which sat on a shelf, a few bookmarks breaking up the stretch of pages.

The town of Lake Saint Croix Beach lay only twenty miles east of Saint Paul and Minneapolis, but it might as well have been two thousand miles away. A handful of families had founded the parish not too long before Roney arrived, and they did so out of pure need. The nearest Roman Catholic church at the time was miles away, and very few of these people had cars, with some having not seen the inside of a Catholic church for

twenty years. Others had never attended a Sunday service. "Religious affil-
iations were soon forgotten," wrote the town's first priest, "and the children grew up as if they lived in darkest Africa."[60] Families eventually
began to meet in each other's homes for Sunday mass while the community slowly raised enough money to construct a church building and rectory. "A table covered with a white sheet served as an altar," wrote that first
priest. "A stove far from adequate supplied a little heat."[61] It was a rugged
kind of Catholicism. "A Mass kit, such as that used by missionaries in foreign lands," the priest continued, "was unpacked and packed before and
after each service. The worshippers knelt on the cold, hard floor."[62] Their
fellowship kept them warm.

Years later, Roney's accommodations, complete with a bedroom, bath-
room, and bookshelves, even a toilet, must have seemed to some of those
founding families like a lavish upgrade for their parish priest, a monumental gesture that far exceeded the community's means, but the assignment was hard for this young man. Roney's years in the seminary had
stimulated him, rousing him from his bed early in the morning and releas-
ing him back to sleep late at night.

In addition to this schoolwork—which he tackled with boyish
enthusiasm—Roney also had the city. A walk down the streets of Saint
Paul and Minneapolis to run a simple errand could mean bumping into a
half-dozen fellow seminarians. And sometimes, when the rigors of seminary life offered the occasional patch of free time, Roney would go to the
movies. In a grand old theater, with ornate brick detail and wood features
that lent the building an almost Tudor-style appearance, Roney would
find a seat near the back of the hall, and quietly lose himself in *The African
Queen* starring Humphrey Bogart, or *An American in Paris* with Gene
Kelly. "I was ordained for the Archdiocese of St. Paul," he would later
write, "and never doubted that eventually I would retire to the city."[63] But
none of it panned out for him.

"In about 1955," Roney wrote, "the Diocese of New Ulm was created
and I suddenly found myself in the most rural diocese of the United States,
with no hope of getting out."[64] Three years after Roney arrived in Lake
Saint Croix Beach, the ecclesiastical districts that organize the Roman
Catholic Church in central Minnesota—and by extension, the lives of
priests—had suddenly shifted. The intention was to redistribute clerical

resources from the city to the prairie with the creation of the Diocese of New Ulm, and the move made good administrative sense, but the decision came from on high and as a shock to those priests with their boots on the ground.

Feeling as if a rug had been pulled out from under him, Roney realized that his vow of obedience to the bishop of the Archdiocese of Saint Paul no longer anchored him to the city that he loved so much; instead, his new allegiance to the bishop of the Diocese of New Ulm now tied him to an expanse of wide-open land to which Roney seemed allergic. "It was a bitter time for many priests," he remembered. "It took me, I know, many years before I overcame the resentment at being kicked out of my home diocese."[65] To the abjection of having been expelled from his ecclesiastical home, Roney might have also added the indignity of never being able to imagine an eventual return, and the looming possibility that Lake Saint Croix Beach, given its relative proximity to the Twin Cities, might very well be his most plum assignment. Maybe it was.

Roney would spend his career quietly shuffling from one remote parish to another, packing and unpacking his books into different sets of shelves on each move, and maybe this solitude could have been for the best. These small towns, one would think, would have kept him far afield from what he had once described from the pulpit, back at the seminary, as the "occasions of sin." There just weren't too many places in Belle Plaine (population 1,708), Walnut Grove (population 890), or Lafayette (population 507) where one could imagine a wicked curiosity welling up inside of Roney, where his soul might have become tempted by desire, distracted by disordered thoughts. This could only have been to his advantage—because Adam and Eve's original sin, he had preached only a few years prior, was not just biting into the fruit but also allowing themselves to drift ever closer to the tree. The pious priest, Roney had recommended, should avoid those places that might tempt him. Far from the glow of the big cities of Saint Paul and Minneapolis, towns like Benson (population 3,678) and even Willmar (population 12,869) seemed bereft of any temptation, of those trees that might bear fruit. For Roney, though, the opposite proved to be the case. Tragically, he spent his time on the prairie not only lingering within sin's occasions, but also biting into the apple.

II Becoming Deviant, 1987–1994

It Took Me Twenty Years to Get Angry

New Ulm, Minnesota

April 7, 1987

Inside the Office of the Bishop, next to the Cathedral of the Holy Trinity, a letter rested atop a mahogany desk. The note had been drafted and then redrafted (only to be typed and then retyped) by April: that young girl who had written a letter to her bishop about Father David Roney years ago and then set its pages on fire, back by the hedges. April eventually wrote another letter some twenty years later, and this time she mailed it:

> Dear Bishop Lucker,
>
> This letter is long over-due. I've composed parts of it in my head many times in the last decade. I will be 30 years old next month. This letter is in regards to some incidents that took place some 20 years ago at St. Mary's Church in Willmar while I was a student at the parochial school.[1]

April's letter is beautifully crafted, defiantly singular in its voice, but it was not the first that Raymond Lucker received in the spring of 1987, nor would it be the last. He had another on his desk. Each seemed to reach toward the next, and these letters were beginning to form a web of credible and (at last) legible accusations against Roney. "I have reason to believe that this is not an isolated incident," one reads.[2] "At your request I can report to you the incidents of the other girls," another letter adds.[3]

Recurring words and phrases knit these notes ever more closely together, creating a chorus of concern. Breaking decades of silence, they began to prod Lucker toward action: "I urge you to exercise your moral leadership in this difficult matter as expeditiously as possible."[4] One letter describes a moment at church when a woman mentioned Roney's abuse to the mother of another young girl: "She registered absolutely no surprise upon hearing this. She had heard this sort of thing before."[5] The letter insists in all caps that "THEY ARE NOT ALONE."[6] April warns Lucker that more letters are on their way: "Father David Roney took advantage of myself and several other girls that I know. I have called these women and they plan to write to you also, to let you know what specifically happened to them and what effect it has had on them. I did not have to look hard at all to find these people, and I feel there are many other women that Father Roney abused in one way or another."[7]

Lucker put his guard up almost immediately. An elderly man with creased jowls and lively, intelligent eyes, he had attended the Saint Paul Seminary a few years ahead of Roney, but Lucker proved to be the far more diligent student. Lucker completed a doctorate in sacred theology from the University of Saint Thomas in Rome and then a doctorate in education at the University of Minnesota. He published in academic journals, fancied himself a Church intellectual, and got involved in the mechanics of ecclesiastical governance. Quickly establishing himself as an expert in the study of Christian formation, Lucker became the bishop of New Ulm in 1975, a post that he would hold for twenty-five years. None of this prepared him to deal with the crisis that these letters precipitated. Instead, he naïvely stood at the pulpit and encouraged his parishioners to have sympathy—for the victims of clerical sexual abuse, yes, but also for the accused. He even asked the faithful to pray for these priests. "They are humans too," he reasoned. "We [priests] struggle over the years with sin, discouragement, anxiety and stress. We have to confront pride, greed, lust, dishonesty and all the other temptations that human beings are subject to."[8] Lucker echoed Augustine's insistence on the moral imperfection of these men, and he doubled down on the theological fact that Jesus was the only person to have ever lived a life free of sin. Underwriting these excuses was also the Church's belief that these men would always be priests, regardless of the sins that they committed.

Lucker's efforts were painfully misguided and fundamentally tone-deaf to the refrain that had begun to build. "Our prayers and love must go out to the priests too," he insisted. "[The priest] offered himself once to the service of God. He must now feel so alone, so wounded, so much in need of support."[9] April felt otherwise: "What finally led me to this point, the revealing of the incidents, was anger (it took me 20 years to get angry), and the fear that others have been harmed and are still being harmed by Father Roney."[10]

Why now? Why hadn't these women said anything sooner? Any one of them could have told their bishop their reasons, had Lucker bothered to ask: guilt, fear, denial, repression. Most of these women also mention in their letters some remorse for having waited so many years to approach their bishop—"We are very sorry it has taken us this long to get the courage to speak up about this"—and their tone is at times self-effacing: "We realize these incidents are minor in comparison to other types of sexual abuse."[11] Some of the letter-writers even verge on self-blame, as if they somehow should have known better despite their young age: "[We] were naive, as I'm sure most children were 20 years ago. We really didn't know what we were touching. We didn't like doing it and it scared us."[12] Others are sympathetic toward Bishop Lucker. "You have my prayers, cooperation, and compassionate understanding," writes the mother of one child. "Please call or write to me if you have any questions."[13] But April is undeterred:

> I have had many different feelings and emotions about what happened: feelings of fright, stupidity, nausea, anger, wickedness. It is hard to sit in church and not remember it, as it happened right *in* the church. There are also feelings of not wanting to hurt Father Roney, as I realize he had done much good for many people. But regardless of this, I feel the most important thing is to make sure that Father Roney's past problems are not current problems.[14]

April's impatience, and the impatience of all these women, is evident in their letters: "Every one of [the women to whom I spoke] said, yes, they felt it was time it was reported."[15] Yet a full account of why April and others wrote to Lucker in the spring of 1987 must make mention of a lawsuit that went public two months earlier. The plaintiff was a young man from Minnesota named Gregory John Riedel and the defendant was Father Thomas Adamson of the Archdiocese of Saint Paul and Minneapolis. The two first met in 1977, when the thirteen-year-old caught this priest's attention at a pool party for altar boys. "What I remember is his aloneness, I guess, with the group—from the group," Adamson later testified under oath.[16] The abuse began in a steam room at the local YMCA, after the two had played a round of racquetball, and it lasted two years, taking place all over town: in Adamson's car, at the rectory, and in gas-station restrooms. He also had sex with the boy in church basements after Sunday mass. "I looked at it more as a sin than a crime," Adamson later admitted to lawyers.[17]

The abuse devastated young Gregory, who went by Greg. By 1982, he had dropped out of high school, had been arrested for sexually assaulting a seven-year-old girl, and had landed in a program designed for sex offenders at a nearby prison facility. After being released from custody, during a heated conversation with his family, Greg broke his silence about Adamson. His parents were shocked. Betrayed by the one person in Greg's life they thought they could trust, his parents pressed the archdiocese for answers, but all they received was a personal check from Adamson for $1,600 to help cover some of Greg's medical bills. One concerned emergency care for a broken jaw. While under police custody, Greg's cellmates had learned of his record as a sex offender and attacked him. In the meantime, Adamson continued serving as a diocesan priest while abusing, by some estimates, more than one hundred children.[18]

Greg's parents cashed Adamson's check and hired Jeff Anderson, a young and brash personal injury attorney who would soon become the country's preeminent lawyer in matters of clerical sexual abuse. Anderson would be the first to sue a parish, the first to sue a diocese, and then the first to sue the Vatican, ultimately sending multiple dioceses throughout the United States into bankruptcy. Collecting 35 percent of every award, across a career that would eventually bleed the U.S. Church of billions of dollars, Anderson would one day become wealthy enough to buy his own private island. Well before all that, in 1984, Anderson filed a lawsuit on behalf of Greg's family, arguing that Church leadership had been negligent in their placement of Adamson.[19] The civil case would take years, but through the process of discovery, Anderson learned that as many as two dozen priests, nuns, bishops, and parish workers had some knowledge of

Adamson's sexual problems. Church leadership had also made clear and deliberate efforts to cover up this abuse by moving Adamson between parishes. Adamson's bishop offered large financial settlements to their families in exchange for silence. They even offered Greg's family upward of $1 million to keep quiet, but in early 1987, after more than two years of private and deeply frustrating negotiations with Church leadership, Anderson encouraged Greg's family to go public with their allegations against Adamson.[20]

The story made television and newspaper headlines across the state of Minnesota, and drew parallels with the events in Lafayette, Louisiana, with Father Gilbert Gauthe. A press release issued by Anderson on February 7, 1987, presented an expansive geography of abuse, with Adamson having preyed on young boys in more than a dozen parishes. The press release also mentioned that Greg and his parents "suffered severe and permanent emotional distress."[21] The press about Adamson resonated with those who had been abused by Roney. April, for one, saw something of her own experience in the news about Greg's case. Exactly two months after the coverage that brought Adamson's story to national audiences, April marshalled the confidence to detail her abuse in her letter to Lucker, which continued:

> It must have been soon after Father Roney replaced Father Cooney that things started to happen. On several of our visits to church Father Roney would be at the church organ. He would call us over to the choir area to talk to him. He would then take our hands in his and start swinging them. Then he would turn us around, our backs to his front and put our hands through the zipper opening in his pants. He wore no underwear. He then made us touch his penis and testicles. If we tried to pull away and remove our hands, he held them there—until *he* decided we could remove them. This happened to myself and [my friend] June, I believe, on more than one occasion. I honestly cannot remember how many times this happened.[22]

The effects of Roney's abuse on these victims' memories—traumatic memories that recede and reappear—are a touchstone of these letters. One woman, years later, had happened to overhear Roney's name at work and then suddenly felt like she had been "hit by a brick."[23] Another began to have nightmares about a room behind an altar.[24] And Carol, that young girl whose mother had caught her pressing a small statue of Christ against her sister's doll some twenty years earlier, ended up running into Roney on the streets of some small town in Minnesota. "He startled me," Carol recalled. "He also looked scared. Not remorseful. Scared. Like I knew something. Like I hadn't forgotten what he had done to me." By then, Roney would have known about the letters, and maybe he was afraid that even more women would put pen to paper; it is also reasonable to assume that Roney knew that the young girls he had abused were now women, and they were resilient. April had always been brave, years ago risking an encounter with Roney to pray and light votive candles at the church:

> After getting up the courage (this was very scary), we would sneak into the church and make sure that Father Roney was not there. We were as quiet as possible, for fear that he would hear us in the church. Sometimes he would come into the church and see us. After these episodes we were escorted to his office in the rectory and treated to a handful of M&M candies from his "famous," giant brandy snifter. I say "famous" because everyone I called remembered this and mentioned it.[25]

What did these women want? Though Lucker might have preferred to feign ignorance in the face of such a question, he knew full well what the answer was. The mother of one woman details the kind of response she would have appreciated from her bishop. In her letter, she mentions that she is "filled with the gnawing uncertainty that, given patterns of exhibitionism and pedophilia, such behavior may not have ceased." She wants to know if "a spirit of openness could be further fostered," and she even provides the bishop with the beginning of a plan, suggesting that he publish "a letter in the Diocesan Newsletter, assuring past and current possible victims that the church is ready to offer support and counseling so that they can rid themselves of this awful secret that they may be carrying."[26] This woman makes the case that breaking the ongoing silence and secrecy around Roney's abuse would provide an opening toward change and healing.[27]

Lucker was certainly capable of moral leadership. He was already something of a rabble-rouser, at least by Church standards. He had long advocated for the ordination of women and of married men, and he had always been a leader on matters of social justice, championing the rights of immigrants and protesting U.S. military interventions in Central

America. He often railed against U.S. imperialism with a message of love: "Jesus teaches us to serve, to love one another, to give, to be last, to become as little children, to turn the other cheek, to forgive."[28] Lucker also spoke with an almost prophetic tone about the diocese's Mission in the war-torn highlands of Guatemala: an expansive religious and social outreach program founded and funded by the Diocese of New Ulm.

Located in a small Indigenous town, the Mission ran a medical clinic, elementary school, and orphanage, as well as a coffee farm whose product could not be Fair Trade–certified because the Mission offered local farmers a price for their harvest that stridently outpaced international standards. Its signature program, however, was land redistribution, an effort that helped thousands of families acquire three acres of property, on which they produced corn and beans to eat and coffee to sell. "In reality," Lucker preached, despite this philanthropic abundance, "we have received much more [from the Mission] than we have given. Our commitment to the Mission [in Guatemala] has reminded us of our responsibility as followers of Jesus Christ to feed the hungry, to clothe the naked, to shelter the homeless."[29] He spoke with pride of his own parishioners, many of them local farmers, who committed a percentage of their earnings to the Mission, sponsored an orphan, and even visited Guatemala amid its ongoing civil war to witness what they considered to be the work of God. Lucker too traveled there with some regularity, so it must have given him pause when a woman ended her letter to him on an ominous note: "My concern extends, of course, to the children of our mission."[30] She knew, as did Lucker, that Roney traveled to Guatemala several times a year to work with the Mission and care for its orphans.

Lucker ultimately balked at the opportunity to lead on the issue of clerical sexual abuse, siding not so much with his priests but rather with the fundamental, deeply theological notion that priests themselves are fallible, and hence that they deserve the same forgiveness and compassion as any other sinner: "We [priests] continually strive through prayer, reading, retreats, spiritual direction and the sacraments to remain true to our commitments," Lucker preached.[31] This sentiment guided Lucker to place April's letter in Roney's personnel file but to refrain from disclosing the abuse to anyone in the parishes where Roney had worked. Lucker also did not initiate an investigation, and he did not make any of the information he had acquired about Roney available to others—neither in the Diocese of New Ulm nor at its Mission in Guatemala. Instead, Lucker entrusted his director of priest personnel, Father William Sprigler, with handling the matter.

Sprigler's note to the mother of one affected child reads, in part, "I received a copy of your letter, which you sent to Bishop Lucker. Please be assured that Father Roney is in a facility for evaluation of the situation."[32] The letter does not give much more information, at least nothing that clarifies what "the situation" might mean or in what kind of facility Roney had been placed. The nature of the evaluation was also left undefined. Overall, the letter is a rather lean response to what had been a very intimate description of sexual assault, submitted by a mother who understandably had expected both more and less from her bishop: more compassion and less aloofness; more transparency and less obfuscation; more openness and less defensiveness. Lucker and Sprigler were confident in their approach, if only because they felt that they were being proactive. A generation or two earlier, Lucker would later note, "We just admonished [these priests] to stop, change their lives, use their willpower. We willingly gave them another chance if they showed some signs of improvement."[33] There was in that earlier moment no discernible plan in place for dealing with sexually abusive priests.

By 1987, however, there was not only a plan in place but also a program up and running for clerics with sexual problems. Thus, at Lucker's orders, Sprigler sent Roney to a treatment facility in New Mexico for a weeklong psychological evaluation. The facility was run by a Roman Catholic religious order known as the Servants of the Paraclete: a ragtag outfit committed to serving and thus saving wayward priests. It was the very same religious order that had treated Thomas Adamson for his sexual problems—and, truth be told, the same facility where Sprigler himself had received treatment for his own sexual misconduct. While serving as a priest in the Archdiocese of San Antonio, Texas, Sprigler sexually abused two young boys in 1976.[34] These transgressions landed him at the New Mexico facility, where he ended up staying for years. He even joined the staff, taken with the mission of ministering to sexually abusive priests, before moving to Minnesota in 1983 to take up the managerial post he held at the time of April's letter. Roney—like Sprigler and Adamson before him, and like hundreds of other clerics from around the world—sought renewal and relief from his "situation" at a retreat center set atop 2,000 rambling acres of New Mexico land known as Via Coeli, "the way to heaven."

Making Up People

Jemez Springs, New Mexico

April 12, 1987

Brittlebush and driftwood.

A bone white crucifix baking in the sun.

Squat cabins on the horizon.

Father David Roney's bedroom was modest, offering him little more than a bed, a desk, and a trifold brochure. The brochure was nothing fancy: black and white, and straight from the copy machine. "You are a priest," it explained, "and you have just arrived at Via Coeli. What's it all about?" An answer immediately followed: "It's all about YOU, really, and about the people who are here to assist you in any way possible while you are a guest-priest with us. It's about the efforts that will be made here to assist you as a human person who is by Baptism a son of God and by Orders a priest of God."[35] The brochure laid out the rhythm of the place, with a clear sense of schedule and even a note on where and when to do laundry. It also let guest-priests like Roney know that they would be kept on a short leash: "Walks to the local post office or stores in the village require permission of your house director. The village proper of Jemez Springs is also ordinarily out of bounds."[36] None of these men enjoyed freedom of movement, and this was by design. It was how Father Gerald Fitzgerald had originally imagined the place.

Fitzgerald, a hard-nosed priest from Boston, founded the Servants of the Paraclete and its Via Coeli Monastery in 1947 to fill an ecclesiastical void. The Roman Catholic Church at the time made no provisions for priests who proved themselves unable to serve in their role. Instead, those who lost their way from substance abuse or a lack of faith ran the risk of not only falling out of favor with the Church but also failing to achieve eternal salvation. This affront to clerical dignity upset Fitzgerald so much that he petitioned bishops across the United States to support what he would later describe as "the M.A.S.H. unit of the Roman Catholic Church."[37]

With the backing of the Archbishop of Santa Fe and some funds from Cardinal Francis Spellman of New York, Fitzgerald purchased an expansive plot of land in New Mexico, upon which sat the ruins of a Franciscan monastery and an abandoned hotel. There, Fitzgerald offered guest-priests, as he called them, holistic programs that promised to rekindle the piety that had once attracted these men to the priesthood. But his center soon began receiving clerics who had been accused of sexually abusing minors. By 1950, priests from thirty-five dioceses and nine religious orders filled his facility in New Mexico past capacity.[38] They crammed into bedrooms, slept on patios, and huddled in cabins. Some priests even hitchhiked across the country for a chance to spend some time at Via Coeli. They were all in search of a transformation, a release from their impulses. Roney was no different.

"Why have you come?" one of the center's many forms asked Roney upon his arrival.

"I need to get my thinking straightened out," he wrote, "to recover some enthusiasm and drive. Others have come here and been healed. I don't know how they were healed, but I am willing to try."[39]

Fitzgerald, in the early years, ran these priests through a veritable gauntlet of spiritual exercises: morning prayers and meditations; the rosary and benedictions; spiritual readings and holy hours on top of the regular church services. Fitzgerald fixated on what he considered to be a misalignment of the human will. These priests were disordered, he insisted, and individuals born of sin can only seek salvation by diligently submitting to the rigors of the Roman Catholic Church. "The will must capitulate to God," Fitzgerald wrote. "The intellect must be captivated by the thought of Him."[40] Not a single member of his team had a graduate degree in psychology, psychiatry, or social work: the program was administered entirely by clerics. Often rejecting the disease concept altogether, Fitzgerald relied on neither the language nor the logic of pathology, instead trafficking in a wandering constellation of moral judgments: "intimacies with the youth," "abnormalities of sex," and "aberrations."[41] Constructing clerical sexual abuse into a problem that only the grace of God could solve, Fitzgerald argued that these appetites could not be cured because they were not sicknesses so much as "weaknesses."[42] Nothing could change his mind. "If [a priest's] compulsions are something he is not morally responsible for both in their initiation and continuance," he once wrote a fellow priest, "then Calvary becomes delusion and redemption worn-out farce."[43] The defining characteristic of these men was a proclivity for "sins with the young," in Fitzgerald's own words, and he never flinched in his opinion of them. "These men are devils," Fitzgerald wrote to a colleague, "and the wrath of God is upon them."[44] The only real solution, by his own account, wasn't even possible: "It were better they had not been born."[45]

By the mid-1970s, however, the Servants of the Paraclete had begun working with local psychologists and hiring resident psychiatrists. They offered a robust approach to spiritual rehabilitation that largely mirrored the work of sexual disorder clinics found in secular settings. Guest-priests such as Roney still attended daily mass, pursued spiritual direction, and prostrated themselves to the Blessed Sacrament, with church bells punctuating the day. In addition to these religious activities, though, many of the priests also received prescriptions for the contraceptive injection Depo-Provera to quell their sexual desires, while others found themselves hooked up to a plethysmograph: a machine with an inflatable cuff that secures to the base of the penis, measuring changes in blood flow while the subject listens to or watches sexually explicit material.[46] And all of them, Roney included, completed a personal history sheet:

Name: David Arthur Roney
Date: April 12, 1987
Current Address: Church of St. Gregory
440—6th St.—P.O. Box 5
Lafayette, MN 56054
Referred to Foundation House by: Rev William Sprigler
Date of Birth: January 3, 1921

Place of Birth: St Paul, MN

Date of Ordination: August 18, 1945

Age: 66

Most Recent Occupation: Pastor—Mission Office Director[47]

The personal history sheet prompted Roney to "give a history of any psychiatric/psychological treatments." He answered, "None."[48] Not once had a psychologist or psychiatrist assessed his thoughts, inclinations, habits, sensations, or opinions. Never had a medical expert tested his personality, recorded his resting pulse, or collected samples of his blood and urine in some effort to name the nature and quality of his sexual disorders. He had never even visited a therapist until his trip to New Mexico, and thus he had never had to endure the consequences of a diagnosis, such as treatment plans or restrictions on work, travel, and proximity to minors. Roney's sense of self had never been contorted by the truth of science, and his identity had never been defined by it. Never once had Roney been prompted to look at himself in the mirror and see anything other than a priest, albeit one who sinned far more often than even he thought acceptable.

Roney's personal history sheet transformed him. With its attention to scientific precision and psychological assumptions about the unconscious, the Servants of the Paraclete converted this quiet and lonesome priest from one kind of person into another: from someone with a moral problem into a sexual deviant. All it took for Roney to take on this new identity was a week of testing, culminating in a diagnosis and a proposed course of treatment. This is not to say that Roney's actions prior to his visit to New Mexico were not sexually abusive towards children. They were. But before arriving at Via Coeli, his actions, though deeply consequential, had yet to congeal into an identity. While there was no precise moment at which Roney became a recognizable sexual deviant—as there had been when he became a priest—one could certainly locate the start of this process in the moment when Roney began to complete his personal history sheet. This self-evaluation constitutes the first thirteen pages of an archive—and a corresponding identity—that Roney would spend the rest of his life trying to outrun: "Give a history of your sexuality: Adolescence was difficult, as it is for everybody. But, probably especially difficult because there was no one to talk to about it. My main problems have always been mental, which is, I think, unfortunate. Sex itself is far more mental than physical, and unfortunately, the mental faculties do not decay as fast as the physical."[49]

The philosopher Michel Foucault in *The History of Sexuality* tells a similar story of transformation, about a peasant named Jouy in 1867.[50] According to Foucault, Jouy was an odd man who slept in barns and stables, living hand-to-mouth while completing odd jobs. At the edges of a French town, at the "border of a field," Jouy played a game called "curdled milk" with young girls. This is something that Foucault mentions rather sympathetically.[51] Foucault calls the caresses that these young girls extended to Jouy, in exchange for a few coins, an "inconsequential bucolic pleasure," describing the game as an "everyday occurrence in the life of village sexuality."[52] Whether Foucault is guilty of an irresponsible nostalgia for some bygone era of sexuality is a worthwhile conversation. More germane to his conceptual concerns, however, is the way that examination, diagnosis, and paperwork transformed Jouy from a person with a moral problem into a sexual deviant.

First, the parents of one young girl reported Jouy to the mayor of the village. Then the mayor reported Jouy to the gendarmes, and the gendarmes presented Jouy to the judge, "who indicted him and turned him over first to a doctor, then to two other experts who not only wrote their report but also had it published."[53] The process changed Jouy, Foucault argues, from a simple man with base desires into "a pure object of medicine and knowledge."[54] He became a sexual deviant. Roney's intake initiated a similar transformation:

List major medical and physical events:
Hepatitis after one trip to Guatemala.
An ear infection that affected my hearing.
High blood-pressure.
Usual ailments of advancing age.

What are your assets/talents/capabilities/strengths?
Quick thinker, if not deep.
Wide range of interests.
Good speaker.
Loyalty.
Understanding human nature.

What are your weaknesses?

Superficiality.

Laziness.

Self-indulgence.

Waste time.[55]

Authorities arrested and examined Jouy in 1867, and this time frame makes sense. The late nineteenth century witnessed a rush of new sciences, many of them interpretive and speculative. There was the rise of anthropology, sociology, psychiatry, demography, criminology, and phrenology, for example, as well as the expansion of biology, medicine, ethics, pedagogy, and political criticism. Each of these disciplines did their best to quantify and qualify the human condition through new modes of description and observation. In the broadest of terms, they aimed at setting standards—at measuring their objects in relation to an idea of what was "normal." Perhaps unsurprisingly, the pursuit of the normal generated an exaggerated interest in the abnormal, with these same experts creating elaborate categories to describe the kinds of people who did not fit within the supposedly "normal" standards of society.[56] The Servants of the Paraclete, in turn, explored the depths of Roney's psyche to determine his abnormalities, with great attention paid to his childhood:

Describe major events of your pre-school years and your feelings about them:
First real memory: coming home from the dentist's office at about age three, maybe four. My mother pulled me in a coaster wagon and bought me a pack of gum—five sticks. I put all of them in my mouth at once. . . . Was probably quieter than most pre-school boys. Liked to pretend I was driving a car.[57]

Philosophically, there are two ways to understand this compulsion to define the abnormal. The first—known as the realist position—insists that if one looks closely and carefully enough, one can find categories of abnormality that appear in nature. According to this view, normal sexual behavior is associated with one set of characteristics, and abnormal sexual behavior corresponds to another set of existing practices. This realist approach extends tremendous confidence to the scientific pursuit of universals. Normal and abnormal sexuality exist, this position holds; one must simply define and document them.

A counter-interpretation, however, builds on what philosophers call a nominalist position: a sense that universals do not appear in nature but, rather, emerge through our efforts to categorize and classify. Thus, experts construct abnormalities, rather than observe them.[58] Foucault, with his attention to the archive, would help popularize this kind of interpretation, which has since generated a well-established philosophical position: that what counts as abnormal is the result of historically specific efforts at description and classification. A crucial implication of this position is that the identities that form around specific abnormalities—the identity of the pedophile, for example—are also constructed and historical.[59] From a nominalist perspective, then, Roney became abnormal through the completion of his intake form, as he grappled with the words to describe his own sexuality within the context of a clinical assessment:

> ELEMENTARY SCHOOL YEARS: Quiet, with outbursts of excessive talking. Rather liked school, but wouldn't admit it. Loved reading. Was sometimes scolded for staying indoors instead of playing outside. Baseball became a passion. In our neighborhood, there were few children, so seldom enough for a full team. . . . As I recall it, I really had no close friends my age.[60]

Similarly, the judge and the doctors who examined Jouy—in their quest to understand in purely scientific terms what kind of person they had on their hands—transformed Jouy into a deviant, just as Roney's completion of the intake form created him anew:[61]

> Describe major events in [high school years] and your feelings about them: Except for one year in public school (ninth grade), these years were spent in boys' school—preparatory seminary. Generally, I liked it. Made good friends. One in particular became quite close. Did well in classes, but not spectacular. A rebellious streak broke out. I didn't obey the rules that much, but was so quiet, hardly anyone suspected. . . . For a year or so, got terribly shy, especially among women. Still am reserved. . . . The absolute insistence on not being with girls was probably unhealthy.[62]

The Servants of the Paraclete deployed psychotherapeutic modes of description to document and define the nature of the priests sent to them but ended up creating new identities for men like Roney. Guest-priests at Via Coeli, for instance, completed a medical examination after the intake form, and it included a pulmonary function and exercise stress test along with a treadmill test and an electrocardiogram. There was also a battery of blood tests with such abbreviations as CBC, SMAC 20, T4, VDRL, UA, FSH, Pt, and PTT, as well as a close look at testosterone levels and the amount of luteinizing hormone in the blood. A pair of psychiatrists completed an interview with each subject—blind to any previous assessments, reports, or evaluations to avoid prejudice. Much of the interview was interpretive, consisting of broad efforts at mapping Roney's unconscious.

Underline any of the below that apply to you at this time:

betrayed	<u>capable</u>	disturbed	peaceful
<u>sad</u>	accepted	<u>helpless</u>	<u>problems with sex</u>
generous	good	dramatic	overly suspicious
depressed	energetic	fussy	<u>obsessive thoughts</u>
<u>clever</u>	<u>empathetic</u>	fascinated	trapped
unfriendly	weight loss	weight gain	unique
<u>embarrassed</u>	ambivalent	<u>lazy</u>	<u>embarrassed</u>
rejected	abandoned	free	miserable
excited	dishonest	<u>exhausted</u>	<u>helpful</u>
understood	<u>inadequate</u>	tremors	<u>hard to concentrate</u>
<u>defeated</u>	foolish	alcoholic	<u>afraid of people</u>
frantic	<u>anxious</u>	unique	unable to relax
tranquil	<u>flexible</u>	<u>humorous</u>	disbelief in God
impulsive	ignored	<u>gentle</u>	spiritual problems
<u>shy</u>	hurt	vulnerable	change mind often
confident	<u>tense</u>	hated	<u>loving</u>
<u>pressured</u>	panicky	blackouts	<u>give information freely</u>

Roney then underwent a series of tests to assess cognitive abilities, personality type, and psychopathologies.[63] There were at least a dozen on
offer, including the Edwards Personal Preference Schedule, Wechsler
Adult Intelligence Scale, and Bender Visual-Motor Gestalt Test, as well
as the Myers-Briggs Type Indicator, Goodenough–Harris Draw-a-
Person Test, and Shipley Institute of Living Scale.[64] Following these
examinations, the staff prepared a written report, which included a
summary of relevant history and presenting problems, test results,
description of personality style and symptoms, and recommendations
for intervention. The report was then integrated with other portions of
the evaluation, including the psychiatric and psychological interviews as
well as directed conversations with a spiritual director and a program
director, the life history survey, health survey, alcohol and drug abuse survey, medical examination, blood tests, physiological survey, and spirituality profile.

The final report provided a comprehensive assessment of Roney, with
suggestions for possible treatment. It formed the beginning of an archive
that affirmed the abnormality of this priest.[65] Through it all, across a full
week of assessment, Roney changed from a man playing games with
young girls at the edge of town into a recognizable and definable sexual
deviant. Roney's deviancy came into being with each question and answer,
each interview and assessment, each observation and evaluation. His
transformation was not sudden, as it was when he became a priest, but it
was complete.

> Describe your behavior [as an adult]: I don't know how to describe this. I
> was a reasonably good pastor and certainly had a good reputation. On the
> other hand, my enthusiasm and ambition gradually declined. Only my
> enjoyment of preaching stayed intact. My spiritual life has never been satis-
> factory. For a time, I tried the charismatic movement. It did teach me to pray
> better, but I could never generate the enthusiasm they required. My lack of
> piety has always distressed me. I tried to improve myself. I guess I went
> through a lot of motions without understanding things.[66]

By the end of Roney's week in New Mexico, the Servants of the Paraclete
had created the very condition that they set out to cure. They presented
Roney with a problem (sexual deviancy) and a solution (a ten-month

program at Via Coeli). In doing so, they provided him with the first ink-
lings of what a new future might look like, leading him to speculate—
however tentatively—about the possibility of permanent escape:

> What is your view of the future? Strangely—to me—administration is no
> longer something I enjoy. Nor do I have a great affection for meetings.
> Retirement is highly unlikely, first, because of lack of money; second,
> because of my mother. Eventually it might be possible to retire in Guatemala,
> but I'm not sure I'm up to the strain of the work there.[67]

Crossroads

Lafayette, Minnesota

May 18, 1987

Roney faced a difficult decision. While in New Mexico, he had seen his fellow guest-priests walking from one building to another. There was Saint Joseph's Hospice (nine beds) for terminally ill clerics, Voluntas Dei Infirmary (twelve beds) for chronically unwell priests and brothers, Villa Regina Mundi (seventeen beds) for those clerics who served on staff, Via Coeli Monastery (thirty-eight beds) for guest-priests such as himself seeking evaluation and treatment, and Lourdes Retreat (twelve beds) for those men of God who had sought treatment for their moral deficiencies and then had made the calculated decision to never leave the compound ever again.[68] Now, having received an official invitation from the staff at Via Coeli, Roney was unsure of whether to take up one of those beds himself for a ten-month program.

> Dear David:
>
> I have enclosed the report that was recently done for you here [in Jemez Springs, New Mexico]. After consulting with the evaluating team, we believe that it would be helpful, at this time in your life, for you to participate in the program here, which begins on July 13, 1987. However, since you did not seem strongly motivated to make this program, we feel that we need to make other recommendations since you may decide not to come.[69]

Roney found the Servants of the Paraclete's commitment to monastic piety appealing. He was, after all, a priest of Fitzgerald's generation, attracted to the mysteries of God's grace and the language of sin. He agreed that the sacramental life of the Church could align his will with the grace of God. But at sixty-six years of age, Roney had little patience for self-reflection and even less interest in the possibility of a breakthrough. The prospects of a weekly class called "psychodrama" or the program's human sexuality seminars and attitudinal healing workshops were far from desirable.[70] He questioned not only the supposed curative power of poetry courses and sharing circles but also, more fundamentally, the idea that he might be sick in the first place. Roney thought it was all infantilizing.[71] A sample schedule had accompanied his letter, and it must have sent something of a shudder down Roney's spine. Despite echoing the *horarium* that Roney had enjoyed at the Saint Paul Seminary so many years ago, the curriculum at Via Coeli differed significantly, ditching the theology of Thomas Aquinas for the psychology of Carl Jung:

Sample Module

A.M.	P.M.
6:30 .... Rising Bell	12:15 .... Main Meal
7:00 .... Bell for Prayers	1:15 .... Art Therapy
7:30 .... Bell for Breakfast	3:15 .... Psychiatrist
8:00 .... Prayer Before the Sacrament	5:10 .... Human Sexuality
8:40 .... Common Morning Prayer	6:00 .... Supper
9:15 .... Psychodrama	7:00 .... Yoga Class
11:30 .... Eucharistic Liturgy	10:00 .... Nighttime Prayer

Roney was not a total cynic. He had flipped through the books placed at his bedside in New Mexico, with their assumptions about the unconscious realm. Together, their titles seemed to tell a story: *Sacrament of Sexuality* (1986), *Make Friends with Your Shadow* (1981), and *Please Understand Me* (1978).[72] He could get behind the idea, at least intellectually, that the conscious mind is like a small island in the vast sea of the unconscious, and that one's conscious awareness grows through the application of innate mental functions like thinking, feeling, sensing, and intuiting. But Roney was far too skeptical to consider ten months of turning inward, of making friends with his shadow from sunrise to well past sunset.

Beyond the question of whether to accept the invitation to return to New Mexico, the letter and the report it enclosed had another awkward consequence for Roney: they saddled him with a diagnosis. He might be able to turn down the ten-month program, as the Servants of the Paraclete fully expected he would, but he could never completely outrun the report, because he was no longer a priest with a moral problem but rather a sexual deviant. Thus, Roney found himself increasingly hemmed in, whether in New Mexico or Minnesota, where his freedom of movement was seemingly as constricted as when he was at Via Coeli. Bishop Lucker had already moved Roney from the town of Willmar to the village of Lafayette, to evade what appeared to be an emerging scandal. The center of Lafayette, itself something of an island, measured only a few square blocks and seemed to drift amid a vast sea of farmland. This isolated and isolating world could have effectively disappeared the aging priest, but the letters Lucker continued to receive threatened to bring Roney back into focus. The bishop was at a loss as to what to do with him.

Roney's evaluation by the Servants of the Paraclete had left him feeling ambivalent about his remaining years. "I am still good at many things," Roney mentioned while in New Mexico.[73] "I am a good preacher; a good celebrant. I am loyal and honest. More than is sometimes good for me. Like many reserved people, when I let go, I go too far."[74] His defensiveness signaled that his time with the Servants of the Paraclete had unnerved him. It had forced Roney to assess his life closely and had left him weary and morose as well as emotionally exhausted. "I am dissatisfied with my spiritual life," he wrote. "Find it hard to pray. I enjoy presiding at baptisms and, strangely, funerals. I would be happy if I never had to preside at a wedding again. I feel old."[75] He also knew that he did not have much capacity for change—for a true conversion. "My future is obviously limited," he wrote near the end of his time in New Mexico. "There is no longer a possibility of large parishes; important assignments."[76] He just wanted to be left alone.

The Servants of the Paraclete did offer Roney a clear path to renewal— even if a return to his unencumbered past was no longer in the cards. After his proposed ten months of treatment in New Mexico, he would have met with the program's social workers. They would have developed strategies for Roney not only to better manage himself in the future but also to find a new assignment. "When necessary," a brochure for the Servants of the Paraclete explains, "the social worker will make the necessary telephone calls and write the necessary letters to help a person find a ministry placement."[77] These placements included positions within the Servants of the Paraclete's own network of renewal centers. By the late 1980s, the order ran dozens of facilities throughout the United States and around the world—in Europe, Asia, Africa, and Latin America—that were increasingly staffed by recovering priests unable to live on their own.

In the end, Roney did not commit to the proposed ten months of treatment in New Mexico. Even still, his life became a flexible, somewhat mobile version of the program that he had refused to complete. For the next two years, from 1987 to 1989, Roney existed under a state of intermittent psychological examination in ways that made him a continued object of medical knowledge.[78] After passing on his chance to spend the better part of a year in New Mexico, working the program and creating a better version of himself, Roney had received the following recommendations from the Servants of the Paraclete:

1. We recommend that you meet regularly (at least once a week) with a qualified therapist, psychologist, or psychiatrist;
2. We recommend that you and this therapist keep in regular contact with Bishop Lucker concerning the progress of this therapy;
3. We recommend that you share the contents of this evaluation with your therapist;
4. We recommend that you meet monthly with a qualified Spiritual Director;
5. We recommend that you attend regularly a priests' support group in the Diocese.[79]

Lucker and Father William Sprigler, who had been copied on this letter, would soon hold a conference call with Roney to discuss the practical and interpersonal benefits of attending the program in New Mexico. This was not an elaborate conversation so much as a brief exchange between colleagues. Sprigler encouraged Roney one more time to give the program a try and to remain open to change. Sprigler himself had found Via Coeli inspiring, and he reminded Roney that he had even committed several years of his own ministry to the Servants of the Paraclete. After his problems in San Antonio with underage boys, Sprigler found his calling first as a guest-priest and then as a staff member with the Servants of the Paraclete, shuttling troubled clerics from the chapel to therapy and then back to the chapel. Sprigler had loved the sense of transformation that this rugged terrain seemed to promise. Each sunset and sunrise enacted nothing short of a miracle—a veritable resurrection that ultimately led to Sprigler's promotion to personnel director in the Diocese of New Ulm.[80]

Doing what he could to convince Roney to at least give the program a chance, Sprigler also mentioned that Via Coeli offered priests such as him a soft landing. The compound had a swimming pool and a nine-hole pitch and putt golf course as well as Ping-Pong tables, card tables, and dart boards. The combination of weekly bingo games, beginner Spanish classes, nearby trout fishing, nature walks, and wilderness hikes made the ten months not just livable but, perhaps surprisingly, enjoyable.[81] But Roney was obstinate, willing to concede some of his flaws but unwilling to do anything about them. In some respects, he considered himself too far gone to be saved. "I think I developed a great tolerance for human beings," he reasoned in New Mexico. "Maybe too much. Eventually one begins to accept everything as normal."[82] Sprigler then pressed the program's more practical virtues, reminding Roney that its social workers could parlay a clean bill of health into a ministerial assignment, albeit one limited to an adult population. The entire program enacted the process of renewal by hitching a cleric to a diagnosis that he could then overcome through treatment, leading to assignments and promotions. Again, Roney declined, insisting that his chance at restoring some sense of self-discipline and personal dignity should come in the great plains of his home state of Minnesota rather than the craggy mountains of New Mexico. Ultimately, Roney submitted to most (but not all) of the prescribed commitments. As much as he might have thought that such a course of activity would help stem the growth of his archival footprint, it had the opposite effect. Roney's decision to pursue outpatient treatment rather than stay in New Mexico would trigger an avalanche of files that would go far beyond the initial report from Jemez Springs, ultimately cementing his new identity as a sexual deviant in painstaking and irrevocable detail.

An Avalanche of Files

Minneapolis, Minnesota

July 20, 1993

There were stacks of depositions, affidavits, and testimonies, plus corre-spondence of all kinds: handwritten notes, formal statements, and the occasional fax. A paralegal named Susan corralled them into files and then organized those files into archives, all at the behest of her employer: a downtown law firm whose client roster included the Diocese of New Ulm. She mostly enjoyed the work, happily finding order amid chaos, but a chance encounter with one stack of files triggered a rush of emotions.

The materials supported a claim of child sexual abuse against Father David Roney, with two documents chronicling the diocese's defense. The first was a confidential report to Bishop Raymond Lucker written by Roney's therapist. The evaluation did its best to close the books on what this therapist claimed to have been a time-specific and very distant chap-ter of Roney's life. The report conceded that Roney "had strong sexual curiosity, not so much for physical experience, but for physical feelings," but the report pushed this curiosity well into the past.[83] "There was a period from the age of 40 to 57," the report reads, "when [Roney's] curios-ity led to the kinds of experiences he has been accused of now."[84] But this behavior had dissipated, the report maintained. Roney's curiosity had run its course. Now well past seventy years of age, Roney was "motivated to move beyond that behavior."[85]

The second set of papers made the unusual argument that the claimant might be mistaken in her accusations against this priest, because Roney at the time of this alleged abuse was far more curious about boys than girls. The claimant, now an adult woman, would not have been his type. Susan knew better—in part because she had been raised in the town of Willmar, had attended Saint Mary's Elementary School, and had even gone to the church's Sunday services, sometimes just to hear Roney preach. Her most visceral reason for objection, however, was the blunt fact that Roney had sexually abused her as a child and, as she had by that point learned, each one of her three sisters.

Unable to find order amid so much chaos, Susan reached out to Lucker. She asked the Diocese of New Ulm to pay for her therapy, and the bishop quickly complied, relieved that Susan did not seem immediately interested in a lawsuit. The problem for Lucker, though, was that the archive that had come to define Roney as a sexual deviant thickened still further once Susan entered treatment. Susan's therapist, for instance, advised her to write an official statement of her abuse, and this document landed in Roney's archive alongside all the others. The therapist then encouraged Susan to write a letter directly to Roney, and this too ended up in Roney's archive. So did Roney's own written response, which Susan requested at her therapist's behest:

Dear Susan,

I cried when I read your statement. It seems incredible to me now that I could have been so selfish, that I could have hurt someone so badly. The consequences for you, for your life, even for your relationship with God, were far greater than anything I could then imagine.

I am deeply sorry for what you have suffered and apologize for any pain I have caused. I never intended harm even when I caused it.

My own life has been irredeemably changed by this. The years of therapy I have taken have opened my mind but not eased my feelings. It is not easy to look back on my life. It is not comfortable to look at the future.

I do not pray for forgiveness. I pray only that you may be given some measure of peace and comfort, that the love of God and the love of other people will surround you and comfort you.

Sincerely,

Father David Roney[86]

Susan found the letter to be as insincere and manipulative as the man she once knew.[87] It was insultingly brief, and it also seemed to position him as the victim of his own appetites. Somehow *his* life had been "irredeemably changed by this." Maybe it was an impression that Roney had gathered from his own therapy sessions. One confidential report to Lucker from Roney's therapist stresses his "obsessive-compulsive personality," how "his father was strict," and how Roney "compares himself negatively to others."[88] At times, the therapist even seems to defend Roney, seeking to reject the imposed label of the sexually deviant priest by emphasizing his humanity. "Dave's identity as a human person," the therapist wrote, "was not experienced enough or affirmed enough for him to have confidence in his own worth." This therapist's report offers Lucker an extraordinarily generous interpretation of Roney: "Dave, as you know, is basically a very good man."[89]

None of this could distract Susan from what she read as Roney's thorough lack of empathy.[90] Susan, with the support of her therapist, requested a meeting with Roney. She wanted to speak with her abuser face to face during one of her therapy sessions. Roney agreed, presumably to stave off the chance of litigation yet again. He even, almost unbelievably, allowed Susan to record the fifty-minute session. The cassette tape that this meeting yielded soon disappeared, having been misplaced when Susan moved from one apartment to another, but its one-time existence speaks to the trove of documentary materials that proliferated around Roney, constructing him ever further as a sexual deviant through reports, letters, and even audio recordings.[91]

The two sat across from each other in Susan's therapist's office, a quiet space with thick carpet and oversized chairs. The tape recorder softly whirred atop a coffee table as Roney fell silent, ostensibly to allow Susan to recount her abuse and the effect it had had on her life. As the meeting ended and Susan began to realize just how little Roney had said, she pressed him with a few direct questions. The first was whether he even knew her name. As a child, Susan had once rationalized her abuse as the dark side of Roney's otherwise bright interest in her. His attention, however destructive, had made her feel special, and she cherished the idea that her parish priest had set her apart from the other children, that he adored her. But Roney, it turned out, had never known Susan's full name, neither

years earlier when Susan was a child nor even at their meeting in her therapist's office. He drew a complete blank. To which Susan, suddenly flushed
with anger, asked Roney whether he still cut holes in the pockets of his
pants. Roney refused to answer, looking away in shame. All he could muster was some comment about soon moving to Guatemala. The diocese's
Mission, which he had visited at least once a year since 1973, would be a
fresh start for him, he told Susan. It would be his last chance for renewal.

Had Susan seen the rest of Roney's file, she would have known that the
Mission had always been, and would continue to be, a place of sexual
transgression for Roney. During his annual visits, he had spent his time in
the Indigenous highlands of Guatemala seeking out children, plying them
with candy and toys, and then spending long afternoons with them—in
the park, at the lake, and in his bedroom. Inconceivably, Roney documented his trips to Guatemala with a monthly column for his diocese's
newspaper. One entry from 1982 is titled "In Love with a Beautiful Girl,"
and the article begins with a confession. "I'm in love," Roney writes, "Have
been for years." The object of his affection is a young orphan. "I fell in love
immediately," Roney continues. "She didn't. Even at that age [of three] she
had a mind of her own and screamed if I came near."[92] His more than one
hundred published articles present a strange tapestry of compulsions. "I'm
partial to the orphanage," he admits. "I suppose it's because children can
love back."[93] He wrote often about children in Guatemala: "Children, it
seems, are much the same in any culture, charming, beautiful, dirty, play-
ful."[94] In these articles, Roney appears oblivious to how incriminating his
writing might one day appear. "Personally," he notes, "I have a high tolerance for dirt. I can hug a dirty child just as easily as a clean one."[95] He even
set some of these children apart. "My favorite child in the orphanage," he
wrote in 1983, "celebrates her eleventh birthday on Valentine's Day so she
has reached an age where it is no longer easy for her to show affection."
Roney often included even the most peculiar of details. "At first it hurt not
to see her as often as usual," he adds about his favorite child, "but we did
have a good talk, and the night before I left, we cried together. We always
do that."[96]

These were not just the musings of an old man. Roney's therapist, in
one report to Lucker, conceded that "Dave did have one incident while he
was in therapy with me. He did touch a woman in Guatemala in an inap-

propriate way."[97] But nothing came of it. "We considered cancelling his subsequent trip to Guatemala," his therapist reported. "[Instead] he went through with it and set boundaries for himself and observed them." The stakes of yet another offense appeared to be relatively low to this therapist, and the possible consequences completely tolerable. "Because of cultural differences," the therapist wrote, "I was not sure of the seriousness of this incident."[98]

Roney's sexually abusive habits in Guatemala had also become a concern for those in Minnesota. The Diocese of New Ulm's newly established Review Board for Sexual Misconduct raised "serious doubts about [Roney's] presence in Guatemala in an unsupervised condition [and his] having access to children."[99] Roney's entire archive is littered with red flags about his annual trips to Central America—so much so that the board reached out to a priest from the Diocese of New Ulm named Father Gregory Schaffer. This aging priest with round features, sloping shoulders, and a broad Minnesotan accent had been running the Mission since the early 1960s and had hosted Roney on each of his nearly two-dozen visits to Guatemala. During one of Schaffer's own stateside trips to Minnesota, he had the following to say to a church representative about Roney, comments that the Review Board for Sexual Misconduct synthesized, enumerated, and then added to Roney's growing archive:

1. . . . Fr. Roney likes to have children around him [in Guatemala]; . . . he prefers younger girls to boys.
2. [Roney] has helped out young girls with their studies (financially), but he also assisted one young man, too. His focus has been on children of the poor and widowed.
3. The 15th birthday is the "coming of age" for females in that culture. Roney has helped out with that celebration for some of the young women.
4. [Schaffer] has never seen Fr. Roney alone with a girl.
5. Roney reads to the children and they gather around him, hug him, sit in his lap etc.
6. . . . [Schaffer] has never heard the women say anything at all about Fr. Roney's conduct. Still, he says that the women may view Fr. Roney as his friend and that might deter them from saying anything negative about him.[100]

The report paints an all too familiar picture of Roney: he liked to have children around him; he preferred young girls to boys; and they hugged him and sat in his lap. The *et cetera* that appears at the end of the report's fifth point screams for clarification. Eventually these facts prompted the review board to ask itself the following question: "Can we assure the Diocese that they are not significantly at risk for a child being abused again? Should his faculties be removed? Should restrictions be placed on his ministry?"[101] To be clear, the question here was whether Roney should continue serving as a priest in good standing or whether he should be put on administrative leave without faculties. The latter option would mean that Roney could not celebrate any of the sacraments in public, nor could he represent himself as a Catholic priest. Roney would still have the ontic capacity to speak in the person of Christ (no one could ever take that away from him), but he would no longer be able to wear the priestly cape or the collar, nor could he stand behind an altar. He would be forced to turn bread and wine into flesh and blood by himself and for himself in his bedroom. The review board debated three options, based on what appears to have been limited information:

A. Do nothing. There has been no mention of such behavior in the past fifteen years; he asserts that none had occurred . . .

B. Continue to allow faculties but restrict his ministry such that he may have no contact with female children 13 years of age and under.

C. Remove his faculties.[102]

Despite the fact that the first option willfully overlooked Roney's conduct in Guatemala—there had in fact been mention of such behavior in the past fifteen years, by his therapist, no less—the Review Board on Sexual Misconduct ultimately chose to follow this course of action, to do nothing: "After due deliberation and further questioning, the [Review] Board by consensus decided to recommend to you [Bishop Lucker] that Fr. Roney's faculties remain in place and that no change in his status be made."[103] The memo does end with a plan of action, should Roney ever move permanently to Guatemala: "I concluded by asking Msgr. Schaffer if he would both keep his eye on Fr. Roney's conduct [in Guatemala] and inform me in a timely fashion of any questionable conduct. He agreed."[104] Case closed.

·   ·   ·   ·   ·

The Diocese of New Ulm, a territory of ten thousand square miles, began to feel rather small to Roney. Word about his abuse had begun to travel from parish to parish, while his archive continued to thicken. In some ways, Roney had never been more unrestricted: his mother, Lulu, had died in the summer of 1993, and Roney had retired from active ministry only ten days after her death. He had even shed most of his stateside responsibilities, having stepped down as the Mission's director of fund-raising. But in other, very practical ways, Roney could feel himself being boxed in with each document that was appended to his archive. Each addition to his file further narrowed his possibilities regarding future assignments.

Lucker was also jumpy when it came to the potential liability that Roney posed to the Diocese of New Ulm. A different confidential report submitted by a church representative wondered aloud where Roney should retire: "Father Roney asked to speak with me this morning and told me some variations of plans he was thinking about for his immediate future. These plans include where he might live and work other than the Pastoral Center."[105] The report's language is stale, bordering on the clinical, but one hears the occasional lilt of anxiety. There was an open question about where to put this priest: "One of the options [Roney] mentioned was living and working in St. Peter [in Canby, Minnesota, population 1,826] with Fr. Harry Behan, but he mentioned that there was a school there and wondered whether I thought he should rule out going there because of his former difficulties—again assuring me that that was in the past."[106] The Diocese clearly did not want Roney near the children of Minnesota. The author of the report explains, "I told him I thought it would be better if he could find some alternative, one without a school."[107]

The fundamental challenge for the Diocese of New Ulm and its bishop was that Roney had become a priest (forever) at his ordination on August 18, 1945, and then became a sexual deviant at Via Coeli in the spring of 1987. The diocese could apparently handle Roney being either a priest or a deviant but certainly not both, and so Roney, with the backing of his bishop, surmised that his sexual deviancy would be easier and more advantageous to unmake than his priesthood. Thus, rather than a church without a school, Roney opted for a town without deviancy:

a place that lacked the conceptual and administrative tools necessary to sustain the concept of sexual abnormality. Roney, with his bishop's approval, made the decision to retire to the diocese's Mission in Guatemala—to evade not just his past, but more profoundly, who he had become.

On the Run

Delta Airlines Flight 1604

March 17, 1994

Cruising at thirty-eight thousand feet somewhere over Ohio, David Roney—lulled into a meditative moment by the din of two jet engines—would have had plenty of time to contemplate all that he was leaving behind in Minnesota. There were the middle-class luxuries that he would likely never enjoy again: hot showers, supermarkets, cable television, decent pizza, American medical care, and bedsheets cleaned by a washer and dryer. He had also always thought that his career would end exactly where it had begun: at the Basilica of Saint Mary in downtown Minneapolis. But this too was no longer possible.

Back when Roney had been living as an associate pastor in the Basilica's rectory—which brimmed with priests in the late 1940s, and hummed with activity as these men came and went—he would have been the first to admit that congregant living strained his nerves. Prior to his ordination, when he was still housed at the Saint Paul Seminary, he had often wished for just a few moments to himself, and sometimes he would wonder if he could endure so much community. To Roney's great relief, however, the expansive rectory at the Basilica offered just the right balance. He remembered being busy, to be sure, but there were also moments of pause. There were nights when Roney found himself happily eating alone in the rectory's industrial-sized kitchen, forking leftovers directly from a cooking pot, his body half-bent over a sink. He appreciated these little reprieves from people, just as much as he enjoyed the occasional dinner with his fellow priests.

In the rectory's well-appointed dining room, with a broad fireplace and a genteel chandelier, they would all sit at a long wooden table and eat big slabs of meat that one of the women on staff had carved in front of them atop a heavy board. Bottles of wine fueled the conversations, with senior priests holding court and telling increasingly bawdy stories as wine gave way to scotch. At the end of the meal, masterfully crafted cakes would inevitably appear. Thickened with buttercream and sweetened with more sugar than the recipe required, these treats came straight from the kitchens of female parishioners who adored these men.

Roney found that he could relax into those evenings, thanks in part to the wine and then the scotch. The ruckus of the other men at the table also sustained him. A guarded person whose instincts tended to keep him quiet, Roney appreciated how the energy of others could draw him out, allowing him to laugh along with the group and maybe even add his own insights occasionally. And for a moment or two, often when he would least expect it, he could sit at that table and suddenly feel (really feel, deep inside of him) like he was a part of something, without having to put much work into it. He rarely had to risk too much of himself. Instead, other priests would strike up the conversations and then push them along with follow-up questions. Some posed debates, offering a polemic about the future of the Church, or just about whether the movie that Roney had recently seen was worth seeing.

Roney loved the city. He also loved the Basilica and its rectory. He had openly pined for them during his years in the Diocese of New Ulm, and had his life turned out differently—had he never acquired that archive that made him up as a new kind of person—he may well have returned to the Basilica in his retirement, becoming one of those older priests telling stories over drinks and cake. But from his seat on a one-way flight to Guatemala, it must have been clear that that door had definitively closed. In the highlands, there would be neither a city nor a basilica nor a rectory packed with priests. He also knew that slabs of meat and homemade cakes would never appear at his dinner table, and there would be no scotch.

Instead, Roney braced himself for something of a permanent retreat in a distant land that he knew and valued but that he had not exactly chosen for himself. He was being sent away, and he knew it, with his superiors telling him in no uncertain terms to get out while the getting was good.

He also flew to Guatemala with some sense of urgency. Records suggest that Roney had been arrested around the time of his trip. He had been picked up for criminal sexual misconduct in the fifth degree: lewd acts with a young child.[108] Several more accusations of abuse were also afoot. One former parishioner claimed that Roney had repeatedly abused him when he was just four years old, and while lawyers for the church worked to expunge Roney's arrest record, promising the police that he would complete even more psychotherapy, consensus quickly formed that Roney had become too much of a liability for the Diocese of New Ulm. He needed to go.

The upside for Roney was that in Guatemala he would not need to complete any more courses of psychotherapy, as his lawyers had just promised the police, because there were no therapists where he was heading. Police officers in wartime Guatemala would also never think to arrest a priest, let alone an American one, regardless of the crimes that he had committed; notably, too, none of these law enforcement officials would have access to Roney's stateside archive; neither would anyone at the Mission, minus Father Gregory Schaffer. From the moment his plane touched down at La Aurora International Airport, Roney would no longer be the person he had first become in New Mexico and then in Minnesota. In Guatemala, he would no longer be a sexual deviant, only a priest.

III A Town without Pedophilia, 1994–2003

Robaniños

San Cristóbal de Alta Verapaz, Guatemala

March 29, 1994

Father David Roney landed in Guatemala on March 17 amid rumors, suspicion, and wild fits of violence. "All U.S. citizens to defer nonessential travel to Guatemala at this time," ordered the U.S. Department of State on March 30. "We urge that U.S. citizens who remain in Guatemala avoid crowds, avoid traveling alone, and exercise utmost caution."[1] Consular authorities insisted that all Peace Corps volunteers should get to the capital city as soon as they could. Their lives depended on it. Outrageous stories had been ripping through the countryside for more than a year, riling otherwise law-abiding citizens into angry mobs and even propelling some of them to attack American tourists.[2] Foreigners—and specifically Americans—had supposedly been kidnapping Indigenous children, murdering them, and harvesting their organs. It was said that these kidnappers (*robaniños*) were then selling the organs on the black market for lucrative sums. No one could substantiate any of these claims, but the rumors took on a life of their own. One of the most common whispers was that someone (somewhere, at some point—though nobody could say who, where, or when) had stumbled upon the body of a dead child. His organs (though sometimes it was her organs) had been clumsily removed and the corpse stuffed with cotton. A U.S. five-dollar bill (but other times it was a

U.S. twenty-dollar bill) had been pinned to the little bloated body along with a handwritten note. It read (in English), "Thank you."[3]

Members of Guatemala's medical community held press conferences to explain the scientific impossibility of these rumors. Their country, these doctors explained, had neither the medical equipment nor the resources necessary to carry out organ transplants.[4] All the while, government officials pleaded with members of Indigenous communities throughout the country to be reasonable. Guatemala's morgues had not processed a single body that matched any of these descriptions, but members of the press fanned the flames of this moral panic with a semblance of journalistic precision. One of the country's most trusted daily newspapers published an article titled "The Black Market for Human Organs Is Flourishing." It even included a graphic that listed the supposed street price of body parts:

Lungs—$100,000	Liver—$150,000
Kidney—$65,000	Heart—$100,000
Heart valve—$3,500	Cornea—$2,500
Heart and lungs—$125,000	Pancreas—$90,000
Bone marrow—$125,000	Bones—$1,500[5]

Diane June Weinstock of Alaska was distantly aware of these rumors when she tried to board a bus from the town of San Cristóbal de Alta Verapaz on March 29, 1994. She had not read the newspaper article, with its horrifying menu of body parts, but it was the talk of the town. Someone had even taped it to the wall of a local store.[6] Weinstock was thus confused, and then quickly terrified, when a crowd of people suddenly gathered around her at the bus terminal. People wanted to know what was inside her backpack, why she had taken so many pictures of children earlier in the day, and where she was going in such a hurry. It had not helped that a woman nearby had suddenly noticed that her young child was nowhere in sight. The woman wondered aloud whether Weinstock had taken him. This is when someone grabbed Weinstock; another person pulled her hair, and one more slapped her across the face. Someone even managed to rifle through her backpack, expecting to find scalpels. A policeman and an American missionary happened to witness the altercation and quickly intervened, escorting Weinstock to the nearest municipal building. "What the hell do they think I've done?" she called out.[7] The policeman and missionary thought that the authorities might be able to resolve the situation, or at least keep Weinstock safe while the crowd cooled off, but more than a thousand people gathered outside the building, and they wanted blood.

The crowd was confused from the get-go.[8] In some of the video footage from that day, as one reporter would later note, a person mentions to whoever had the camera that they are after a man. No, says another, it is a woman. Then another in the crowd says, "It is a man who turned into a woman."[9] Later, someone started throwing rocks at the building while others broke through a fence. A few kicked down the front door and then someone set the building on fire. The police officer and the missionary who had first helped Weinstock, along with everyone else inside the building, fled for their lives while Weinstock did her best to hide in a back room. But they found her. Armed with clubs, tools, and machetes, a crush of men beat, stabbed, and raped Weinstock, leaving her in a coma, and then dragged her limp body out of the building. Preparing to burn her to death with a few gallons of gasoline, the mob receded only after having mistakenly assumed that she was already dead.

The attack made international news, with gripping stories published in the *New York Times*, *Washington Post*, and *Los Angeles Times*.[10] Weinstock's attack attracted worldwide attention because of her violent brush with death. She barely survived the attack and was soon airlifted to safety, making only a partial recovery after years of medical treatment in her home state of Alaska.[11] The more compelling journalistic angle, however, was that Weinstock was not the only American who had been accused of stealing children in the highlands of Guatemala. Dozens of similar reports had been gathering over the previous year. Only a few weeks earlier, a different mob in a different small town attacked a police station that held a different American woman accused of stealing children for body parts. In the town of Santa Lucía, hundreds of Guatemalans threw rocks at the police station, set a police car and then a pickup truck on fire, and eventually stormed the building. They never reached the young American woman, but the crowd injured fifteen police officers and thirty-four residents.[12]

While these rumors of organ theft never aligned with reality, the hysteria fueling them was not entirely without basis. The Guatemalan American author Francisco Goldman probably said it best when he told a *Washington Post* reporter that "Everything about the baby-parts story is true, except for gringos and baby parts." The rumors had a certain basis in fact. "Children get stolen all the time in Guatemala," Goldman explained. "But not for their organs and not by foreigners. The Guatemalans steal them for adoptions."[13] There was at the time a lucrative and loosely regulated market for international adoptions in Guatemala, with the number of Guatemalan children adopted by American parents having nearly doubled by the time Roney moved to Guatemala. In 1994, Guatemala was second only to South Korea in the number of children adopted by American parents, and most of these children came from the rural highlands under suspicious circumstances.[14] Many of these adoptions might as well have been kidnappings.[15]

The private orphanages (*casas-cuna*) that structured the industry positively reeked of corruption. Stories piled up in the popular press of poor Indigenous women duped into giving up their newborn babies for adoption, many of them plied with cash payments, while the orphanages themselves tended to be described as clandestine sites located in shadowy parts of the capital city.[16] More than a month before Weinstock's attack, a government official even connected these orphanages to the supposed sale of body parts in a widely read newspaper article. "There exists a good number of clandestine *casas-cuna* that are used for the future sale of children's organs, the majority of whom have been kidnapped." The article relied on conjecture. "Sold as 'spare parts' for other infants with physical defects, Guatemalan children and foreign undesirables have been shown and proved to obtain juicy profits—in U.S. dollars—through the sale of this human merchandise."[17]

Another set of rumors insisted that the Guatemalan military had its hands in the kidnapping and organ trafficking business, and this may explain why the stories about *robaniños* tended to be so graphic. By the mid-1990s, Guatemala had already been at war with itself for thirty-six years, with most of those impacted coming from small towns such as San Cristóbal de Alta Verapaz and Santa Lucía, as well as the village where David Roney's new home at the Mission was located.[18] Only a few years earlier, in fact, while driving from the Mission to the capital city, Roney had been caught in the middle of a firefight between guerrillas and soldiers. "A cloud of smoke appeared on the road about fifty yards ahead of us," he wrote: "A mine had gone off, just missing one of the army vehicles." Roney, by his own account, "huddled on the floor of the car" amid "the sound of automatic rifles" and of "a spotter plane that the army sent in to direct the fighting."[19] Violence had become a way of life.[20]

The military often perpetrated this violence against Indigenous Guatemalans in public settings, with mutilated bodies paraded through streets, hung from trees, and left to rot in the Central American sun. Soldiers cut fetuses from the stomachs of pregnant women and bludgeoned children to death in front of their parents. Massacres and mass graves studded the countryside. These grotesque acts of violence explain not only the Indigenous peoples' complete lack of trust in either the American or the Guatemalan government, but also their sharp turn toward popular justice and sometimes vigilantism. As Guatemala's civil war ended with the signing of the 1996 Peace Accords, people turned on each other, and attacked, maimed, and murdered hundreds based on suspicions of theft, murder, and even witchcraft. Many of these terrible acts were also in response to the reported abduction of children.[21]

Roney moved to Guatemala smack in the middle of this moral panic. His plane touched down only ten days after the riot in Santa Lucía and just twelve days before the attack on June Weinstock in San Cristóbal de Alta Verapaz. Amid waves of rumors that seemed uncannily targeted to his profile, Roney quietly shepherded himself and his single suitcase through customs and then boarded a private van headed to the Mission. The trip was entirely without incident. No one tried to pull Roney's hair or slap him in the face or search his suitcase for scalpels. Instead, Roney slipped through this otherwise tightly woven net of popular justice. Although he would soon spend his days taking thousands of photographs of children, and even participate in an informal adoption that might as well have been a kidnapping, he avoided being labeled a baby snatcher. There, at the Mission, he was an American priest and nothing more.

All Roney suffered upon arrival was the four- to five-hour van ride from the airport to the Mission. The route had its share of switchbacks and stretches of unpaved road, sheer drops and hairpin turns, and near the end of the journey, Roney's driver would have parked, as drivers invariably do, at one of the route's many look-out points—to let Roney catch his breath, stretch his legs, and enjoy the view of Lake Atitlán. Perched hundreds of feet above Central America's deepest and arguably most majestic body of water, Roney would have seen the region in its entirety: its active volcanos and lush forest, small towns and soaring clouds, and fishermen paddling across blue waters to eke out a living. It is a stunning sight that the British author Aldous Huxley once described as "too much of a good thing."[22]

A little later, after descending the mountainside at a gradient that would make anyone nervous, Roney boarded a simple motorboat that carried him several kilometers across the lake to the Mission: a constellation of modest buildings and a sturdy, white-walled church that hugged the banks of Lake Atitlán. With sun in his eyes and lake water spraying his face, Roney's guide eventually cut the engine to let the boat drift safely toward a dock lined not just with grateful townspeople but also with dozens of children: all of them waving, laughing, and singing a church hymn. The Mission tended to greet its visitors with a bit of fanfare, laying it on particularly thick for American priests: welcome parties would even serenade visitors with the word *hola,* sung to the tune of "Amen" from the 1963 movie *Lilies of the Field.*[23] As these well-wishers gathered Roney's belongings, shouldering his only suitcase with the strength and agility of those who labor for a living, children crowded around him, at first clinging to his legs and then giggling with sheer joy when it turned out that this skinny priest from the United States had pockets full of candy.

At that moment, against the immediate backdrop of angry mobs, international adoption rackets, and a genocidal civil war, Roney's whole retirement stretched out ahead of him. He had just left his increasingly encumbered life in Minnesota to find himself ensorcelled by the sight and touch of small children, smiling and laughing, who seemed to want nothing more than to follow him everywhere he went; who would soon love above all else to spend a morning and maybe even an afternoon with him while their parents labored on their farms or, more commonly, worked for scandalously low wages on someone else's property; and who craved the attention of an American priest who liked to waste his afternoons at the lake, swimming and splashing in the water and then drying himself in the sun.

On the day of his arrival, before any of those trips to the lake, Roney's welcome party walked him only a few hundred meters from the dock to a simple but sufficient one-bedroom house. Its concrete walls, always cool to the touch, first reminded Roney of the simple setup he had endured at Lake Saint Croix Beach back in the early 1950s: squat ceilings, narrow windows, and mismatched furniture. This new place did have a distinct advantage over the rectory back in Minnesota: his new home in Guatemala was located right across the street from the Mission's elementary school and only a few blocks from its bustling orphanage. There, in the quiet of his new house, with only the nearby laughter of schoolchildren to distract him, Roney unpacked his suitcase and then he sat at his kitchen table to scratch out a shopping list of all the items that would soon make him a favorite with all those kids: candy and toys, bicycles and board games, and every Disney movie that he could get his hands on. Indeed, he must have thought to himself—like Huxley describing Lake Atitlán—that this was "too much of a good thing."[24]

A Totally Innocent Person

Sololá, Guatemala

October 24, 1995

Inside the town's church, among long sloping shadows, Father David Roney held a little girl in his arms as she desperately tried to free herself. She was pulling, kicking, and screaming. "I don't remember any of it," Justina admitted decades later. "All I have is a photograph." Not yet three years old, with big brown eyes and a round, tear-streaked face, Justina could not be convinced—although many tried—that she needed to let Padre Davíd, as Roney was known in Guatemala, pour water on her head and rub oil onto her chest. "I must have been worried that my [baptismal] dress would get dirty," Justina later reasoned, and who could blame her? The gown was silken and intricately embroidered; it was also one size too small, but it was hers.

Two years earlier, just before Roney arrived in Guatemala, a nine-month-old Justina appeared on the steps of the church. Her mother had died while giving birth to her, in a remote clinic completely ill equipped to stop the bleeding, and her father—a thin and rather weathered man—struggled against abject poverty and alcoholism in a cornstalk house. Soon after his wife's death, in an act that would later be remembered by Justina alternately as her greatest loss and her only blessing, this poor man handed his daughter over to the Mission. He was sick with drink that day.

The Diocese of New Ulm opened the Mission in 1958, in response to the Vatican's concern that most Guatemalans rarely ever saw a priest.[25] It was a clerical shortage that had been years in the making. In the early 1820s, as the Guatemalan government restructured its economy towards the cultivation of coffee, notions of order and progress guided efforts at reform.[26] These included large-scale projects such as the construction of roadways and ports, but also efforts to undercut the Church's power and authority. Anticlerical programs seized Church property, expelled foreign clergy, and abolished religious orders, with the country's president even going so far as to recruit Protestant ministers from the United States to de-Catholicize and thereby "civilize" the country.[27] Reverend Edward Haymaker, a graduate of the Yale Divinity School, arrived in 1887 to—in his words—turn Guatemala into "one of the greatest little countries in the world" by replacing "Romanism, which subject[s] the masses to pauperism, illiteracy, [and] superstition" with a supposedly "modern," Protestant emphasis on things like "sanitation, motherhood, education, [and] thrift."[28]

These anticlerical programs radically reduced the number of Roman Catholic priests in Guatemala.[29] By 1870, there were only ninety-four priests for a country of two million people, and fifty years later there were just eighty.[30] With one Vatican diplomat describing the state of Roman Catholicism in Guatemala as "deplorable," the most dramatic disparity was between city and country.[31] In the rural highlands, for instance, the priest-to-parishioner ratio dropped as low as one priest for every 88,000 Catholics.[32] This raised concerns within the Catholic Church about the souls of ordinary Guatemalans. A Dominican friar who toured the countryside in 1914 remarked that many Guatemalan couples lived in what he called "concubinage," a sinfully unmarried state, because of their limited access to the sacrament of matrimony.[33] There were not enough priests to perform baptisms, confessions, or first communions, and hardly anyone observed last rites. Perhaps most frightening of all, from a Catholic perspective, was the fact that the Church was becoming incapable of reproducing itself, with Guatemala's seminaries ordaining just eight priests between 1914 and 1920.[34]

Pope Pius XI (1922–1939) intervened by transferring priests from the United States to Guatemala.[35] Pope John XXIII (1958–1963) then doubled down on this intervention by calling on the U.S. Church to send a full

10 percent of its clergy to Latin America.[36] With seminaries across North America brimming with young aspirants, U.S. bishops forged a set of social relationships that quickly connected the two countries. These sometimes took the form of full clerical placements, with U.S. priests pastoring Guatemalan parishes, but the church's endeavors also included more informal arrangements, such as mission trips, clerical exchanges, solidarity movements, sponsorship programs, volunteer opportunities, and, as in the case of David Roney, semi-active retirements. The intention was to recruit and train a new generation of Guatemalan seminarians, but the net effect was near dependency on the sacramental labor of foreign clerics. Priests from the United States staffed Guatemala's seminaries and schools while performing baptisms and confessions at increasingly expansive scales. While this reliance frustrated bishops in the United States, Guatemala's numbers did improve. A little more than twenty years after the first U.S. priests arrived in Guatemala, this relatively small Central American country boasted 531 clerics, with 434 of them foreign-born.[37]

The good people of Minnesota did their part by opening their own Mission in Guatemala, hoping to rebuild the country's priesthood and save those newborns who had come to be known in the 1950s and early 1960s as "pagan babies." This Catholic shorthand—now piercingly insensitive—referred to the unbaptized children of Asia, Africa, and Latin America. Roman Catholic elementary schools across the United States raised money for foreign missions by asking young children to donate some percentage of their allowances to support missionary priests from the United States in their efforts to baptize these so-called pagans. It was an incredibly popular movement. Even Carol, that young girl whom Roney had abused at the rectory, distinctly remembers squirrelling away nickels and dimes so that some orphan in Guatemala could go to heaven.[38] "I think I named my orphan Mary," she recalled. These Minnesotan children would in addition receive a decorative certificate from their parish priest. "We trust," one reads, "that you will not suffer with indifference that so many pagan babies should be deprived of the grace of Christian rebirth."[39] Ostensibly signed by Pope Pius XII, these certificates attested to a missionary intervention that was not a matter of life and death so much as life after death.[40]

Roney's first encounter with Guatemala, or at least the idea of Guatemala, came amid this Church-wide anxiety over baptisms. While serving as a pastor in the small rural towns of central Minnesota, throughout much of the 1960s, Roney was often tasked with visiting the elementary school to speak to its students about the diocese's Mission in Guatemala. Although he knew priests who had worked in Central America, Roney had not yet been there himself. He nevertheless felt capable—entirely comfortable, really—imagining for Carol and all the other young students the conditions under which these Guatemalans lived and their desperate need for the sacraments. All Roney had to say was that the residents of this small town in the volcanic mountains of Guatemala lacked not only plumbing, electricity, and phone lines—the very luxuries that made life in Minnesota so pleasant for these schoolchildren—but also access to eternal salvation: to the sacrament of baptism.

Roney was also known to break frame on occasion, in some effort to speak frankly with these children. Casually resting against the teacher's desk, he would suggest in a sincere, candid tone that "adoption" was a polite euphemism, as opposed to the theologically more precise term of "ransom." These students in Minnesota did not technically adopt unbaptized children in Guatemala. Very few of the Guatemalan children were orphans and none of them lacked a name. The entire premise seemed to offend Roney; from time to time he called the whole thing silly. It would be more theologically accurate, he explained, to say that these nickels and dimes freed children from the bondage of original sin through the sacrament of baptism. This is what a theology of atonement argues, he explained. None of it would have made much sense to these kids in Minnesota, but Roney persisted: The devil holds the soul of a baby hostage until baptism sets its soul free. This is where the language of ransom originated. Roney thus taught the children that their five dollars amounted not to an adoption fee but to a sum of money paid for the release of a prisoner.[41]

Cribbing from sermons he had heard from more experienced missionaries, Roney explained this bondage in colorful terms, telling these young students in Minnesota how the Indigenous peoples of Guatemala relied not only on a network of shamans to bless their crops but also on a motley crew of saints that they superstitiously imagined in the likenesses of their own gods. He described men and women drinking and dancing in front of statues of Saint Jude and completing animal sacrifices on church steps.[42]

Roney had learned all of this from missionary reports from rural Guatemala, in which priests from the United States complained that the local holy days amounted to "nothing less than pagan bacchanalian orgies." The Indigenous faithful would play marimbas in the main plaza and engage in what the American priests described as an endless cycle of "drunken shouts, howls and shrieks" throughout the night.[43]

This raucous image of Guatemala remained Roney's only idea of the country until his first trip there in 1973, with a gaggle of nervous parishioners. He and the others traveled from the airport to the Mission, along those harrowing cliff-top roads—through the kind of ridges that must have seemed unimaginable to those born and raised on the great plains of Minnesota. Roney's idea of a nation full of disorderly believers and pagan babies gave way to something slightly more substantive, more textured, and in the end, more deeply felt: a vision of a people who needed him, a people whom he could save. "I fell in love immediately with the people and with the mission program," he would later write. "The next year I went down with another group; then another."[44] He was hooked. "I have never let as much as a year go by between visits. It was my vacation, and now, it is my work."[45] While in Guatemala, he would perform baptisms, weddings, and confessions at scale, and he would participate in the Mission's ever-proliferating social projects. Roney also spent his time in the highlands compulsively courting the attention of very young boys and girls. He served as the godfather (*padrino*) to at least two dozen children, many of whom would insist years later that she or he was Roney's only godchild (*ahijada*). He also spent time with hundreds more.

In the Mission's courtyard, under the shade of towering trees, he would tell groups of children fantastic stories, lead them in song, and play along with their silly games in halting Spanish, at times running around like a child himself. "I love to read stories [to the children in Guatemala]," he wrote, "especially the classic fairy tales, like Little Red Riding Hood, Goldilocks and the Three Bears, and The Three Little Pigs. And if I must say so, I read them well, giving to the ferocious wolf the appropriate tone of snarling menace."[46] These kids adored Roney. They often fought for his attention—and the ice cream, candy, and toys that came with it—but none of them could ever compete in Roney's mind with the incandescent charm of Justina.

Roney cherished this young girl. Maybe it was because Justina never really fit in, and neither did Roney. When her biological father first handed Justina over to the Mission in 1993, no one really knew where to put her. She was far too young for the orphanage, which the Mission had opened several years earlier to care for those children who had lost their parents in the country's ongoing civil war. The orphanage was an obvious godsend, an absolute gift to the people, but it was not the right place for a toddler. Rather than share a bunk with an older orphan and possibly flounder for lack of care, Justina enjoyed the affection of the women who worked at the Mission as cooks and cleaners, routinely spending her nights at their houses. These women made do, out of the goodness of their hearts, passing Justina from one set of arms to another, but there was no real sense of routine. During the workday, Justina often got in the way, crawling about the kitchen and then stumbling her way through the church grounds. In those early years, Justina always had eyes on her, sometimes dozens of them, but she never had anyone's full attention—until Roney moved to town in the spring of 1994.

The most innocent explanation for Roney's interest in Justina is that he did not have much to do. Before moving to the village, Roney had resigned from his stateside role as director of the Diocesan Mission Office and settled his affairs after his mother Lulu passed away. It was an absence of responsibility that Roney had pined for during the most professionally demanding moments of his career, when he would daydream about not just a vacation but more profoundly a release from the rigors of church and family life: a complete break from it all. The felt reality of such freedom, though, unnerved him. At one point, Roney decided to re-create his seminary's daily schedule at the Mission, apparently nostalgic for the effervescence of community living. He could still remember, even half a century after graduating, meeting every morning at 5:30 a.m. in the first-floor chapel of his dormitory to begin canonical hours. Roney could still feel the warmth of standing shoulder to shoulder with his classmates, without an inch of free space to be found, as they hit their marks with almost military precision. But it was hard to sustain such discipline without an army of fellow aspirants, and even harder in the highlands of Guatemala. The town's elevation made the mornings far cooler than expected and the warmth of his bed was therefore far more tempting than he could have anticipated. In those early hours, as the sun itself seemed to struggle to rise above the massive volcanoes, Roney admitted to himself that the mystery of it all had faded. He was still a priest, he told himself, but not a monk and certainly not an ascetic.

Roney soon doubled down on efforts to meet the sacramental needs of the countryside, volunteering his time with the Mission. This seemed to give him a renewed sense of purpose. For an American priest accustomed to drinking alone in the rectory every night and stealing little bits of intimacy from schoolchildren during the day, there was an almost electric vitality to celebrating mass and wrestling over questions of life and death with the families of this small town. He also administered last rites and delivered funerals for a people in need, and this feeling of purpose stuck. It was a sense of community that clearly captured Roney's attention at an almost existential level, delivering him a sense of ministerial purpose that he had long seemed to lack in Minnesota. There was also something obviously exciting about being so far away from what he and his fellow priests from the United States would have considered civilization. Plumbing, electricity, and phone lines might have made life in Minnesota comfortable, but these relative luxuries also came with a constellation of societal norms and ecclesiastical expectations—not to mention juridical and psychotherapeutic standards—that the Mission's remoteness seemed to suspend for him as an American priest. In the highlands of Guatemala, Roney knew at a theological level that the baptisms he was performing would save these pagan babies from the pain of original sin. But Roney also knew that he too had been set free.

Emboldened by this newfound freedom. Roney began to care for Justina, who often raised a ruckus only a few feet from his front door. Given how many times Justina seemed to spill out of the church grounds into the town's (admittedly slow-moving) traffic, it made perfect sense to the women who worked in the kitchen that this priest would look after Justina from well before dawn until well past sunset, and not just from Monday to Friday but also on Saturdays and Sundays: feeding her, bathing her, and putting this small child for naps in his own bed. "He never used a sponge or a cloth," Justina would explain decades later to lawyers in Minnesota. "He always washed me with his hands. With his bare hands." Roney read books to Justina, and sat with her while she learned to count, say the alphabet, and eventually read. He also provided financially for her in ways that no one else did. In addition to the toys and bicycles which Justina treasured, Roney also offered money for tuition payments and schoolbooks, clothes and birthday parties, elaborate meals and medical care. For a child born into abject poverty, Justina enjoyed a standard of living that made her the envy of nearly everyone. By all accounts, including her own, she appeared to be the luckiest girl in town.[47]

Justina was in awe of Roney. One of her clearest memories is of sitting under the church's altar while Roney celebrated mass, surreptitiously watching the congregation standing, sitting, and kneeling at her new father's whim. She even called him "Papá" as a term of endearment, signaling to everyone in town that Roney was the only person in the world willing to watch over her and set her apart, to honor her and sometimes even fight for her. This bond endured nearly uninterrupted from Justina's infancy to Roney's death on January 27, 2003. The only hiccup came when Justina's biological father returned in 1995, a year and a half after handing her over to the Mission and a few months after Roney had started to take care of her full time. Her birth father had had second thoughts, and after some discussion, Justina again began to live with him. But this only lasted a few weeks. As Justina remembers, Roney visited her one day, saw the state in which she was living—barefoot, dirty, and hungry—and promptly brought her back to the Mission for good. Roney's long-time housekeeper in Guatemala, decades later, would tell the story slightly differently. Justina was indeed hungry and did not have shoes, and her biological father was in no state to care for her. There is no doubt about any of this. But Roney also missed Justina terribly: apparently, he would sit alone in his house for weeks, at times weeping into his hands. He was completely distressed until one day he stood up from his chair, marched his way clear across town, and took her back. This one-sided battle between a poor Indigenous man and a North American priest settled for Justina any question about paternity. Roney was now her father.[48]

Roney baptized Justina on October 24, 1995, soon after bringing her back to the Mission, and he paid in full for the party that followed the sacrament. The event was nothing special—just some cake and coffee plus a few balloons and a present—but it all seemed to ignite in Roney a new spark of joy. Holy baptism, as this priest had often explained in sermons, draws its meaning from an association with the death and resurrection of Jesus. Baptism is the end of one life and the beginning of a new one. It is the annulment of one's sins and the rise of a totally innocent person. Like his new daughter, of course, Roney had also ended one life and begun a new one: in his case, when he moved from Minnesota to Guatemala. At the Mission, he too was innocent anew, effectively cleaved from his archive back home.

No Hay Pedofilia

Sololá, Guatemala

December 1, 1995

A pair of American volunteers were starting to wonder aloud about how Father David Roney spent his days in Guatemala. Most of the short-term missionaries from Minnesota had not noticed anything. They were teenagers whose parents had paid upward of thirty dollars a day so that their sons and daughters could live for a week or two at the Mission on the equivalent of one dollar a day—all for the piety-building privilege of digging ditches and clearing fields in the Central American sun and then soldiering through cold showers and sleeping on stiff cots at night. These volunteers gave little thought to Roney's activities. Two retirees from Willmar, though, had started to talk. In the fall of 1995, this married couple had come to the Mission to live out the Gospel for a year. They were no strangers to Guatemala. The two had traveled nearly a dozen times to the Mission over the course of several decades and had already spent a full year there in 1977. The two also knew Roney well. The woman had been the secretary for Saint Mary's elementary school back in Willmar when Roney served as the parish priest, and she was aware of his abusive appetites. Her husband had once worked with the school's band director to confront Roney over the suspicions that he was molesting children. But nothing had come of their intervention. "My husband and I were concerned about a possible scandal with the Church," she later admitted about their concerns about Roney back in Minnesota, "and wanted to avoid that if possible."[49] So they had kept quiet.

In Guatemala, the two saw Roney regularly at church services, as well as while walking the village streets. He always had children at his side, and Justina was usually in the mix, sometimes in Roney's arms or even on his hip. It got this married couple talking. "I learned that Father Roney was planning to adopt . . . an orphan girl," the wife later wrote. "I knew that she spent her days at Father Roney's home." This volunteer from Minnesota began to worry. "Knowing Father Roney's history as I did," she continued, "from discussions with parents of children who had been sexually molested by Father Roney, I was very upset when I found out that Father Roney had this child staying with him and was planning to adopt her." She added, with what was either extreme understatement or inconceivable naïveté, "I was afraid that something inappropriate might be going on."[50]

Word eventually got back to Bishop Lucker. During a meeting at the Cathedral of the Holy Trinity, amid the early rumblings of a winter storm, he scribbled some notes on a yellow legal pad. They were intended for his eyes only, a simple record of his meetings for the day, but they eventually ended up in the hands of lawyers. Much of what Lucker wrote is illegible, a wild nest of shorthand, but one stretch of cursive reads as clear as day: "This new report of Roney 'raising' this little girl is a concern to me."[51] Lucker had heard about the baptismal dress, the gifts, and the many hours that Justina spent under Roney's direct care. It had all given Lucker pause, even reason to raise an eyebrow, but he did not do anything about it—in part because of the occasional and rather incomplete reports that the bishop received from the Mission, but more importantly because he grasped something extremely important about Roney's situation. The problems Roney faced in the United States did not, in a very real sense, exist in Guatemala. The Mission was not just a distant place in the world— one conveniently located on the other side of volcanoes and an expansive lake. It was also a place far removed from North America's medicalized definitions of sexual deviancy—a place where clerical sexual abuse, as a category of criminal behavior, could not yet be named or recognized.

Only a few years earlier in Minnesota, credible accusations of sexual abuse had triggered a clinical intervention that not only made Roney into a sexual deviant but also sustained his diagnosis with an ever-thickening archive: psychological examinations, medical tests, confidential reports, and even the occasional cassette recording. These materials connected a consequential identity to Roney's once undefined actions, quickly circumscribing his life and defining his future. It was a story—by now a familiar one—of how a person can get made up into an entirely new kind of person.[52] Michel Foucault's object of study, Jouy from the French countryside, had endured something similar a century earlier for giving "a few pennies to the little girls for favors."[53] Jouy's transformation from a transient farmhand to an object of psychological and legal intervention depended on what Foucault called "a whole machinery for speechifying, analyzing, and investigating."[54] This included psychiatrists, psychologists, and social workers as well as judges, law enforcement, and psychiatric hospitals. All these actors and bureaucrats "made" Jouy in France into a sexual deviant, and a parallel process would eventually "make" Roney in the United States into the same.

None of this happened—or even could have happened—in the highlands of Guatemala because there are practical limits to an identity such as sexual deviancy. It can only emerge in certain times and places, and the Mission in 1994 was not one such time and place. In sending Roney to Guatemala, Bishop Lucker exploited the limits of sexual deviancy to unmake the person the Church had made in New Mexico. One element of Roney's unmaking involved juridical arbitrage: the phenomenon of criminals seeking refuge and retirement abroad to avoid prosecution in their native jurisdiction. In this sense, Roney was no different than many other outlaws. His criminal acts in the United States had not only been committed in another jurisdiction, but they were in fact largely absent from Guatemalan law. The sexual abuse of a male minor, for example, was not a criminal offense until a reform of Guatemala's penal code in 2009. Prior to this change, the most proximate crime was the production of pornography, which carried a fine of approximately US$50.[55] Moreover, this Central American country's civil war had also created the perfect cover for Roney's crimes. In a land scarred by mass graves, political assassinations, and angry mobs, where the intellectual architects of the country's genocide would never see the inside of a prison, no one in Guatemala had the political capital or time to question (let alone accuse of wrongdoing) an American priest who had quietly committed himself to the country's children. Wartime Guatemala provided Roney with a space of near impunity.[56]

The more profound element of Roney's unmaking, however, was a parallel process best described as *ontological arbitrage*. Just as the discrepancies that exist between competing legal codes can be leveraged by criminals to avoid accountability, so too can criminals leverage the differences between distinct cultural and social settings to avoid being recognized as criminals in the first place. Foucault explains that although French authorities arrested and examined Jouy in 1867, authorities neither would nor could have done the same just a few decades prior. This had everything to do with the proliferation of expertise throughout western Europe in the mid-nineteenth century, from psychology and psychiatry to criminology and sociology. These new modes of observation solidified new ways of being, making it possible for the village misfit to suddenly become a sexual deviant.[57] In France, during the latter half of the nineteenth century, Jouy found himself in a time, place, and setting where authorities had the capacity to lock him up in a psychiatric hospital for the rest of his life because of who he *was*, ontologically, not just because of what he did or how he behaved.

The cultural and historical specificity of making up people is why travel can be such a diabolical antidote to the kind of diagnosis that Jouy received.[58] Relocating to a different place and a different social setting can effectively unmake the very person that someone has become. Jouy could have unmade his deviancy by fleeing France for a place without the requisite "machinery" for "speechifying, analyzing, and investigating" his abnormality—a place without the ontological conditions that would allow someone to become a sexual deviant.[59] He could have achieved this effect almost anywhere in the world in 1867. Some places such as France had begun to mobilize along the binary of normality and abnormality, but grand sites of therapeutic intervention were still very rare. Few places beyond France at that time had psychiatrists, psychologists, and social workers. Even fewer had judges, law enforcement officials, and psychiatric hospitals empowered by the science of sexual deviancy. All Jouy would have had to do was find a place where what Foucault refers to as "inconsequential bucolic pleasure[s]" were still "everyday occurrence[s] in the life of village sexuality."[60]

Jouy was not the only one who could have found advantages in a change of scenery, as Foucault himself likely knew all too well.[61] In 1968, a century after Jouy's arrest, it is rumored that Foucault found refuge in Tunisia, escaping accountability for the very sexual acts that he had theorized so well, despite insisting to many of his colleagues that his interest in the former French colony was primarily intellectual. "Tunisia, for me," he would write, "represented in some ways the chance to reinsert myself in the political debate."[62] However, there is reason to believe that he might have also leveraged Tunisia's stark absence of experts, authorities, and archives to sexually abuse prepubescent children. Foucault allegedly paid to have sex with eight-, nine-, and ten-year-old boys at a cemetery in the town of Sidi Bou Said, north of the capital Tunis, and he was apparently flagrant about these sexual encounters. He is reported to have abused children atop gravestones under a full moon. Yet nothing came of these allegations. There is no publicly available police record covering Foucault's alleged behavior in Tunisia. Neither is there any evidence of any "judicial action, medical intervention, clinical examination, or theoretical elaboration."[63] This may mean that the rumors about Foucault's sexual abuse of children are categorically false—that it may never have happened. However, the lack of any record may also evidence the absence of any "machinery" in Tunisia that could have set the ontological conditions for someone such as Foucault to become a sexual deviant and face the consequences of his actions. Either way, Foucault, in very practical terms, was never a sexual deviant in Tunisia. He may have had sex with children, and some insist that he did, but these alleged abusive acts never sparked the interest of a Tunisian expert or authority and consequently never formed into an archive of any consequence. If Foucault's move to Tunisia was an act of ontological arbitrage (in addition to juridical arbitrage), then it successfully safeguarded his academic celebrity not just in his native France but also across dozens of other contexts where the category of sexual deviancy is both recognizable and consequential. Without the right kind of experts, authorities, and archives in Tunisia, these rumors have remained nothing more than rumors.

Roney too, at least while he was in Guatemala, was never a sexual deviant. His move to the Mission allowed him to shed nearly all his personal belongings (which he stored stateside but never retrieved), as well as to leave behind his diagnostic archive (which also ended up collecting dust in Minnesota). While seemingly every encounter in New Mexico and Minnesota had once added to Roney's file with reports, letters, and recordings of his misdeeds and diagnoses, an obvious and observable disconnect occurred once Roney retired to the Mission. There was a clean break, a full stop, between the densely documented scandal in Minnesota and the sheer absence of any archival footprint in Guatemala. This chasm between North America and Central America unfortunately provided Roney with an unchecked level of freedom.

.   .   .   .   .

A few days shy of Justina's fifth birthday, Roney chartered a private boat to carry the two of them clear across the lake to a popular tourist town. He had packed them an overnight bag with bathing suits, pajamas, and toothbrushes. A photograph from that day has them sitting on the boat side by side. Wind whips at their hair, and they are both smiling ear to ear. They were going on holiday, Justina remembered years later, and she couldn't wait.

Justina had never been on vacation and neither had anyone she knew. Roney was obviously familiar with travel. So too were the handful of other American priests who lived at the Mission. There were also hundreds of volunteers who passed through town every year. Those earnest folks from Minnesota would often reframe their middle-class adventures as service rather than sightseeing, but their time in Guatemala was a form of tourism all the same. Most of Justina's friends, however, had never left town and neither had their parents, at least not for the sole purpose of pleasure. They had plenty of celebrations and other reasons to walk away from the fields to enjoy each other's company, but no one had the money (and thus no one had the inclination) to leave town, check into a hotel, and lounge poolside for a few days.

In his retirement, Roney had both the money and the inclination to pay for a few nights at a three-star hotel for the sole purpose of pleasure.[64] The hotel he chose sits at the edge of the lake, with stunning views of the volcanoes. It also offers its guests an overpriced but consistently good restaurant. Its fastidiously manicured grounds provide hammocks and a large swimming pool complete with a water slide that twists and turns all the way down. One of Justina's brightest memories from this trip is of the pool. Too small to go down the slide, she remembers floating on something round as older kids shot down its slippery surface and crashed into the water. The rhythm of all this mayhem—yelping, splashing, laughing—struck Justina as the most magnificent comedy she had ever seen. "I also remember him later helping me out of my swimsuit," she added, "and realizing that we were the only two people sleeping in the room."

In Camera

Sololá, Guatemala

October 1973 to January 2003

David Roney carried a point-and-shoot camera almost everywhere he went in Guatemala. In part, he wanted to document life in the highlands, from the colors and customs of its Indigenous communities to the breathtaking vistas that the lake and volcanoes offered. Roney also had an obvious eye for the quieter moments of village life. Some of his subjects in Guatemala pose for the camera, obediently standing at attention, but many more seem to be completely unaware that Roney had been watching them. In his vast trove of images, taken between the spring of 1973 and the winter of 2003, there are photographs of children sleeping, children swimming, children playing, children sitting, children eating, children running, children reading, children laughing, children praying, children walking, and children coyly peeking out from behind a tree or an adult's leg. His nearly ten thousand images present a world bereft of adults: Roney's vision of Guatemala is populated almost entirely by children. He is the only recurring character over the age of twelve.

None of Roney's photographs are pornographic. Their focus on young children lends his archive an unsettling affect, but the content of his images is rather banal: birthday parties, soccer matches, and first holy communions. There are also innumerable images of Justina, but his crimes never appeared on camera. Instead, his photographs evidence how successfully Roney had escaped his past, and how many children were put at risk as a result. For a priest once advised to avoid clerical assignments in Minnesota with elementary schools, "because of his former difficulties," Roney's photographs in Guatemala depict a completely unencumbered life.[65] He had absolutely no restrictions on his movement. "I always walk around the school," he wrote about his visits to the Mission: "[I try] not to disturb the classes but [I am] secretly delighted when children wave through the windows."[66] That Roney felt sufficiently confident to write about these feelings in his diocese's newsletter indicates just how free he perceived himself to be in Guatemala—entirely beyond suspicion. He later wrote how the orphans giggled every time he pointed his camera at them and that their reactions prompted him to take even more photographs. Roney ended up storing these images at home, in his private collection. "There is one box," he wrote in 1989, "just for the orphans."[67]

.   .   .   .   .

It was not unusual at the time for clerics to have cameras. Prompted by concerns over celibacy and what some described as a rash of loneliness in the American priesthood, bishops across the United States encouraged their priests to enjoy their free time and seek out some rather standard hobbies. These included gardening, golf, and card games, but photography was probably the most popular avocation for priests by the time Roney first traveled to Guatemala. Clerics had even begun angling their cameras toward subjects that spoke to more introspective questions, lending this increasingly affordable technology spiritual significance. Priests would seek out the presence of God in wide-angled photographs of sunsets, mountain ranges, and lonely city streets, often allowing the wonder of His creation to reveal itself in dramatic black-and-white images. The American monk Thomas Merton, a contemporary of Roney's, became something of a Church-wide ambassador for this practice of contemplative photography. Taking up the art form late in life, Merton understood his camera as an opportunity to see rather than merely to look at the world, to meditate on what his faith took to be some of the most ineffable mysteries of life.

Turning the darkroom into a confessional, photography allowed Merton to develop his own self alongside his photographs.[68]

Roney's efforts to strengthen his faith were a little more halting. He was constantly in search of new ways to revive his dwindling level of devotion and apparently turned to photography as yet another avenue for theological reflection. But nothing seemed to work. "My enthusiasm and ambition gradually declined," he added while under the care of the Servants of the Paraclete. "Only my enjoyment of preaching has stayed intact."[69] Despite photography's failure to restore his ebbing spiritual commitment, the medium empowered Roney to engage the world with newfound confidence. He had always been, in his own words, a "terribly shy" and "reserved" person, and he often blamed this on his years at the seminary.[70] Yet some of this restraint seemed to melt away when he had a camera in his hand. The device gave him the permission he needed to linger at the edges of society, to be both present and absent at the Mission. He would sit for hours underneath a tree at the elementary school or wander through the orphanage over an entire afternoon. His camera drew him out into the world, and did so in ways that focused his desires, normalized his gaze, and further insulated him from the potential suspicions of volunteers from Minnesota.[71]

Given the poverty and the violence, let alone the country's natural beauty and vast array of Indigenous cultures, Roney could have played the part of humanitarian photographer or war correspondent. He could have even imagined himself as a freelance photographer for *National Geographic*. Other priests in Latin America certainly tried their hand at each of these pursuits. Roney, though, spent his days photographing a fantasy that he clearly wanted to inhabit. One photograph is of Roney and a six-year-old Justina. They are in his house on the day of her first holy communion, with Roney sitting in a straight-back chair and turning his head toward Justina, who is standing next to him. She wears a skirt and blouse as well as a white veil and white gloves. The veil and the gloves were standard at the time, meant to symbolize humility, reverence, and modesty before God. "He asked me to look him directly in the eyes when we took the picture," Justina remembered years later. "I do not know why, but we had to take that same photograph several times." Roney wanted to get the composition right, and this meant having the two of them appear, at least superficially, like newlyweds.[72] Roney has his arm around Justina's waist, and they stare into each other's eyes. He smiles intensely toward her and, as instructed, Justina returns his gaze while managing her flowing veil with her gloved hand. "I remember thinking it was strange that he wanted me to look into his eyes," Justina later commented. "It didn't make sense to me." In fairness, most of Roney's images do not make sense, at least at first blush. They only come into focus when placed within the context of Roney's abusive appetites.[73]

Roney's photographs allowed him to curate a world where children scampered about playgrounds and stared deeply into his eyes.[74] If his slides of Rome and the Vatican—the images he used to peruse back in Minnesota at the rectory with a glass of scotch—were about a life once lived, then this parallel set of images from Guatemala provided Roney with a vision of how Edenic life could be, especially when he was able to live without the burden of a diagnosis.[75] It was also a place seemingly without any limits on his behavior. There was a time, of course—a long stretch of time—when Roney had worn a clerical cape back in Minnesota. The cloak allowed him to create a bit of cover while he pressed very young girls and boys against his erections or lured small hands into his pockets with holes cut into them. But Roney never wore a cape in Guatemala. It was too warm, for one, but it was also totally unnecessary. What was there to hide? His actions in town were beyond suspicion, illegible as anything but ordinary care and devotion. Instead, Roney's garment of choice in Guatemala was not priestly at all. It was a novelty t-shirt that he had made with the help of a local vendor. While walking the town with his camera, visiting the orphanage, or even just spending some time on the school's playground, Roney would wear this t-shirt for all to see. It was white and featured an oversized photograph of Justina on the front. She is very young in this image, maybe two years old, and stares blankly into the camera. It is clear that someone on the other side of the lens is trying to get her attention, to make her smile, but all she musters is an empty stare.

·   ·   ·   ·   ·

Roney developed his rolls of film in Guatemala City. This was neither an easy nor an inexpensive task for him. It involved significant amounts of effort and money, but he sacrificed both so that he could hand out his photographs as gifts to people in Guatemala. It was a seemingly generous gesture, allowing those living in the highlands to attain some visual record of their lives, but Roney's attentions were not evenly distributed. He clearly had a type: young girls who had at least one unstable or absent parent. Nor were his gifts motivated by generosity alone. Photographs allowed Roney to build trust with these families, enter their homes, and gain access to their children. To track down Roney's photographs is to quietly map the history of his abuse, block by block, house by house, with each image pinpointing a potential site of his transgressions. One cannot imagine the feeling of relief that washes over the ethnographer when the members of a given family reply that they only have an image or two of his. It is the clearest evidence that Roney passed over their house and their children. The opposite is also true. It is heartbreaking to enter a home and see hundreds of his images taped onto walls and carefully stacked inside boxes, with the most cherished of them tucked into a family bible. This excess of images can make even the warmest home feel like a museum to clerical sexual abuse. "Father David was my godfather [*padrino*]," explained one woman, her wall postered with a thicket of his photographs. There were more than one hundred and fifty of them. The images on her wall were simple snapshots of her and her sisters playing tag, marching in a band, and opening some Christmas presents that Roney himself had delivered on the morning of the twenty-fifth. Nothing about these scenes suggested the violence that these photographs had facilitated.[76]

The photographs Roney took in Guatemala have been passed down from one generation to the next as heirlooms. One family considers itself in debt to Roney because of a particular image that has remained in their possession for almost half a century. The image is of a mother and father, their four daughters and one son. They all sit together in two rows, with the youngest three up front and on the floor. The parents bookend the top row, sitting on either side of their two oldest daughters. It is a beautiful photograph, an effortless execution of middle-class portraiture softened with a heart-warming degree of informality. While the father stares straight into the camera without smiling, the youngest children at his feet break frame, laughing alongside each other. The mother, top right, has also cracked a bit of a smile that might soon trip into laughter. Tragically, the woman in the photograph died of cancer soon after Roney took the picture and well before any of her children could form a lasting memory of her. The young girls, now adults, treasure this lone photograph because it is the only image they have of their mother. "We wouldn't know what she looked like without it," one of them explained.[77] When they think about their mother, dream of her, or even pray to her, she looks like the woman in this photograph. She is relaxed, matronly, and always about to laugh. "I'm so grateful to Father David for this photograph," their father later added.

Roney gifted hundreds of photographs to the people of this small town, allowing them the rare chance to see (and later remember) themselves. It was a lavish, charitable practice that seemed to come straight from Roney's heart, but it was also strategic. He clearly used photographs to ingratiate himself with these families, to put these poor men and women into something of an emotional debt; then, he would continue to ply them with images until he had full access to their children. Roney, for example, continued to take photographs of that woman's four daughters long after she died, becoming the godfather of each one of those little girls. Their father appreciated the priest's interest and support, which began with the occasional image but later included money for medical expenses and tuition payments. Forced to work long hours in the fields, the father of these four girls considered himself blessed to have his children under the careful watch of such a generous American priest. "When I was working in the fields," the father later remembered, "he would take the girls to the lake. Sometimes Father David would spend the whole day with them at the lake."

·   ·   ·   ·   ·

Roney's photographs have a timeless quality to them, in large part because his subjects always seem to be about the same age. He photographed the Mission and its town for thirty years and yet the children in his images remain forever young. His trick was that he would lose interest in kids once they entered adolescence, forever retraining his gaze on those between the ages of five and twelve, but the strategy could only do so much. He often seemed slighted by the effects of time, as if his children of interest had somehow betrayed him by simply growing older. "For years

we were very close," he wrote about one orphan in 1986. "She [once] preferred to hold hands as we walked around town." But time waits for no
one, Roney had learned. "As she approaches her fifteenth birthday," he
wrote with something of a sigh, "she has become painfully shy." She now
refused to hold his hand in public, and Roney was crestfallen: inconsola-
ble. "People tell me she's pretty," Roney wrote with a huff. "I neither know
nor care."[78]

This was not the case with Justina. Roney was not about to let her go.
He was completely committed to her, even as she began to mature before
his eyes. Once cherubic, with chubby cheeks and soft hands, she had by
the turn of the millennium become lean from swimming in the lake and
running around the playground with her friends. Roney could no longer
carry her in his arms: Justina had grown much too big, and he was now far
too old. At the same time, Justina was becoming more independent,
attending elementary school and then running off to play with her friends
in the afternoon. Heartbroken by the passage of time, Roney could not
bear to let his fantasy of Justina go, and his photographs of her were
clearly not enough for him. Thus, he turned to a local sculptor who worked
in stone, commissioning a life-sized statue of Justina at about four years
of age. The statue, which has stood in one of the Mission's courtyards for
decades, is forty inches tall and weighs no more than fifty pounds. The
Justina of this statue wears overalls with suspenders over a short-sleeve
shirt. She is barefoot, her hair in pigtails, and stands upright, on her own
two feet, but not at attention. Her body curls ever so slightly inward, and
her eyes are closed. She looks vulnerable, as if she wants someone to pick
her up—to save her, to take her away.[79]

Orphaned Again

Sololá, Guatemala

January 27, 2003

Father David Roney had not been well for months. At 82 years of age, his heart had begun to fail, and he was struggling to breathe, often coughing and wheezing his way through the night. Already having troubles walking on his own, his growing reliance on a series of increasingly cumbersome oxygen tanks eventually planted him in the same overstuffed recliner in which Justina once napped as a toddler. Now she spent her days sitting next to him as he faded in and out of sleep, holding his hand and wondering to herself how she was ever going to live without him. She was eleven years old and knew that she would soon be an orphan again.

Roney had made provisions, of course, entrusting Justina's future care to one of the women who had worked at the Mission for decades. She was strict but fair, a community leader and trusted mother of three. He had also set up a financial trust for Justina. On her eighteenth birthday, she would receive US$10,000.[80] This was a magnificent sum of money in the highlands of Guatemala, where the average annual salary rarely cracked a tenth of this figure. Roney had also paid in advance for Justina's quinceañera celebration: not just the hall, food, and dress but also a gold necklace that his fellow American priest at the Mission, Father Gregory Schaffer, would present to her on the day of her fifteenth birthday. Finally,

Roney told his long-time housekeeper that the toys, stuffed animals, and towering stacks of Disney videos that littered his living room would all go to Justina. They were for her, he insisted. No one else.

Roney had other reasons to take stock of his life. Only a few months earlier, Bishop John C. Nienstedt, the successor of Bishop Raymond Lucker, wrote a letter to Roney. The bishop explained that the Diocesan Sexual Misconduct Review Board had met "to discuss multiple allegations that have been brought against you since 1987" and that after considerable discussion, the Board "voted unanimously to recommend that you not be allowed to continue pastoral ministry as a priest in good standing." Roney could no longer present himself as a priest in public. "I very much regret the necessity of this canonical action," Nienstedt added, "which you have brought about by your own activity."[81] A stateside colleague from the Diocese of New Ulm then called the Mission to confirm on behalf of the bishop that Roney had received the letter and its decision, but it is unclear whether Roney ever got the message. "Our telephone conversation was very poor," the colleague reported to Nienstedt, "and [Roney's] hearing aid was sounding."[82] Amid broken speech and bursts of noise, with two old men yelling at each other from opposite ends of a continent, Roney effectively vanished.

The highlands of Guatemala allowed Roney to exist beyond the reach of his archive and its consequences. No one at the Mission other than Schaffer knew about the Diocesan Sexual Misconduct Review Board's decision—it worked at the time under the conditions of complete secrecy—but Roney also knew that time was running out for him. His life was clearly coming to an end, and thus, Roney must have known, at least at some level, that he was saying goodbye to Justina when he boarded a private ambulance on January 27, 2003. His health had become far too complicated for the doctors at the Mission, and so he decided to seek out a more sophisticated level of care in the capital city. He had already made several appointments with specialists, each one promising him treatments that would give him a few more years of life, but he never made it. While en route to Guatemala City, along those curvy roads and stomach-turning switchbacks, Roney's heart skipped a beat and then stopped altogether.

A funeral home in Guatemala City prepared the body that same day for its immediate return to the Mission, laying the corpse atop a bed of ice, dressing it (despite the Review Board's decision) in liturgical vestments, and coloring its face with a bit of makeup. Roney had become especially pale toward the end of his life. A hearse then drove the body back to the Mission, where hundreds of mourners greeted Roney's remains with a level of simultaneous reverence and revelry usually reserved for saints and celebrities. There were drums and incense as well as fireworks and dirges. His body then lay in state at the foot of the church's altar until a crowd of at least three hundred well-wishers shouldered the coffin and paraded it through the streets of this small town, slowly wending their way toward the cemetery. Too young and far too short to lend her own shoulder to the procession, Justina insisted on walking closest to the casket, not once letting her hand slip from its brilliantly smooth exterior. She only lost contact when the mourners slid the coffin into a tomb that Roney had purchased for himself years earlier. They then sealed it with a bronze plaque that he had ordered around the same time. As Justina stood at the lip of her father's grave, reading its inscription for the first time, men pounded the plaque into place with rubber mallets while she thought to herself, amid waves of panic, "What now?"

Reverend David Arthur Roney

Those who followed the footsteps of Christ on earth
now rejoice in Heaven; and because they loved Him until
they died for Him, they now celebrate with Him for eternity.

Born 3 January 1921

Died 27 January 2003

IV At the Margins of
Victimhood, 2003–2017

An Accelerating Conversation

Central Minnesota

January 30, 2003

Father David Roney's stateside obituary is really nothing more than a handful of facts strung together in chronological order. It doesn't offer a single descriptive adjective. One gets the sense that the Diocese of New Ulm wanted Roney's death to go unnoticed, to fade into the ether as quietly as possible, but his obituary's publication in one of central Minnesota's daily newspapers didn't just get people talking. It got them angry. The obituary reads, in full:

> Reverend David Arthur Roney died on Monday, January 27, 2003 at the age of 82. A Memorial Mass will be celebrated Monday, February 3, 2003, at the Cathedral of the Holy Trinity in New Ulm, MN at 11:00 a.m. The Mass of Christian Burial was celebrated Wednesday, January 29, 2003 in Guatemala, with burial in the Church cemetery. Father Roney was born January 3, 1921 and was ordained at the St. Paul Cathedral on August 18, 1945. He entered the Diocese of New Ulm in 1957. He retired from active ministry on June 16, 1993 and had been living in Guatemala since 1994.[1]

A woman who would soon enter the legal record as "Jane Doe 43C" stumbled upon the obituary at her kitchen table while drinking her morning cup of coffee. In an instant and without warning, she found herself pressed up against memories that she had spent decades trying to evade. They came in waves. She remembered being the new girl in town and not knowing a soul, that all the other fifth graders already had friends and they told her as much. She also remembered waiting for her bus in the school's entrance or the church's vestibule. She'd pray for it to arrive early, but her bus was always last and often late. Finally, she remembered Roney waiting with her. He would kiss her, tell her that he loved her, and then force her to reach into his pockets and through the holes that he had cut into them. It had all made her feel, in her own words, "worthless and dirty," and so she began to "close off and disappear."[2] This meant hiding her years of abuse—from her family, her church, and most significantly herself—until she read Roney's stub of an obituary, became absolutely incensed that he would be honored at all, and called the law offices of Jeff Anderson & Associates in downtown Saint Paul, Minnesota.

Her phone call came amid an accelerating conversation about clerical sexual abuse in the United States. A year earlier, in January 2002, *The Boston Globe* had begun to publish a series of investigative reports on the Archdiocese of Boston, exposing how top church officials protected abusive priests, stonewalled the media, and paid off dozens of people.[3] *The Boston Globe*'s forty-plus articles led not only to the criminal prosecution of five Roman Catholic priests and the processing of hundreds of other criminal cases but also to a high point in public awareness about clerical sexual abuse. Certainly, there had been national scandals before 2002, with coverage of Father Gilbert Gauthe in Lafayette, Louisiana, and Father Thomas Adamson in Minneapolis, Minnesota, grabbing headlines in the 1980s, but Boston was different. *The Boston Globe*'s coverage proved so relentless and the charges against the Archdiocese of Boston so egregious that bishops throughout the United States realized that they needed to mount a national response. They could not, as they had done in the past, offer a series of apologies, pay for some therapy, and then blame the media for blowing it all out of proportion. Instead, these bishops decided that they needed to take control of the scandal as best they could.

In June 2002, 285 bishops met at the Fairmont Hotel in Dallas, Texas. As cameras clicked and flashed, these Church officials made a series of carefully curated, deeply stylized confessions to an audience of more than seven hundred journalists. "We did not go far enough to ensure that every child and minor was safe," a bishop conceded to a crowded conference hall. "We failed to take the necessary steps."[4] Other bishops followed with similar talking points, engaging in unusually public acts of remorse. Used to hearing their parishioners' confessions and prescribing acts of penance, these clerics were now suddenly the ones performing those rituals of reconciliation, guided by crisis consultants and public relations experts.[5] "We worried more about the possibility of scandal," the same bishop admitted, "than bringing about the kind of openness that helps prevent abuse."[6]

The three-day event in Dallas also included the voices of those directly affected by clerical sexual abuse. "I remember him doing things to me that had never been done [to me] before," recounted one man. "He told me it was OK. [He told me] it was part of growing up."[7] The bishops listened intently, many leaning forward in their seats and even burying their heads in their hands. One bishop later commented to the press that the testimonies were "terrifically overwhelming," and he was right.[8] "I could describe nights curling up in the fetal position and sobbing hysterically," explained another man, "and eventually having to get up and change the bed sheets because they were soaked with tears."[9] Unsettling sound bites such as these punctuated the bishops' time in Dallas, with many of these statements broadcast live on cable news outlets and then replayed on the nightly news. It was a theater of contrition that ultimately helped to frame the announcement of a new set of procedures for addressing allegations of clerical sexual abuse.[10] These were guidelines that would soon come to be known in Roman Catholic communities throughout the United States as "the Charter."

The *Charter for the Protection of Children and Young People* provides guidelines for reconciliation, healing, accountability, and the prevention of future acts of abuse, with its primary purpose being the creation of a safe environment for children.[11] The Charter also includes a pledge to report all allegations of sexual abuse to police, a policy of zero tolerance when it comes to this abuse, and a stated commitment to never reassign an offending cleric to another parish. After an investigation in accordance with canon law, a cleric found guilty of sexual abuse would not be removed of his ontological capacity to be a priest, since this is not theologically possible, but would instead be permanently removed from ministry. Finally, the Charter inaugurated a national Office for the Protection of Children and Young People. The office would not only audit dioceses' compliance with the Charter but also inaugurate a thicket of bureaucratic procedures aimed at keeping the language of personal boundaries and a healthy suspicion of authority top of mind within Roman Catholic parishes, schools, hospitals, seminaries, and charities. These procedures included trademarked videos and workbooks along with in-person programming sessions and certification programs that promised "five easy steps" to prevent clerical sexual abuse. With titles such as "Protecting God's Children®" and "Teaching Boundary and Safety,™" these Church-produced prevention programs delivered their lessons in "digestible bites"—aiming to prevent wrongdoing and promote "right doing."[12] Facilitators also defined child sexual abuse for their participants, encouraged its reporting to law enforcement officials, discussed how to screen and then select for employees and volunteers, celebrated victim advocacy, and published pastoral codes of conduct.

The National Catholic Risk Retention Group, Inc. published the first pastoral code of conduct on March 17, 2003, and this made good business sense. This limited liability association provides dioceses throughout the United States with comprehensive insurance and risk management programs, having opened for business in the 1980s amid two national crises. The first was the clerical sexual abuse scandal in Lafayette, Louisiana, centered on the predatory behaviors of Gilbert Gauthe and some of his fellow priests. Their abusive acts opened dioceses in Louisiana and beyond to unanticipated levels of legal liability. People across the nation started to sue priests, parishes, and dioceses for ever-larger financial settlements. The second crisis, occurring roughly at the same time, was the near collapse of the American insurance industry, with *Time* magazine clocking the mood of the nation with the wry headline of a 1986 cover story: "Sorry America, Your Insurance Has Been Canceled."[13] The headline applied to a range of nonprofit and commercial entities but proved to be especially relevant for the Roman Catholic Church in the United States. After the scandal in Lafayette, insurance companies had begun to include exclusionary language in their liability policies, eventually denying coverage for claims arising from sexual contact between priests and parishioners.

U.S. bishops scrambled to find policies that would cover the risk and liability of clerical sexual abuse, but in the end, they could find neither comprehensive nor affordable coverage. Left completely exposed by the abusive appetites of their own priesthood, bishops across the country turned toward National Catholic, but it was coverage that came with significant compromise. National Catholic would insure dioceses and their parishes, with policies that would eventually cover roughly 80 percent of all future abuse settlements, but bishops and their priests would have to take an increasingly preventive and proactive approach to sexual misconduct. This meant talking about clerical sexual abuse—openly, and seemingly all the time.[14]

The unintended effect of the Charter, the newly inaugurate Office for the Protection of Children, and these insurance policies, with their prevention programs and codes of conduct, was to make the scandal of clerical sexual abuse an even more uncontrollable phenomenon for bishops in the United States. Rather than managing the situation by naming the sin in Dallas and then taking some level of responsibility with the Charter, all in the hopes of pushing the topic deep into the past with the right kind of programming, talk of clerical sexual abuse ended up creating even more talk of clerical sexual abuse.[15] It proliferated. For one thing, those in the United States began to learn about these violations of trust from investigative journalists and even from the Church itself, through its own prevention programs. But they also (and far more profoundly) had the vocabulary to reread their past experiences with priests in the context of this ever-multiplying talk of abuse. They finally had the necessary language to become victims and survivors.

After reading Roney's obituary, the woman known as Jane Doe 43C called Anderson's office because she was angry. But she was also empowered by a new way of being that had not previously been made available to her.[16] By her own account, this woman had "discussed the generalities of the incidents" with her mother in 1980, a full decade after Roney had abused her.[17] She also mentioned something to her boyfriend at about the same time and then to her husband years later in 1995, but these conversations didn't amount to much and for good reason.[18] For one, they leaned on intimations and knowing glances. She didn't entirely know how to describe what Roney had done to her years earlier. More importantly, her comments were delivered and heard in a context where her experiences could not be immediately linked to a legally substantial and therapeutically recognizable identity: the identity of the victim of clerical sexual abuse. Few people in 1980 or even in 1995 knew how to respond to her experiences with Roney, or even what to call them. It was only in the winter of 2003, after the events of Boston and the meeting in Dallas, that this woman could describe Roney's obsessive interest in her as grooming, his sexually invasive touch as abusive, and her years of nightmares as the symptoms of that abuse. Only in the winter of 2003—serendipitously, on the heels of Roney's death—could she begin to understand herself as having been a victim and then a survivor of this priest's abuse.

Importantly, the woman known in the legal record as Jane Doe 43C was not alone in her transformation. In 2003, Anderson's law offices began to field more than a dozen phone calls every day from men and women, each of them stepping forward for the first time in their lives. This created more work than Anderson and his team of lawyers could handle. "I'm managing 150 cases [of clerical sexual abuse]," Anderson mentioned to the press with some exasperation, noting that if he had the time he could "probably manage another 150."[19] This included a growing cohort of survivors with credible accusations against Roney, with Jane Doe 43C soon meeting in person with women now known in the legal record as Jane Doe 43A, Jane Doe 43B, Jane Doe 43D, Jane Doe 43E, Jane Doe 43F, and Jane Doe 43G. In the winter of 2003, alongside many others, these survivors began to form a joint action lawsuit against the Diocese of New Ulm.[20]

The growing number of people coming to understand themselves as survivors in and around 2003 could have been financially cataclysmic for the Diocese of New Ulm, but Minnesota's statute of limitations safe-guarded the Church. In 2003, a sexually abused child in Minnesota needed to file a claim within six years of the assault or by the age of twenty-four, but this was rarely enough time for a person to gather enough per-spective and the courage to speak out. Carol, for example—that young girl who had pressed a statue of Christ up against her sister's doll decades earlier—had read Roney's obituary and had called Anderson's law offices, but she had waited too many years to file a claim. "I called Anderson's office, but he said that he couldn't do anything for me," she explained years later. Minnesota's statute of limitations provided the Diocese of New Ulm with a levy against a rising tide of claimants, one that allowed Bishop John

C. Nienstedt—Raymond Lucker's successor—and his team of lawyers to frame Roney and others as abusive outliers rather than as the direct responsibility of the Church. The attorney representing the diocese told the local press in Minnesota that "without sufficient evidence to admit or deny, we're taking the position that the diocese is not legally responsible or liable or negligent."[21] Roney was a sexual predator, Nienstedt conceded, but he acted alone.

Anderson, working alongside a groundswell of advocates and activists, took matters into his own hands. He spent the next decade further accelerating the conversation on clerical sexual abuse in Minnesota with the goal of amending the state's statute of limitations. He sought a constitutionally mandated window of time during which survivors of clerical sexual abuse could file civil lawsuits against the dioceses of Minnesota regardless of when the abuse occurred. Anderson's efforts were loud. They were brash. At times perpetuating the many clichés of personal injury attorneys in his dogged pursuit of new clients, Anderson relied on a steady drumbeat of press conferences, photo opportunities, and media appearances to get the public's attention. In one, the two women initially known as Jane Doe 43A and Jane Doe 43B spoke to a room filled with journalists, photographers, and reporters. A photograph of David Roney was prominently displayed. "I originally filed as a Jane Doe," one of them explained, "but I guess I decided I could be brave enough to use my name." She held a photograph of herself at about the age when Roney had abused her. She is nine years old in the image, wears a blue sundress, and smiles brightly for the camera. "This man was God to us," she said with her mother at her side. "I looked up and all I saw was that white collar." Anderson then recounted the timeline of Roney's case, focusing on the abuse the two women experienced. "The bishops became clearly aware that this guy was a serial molester," Anderson told the press. "[They] allowed him to continue in ministry, moved him to various parishes, and ultimately out of Willmar to Guatemala where he continued in ministry in good standing." The facts spoke for themselves, Anderson insisted: "What we have learned, at least by our count, [is that] at least twenty kids, both boys and girls, were molested by this offender." With the known number of Roney's survivors in Minnesota eventually doubling, these two women ended the press conference with a talking point that would soon serve as Anderson's principal legal argument: "Father Roney was our predator," one of them said, "but the diocese is the monster."[22]

.   .   .   .   .

Everything changed on May 24, 2013, in a magnificent *whoosh*. The Minnesota House of Representatives signed the Child Victims Act into law after years of raucous organizing and vociferous debate. It created a three-year window for those abused as children to file civil suits against their abusers and the institutions that harbored these criminal actors, irrespective of when the abuse took place. Over the next three years, until its expiration on May 16, 2016, the Child Victims Act would result in more than 550 claims against Roman Catholic priests, force an archbishop to resign, and send multiple dioceses into bankruptcy.[23] More than one hundred credibly accused priests from Minnesota would also be publicly named during this three-year period, in large part because people finally had access—in the words of Michel Foucault—to the "machinery for speechifying, analyzing, and investigating" necessary to become victims.[24] This included psychological assessments, courses of outpatient therapy, and a bevy of legal forms, from survivor testimonies to proofs of claim to damage questionnaires. All this reporting ended up bringing about more victims. It created them at unanticipated scales of production, not because of sensationalism or self-deception but rather because of a framework that finally made victimhood a clearly legible category, one that invited the people of Minnesota to connect their past experiences to a now recognizable social identity. "Anderson's office called me," Carol remembers, "and so I started putting pen to paper. I made some notes. And then I wrote about my abuse."

Notably, this process of becoming a victim was just as culturally specific as the process of becoming a perpetrator of clerical sexual abuse, a fact that can only be truly appreciated when juxtaposed with the experiences of those who found themselves at the margins of victimhood: those who had experiences best understood today as clerical sexual abuse but who could not access the social identity of a victim of such abuse. This was certainly the case with Justina. None of this stateside talk of clerical sexual abuse ever made it to the highlands of Guatemala, neither at the point of

Roney's passing in 2003 nor with the signing of the Minnesota Child Victims Act in 2013. The Diocese of New Ulm never made a public statement in Guatemala about David Roney, never established its own office for the protection of children and young people in Guatemala, and never adapted any element of the Charter in the United States for children in Guatemala. "No one ever told me about his history of abuse," Justina would explain years later. "I knew nothing. I had no idea about the lawsuits. I had never heard of the [Child Victims] Act. No one ever told me anything." The diocese protected its own interests above all else.

There were also practical obstacles, of course, to Justina accessing any of this information. She lived in a remote town. Well beyond the earshot of Anderson's organizing and the Church's parade of stateside concessions, literally on the other side of a volcano, Justina in one sense never had the chance to become a victim of David Roney's abuse. Yet strangely enough, given a Church-sponsored trip that she took to Minnesota in April 2012, Justina might have had just as much of a chance as anyone in the United States.

In the Dark

Central Minnesota

April 9, 2012

A blood-red silo.

Wind whipping in from the west.

The uncertain grayness of northern sky.

Nineteen years old, Justina was curled up in the backseat of a slightly dented sedan when she arrived at the farm. The purr of the car's engine had mixed with the indecipherable murmur of talk radio to lull her to sleep. The old man who had picked her up at the Minneapolis–Saint Paul International Airport, with a handwritten sign that read "Justina" in thick black letters, was a volunteer from the church. Though eager and earnest, ready to serve in any way he could, he did not speak a word of Spanish. Once they smiled at each other, shook hands, and then laughed uncomfortably after he tried to pantomime something about the weather, Justina finally had the chance to realize just how tired she was.

Her trip from the highlands of Guatemala to central Minnesota had begun days earlier, in the dead of night. There was, first, that four- to five-hour van ride from her home to the capital city, and then a pair of international flights. In each of the airports that she entered and then exited— first in Guatemala City, then in Atlanta, and finally in Minneapolis—she was faced with a crush of questions. Customs officers, security guards, and airline stewards seemed to constantly ask Justina for her passport or her visa or her boarding pass. She found the seeming urgency of each request overwhelming, with every encounter startling her anew. At one point, while handing her passport to an agent in Atlanta, Justina noticed that her hand was shaking.

The air travel itself was otherworldly, however, more magical than she could have ever imagined. It filled Justina with the kind of euphoric optimism that international travel can sometimes evoke. Before her first ever flight, from Guatemala City to Atlanta, Justina even marshalled enough pluck to ask the passenger sitting next to her whether she could have the window seat. Justina wanted to see the world as she had never seen it, from on high and through a bank of clouds. It was magnificent.[25] To this day, she swears that she spotted her town a few minutes after taking off, her lakeside village quietly nestled on the banks of Lake Atitlán against the backdrop of lush landscape. The experience of soaring thousands of feet above her home, of racing past her neighbors as they quietly went about their day, also lent Justina an unexpected vantage on life. It is a perspective she sometimes revisits when she is overwhelmed with anxiety or has trouble falling asleep: a visceral, deeply existential sense that the world is vast and that we are all so fantastically small.[26]

Father Gregory Schaffer had hoped that Justina would enjoy her trip to the United States. After almost fifty years of directing the Diocese of New Ulm's Mission in Guatemala, during which he had seen Justina grow up largely under the care of Father David Roney, Schaffer had returned to central Minnesota in early 2012, at first to seek medical treatment for an aggressive form of cancer and then, once his doctors delivered a terminal diagnosis, to prepare himself for death. Doing so meant sending for Justina, as well as for the woman who had taken full responsibility for her after Roney died in 2003. Schaffer had added a few outreach events to Justina and her guardian's itinerary in Minnesota, in the hopes of raising some awareness and funds for the Mission.

Justina visited a pair of churches during her time in Minnesota at Schaffer's request, the second parish even more rural than the first. Speaking through a translator, she and her long-time guardian told a chapel full of parishioners about their country's thirty-six-year civil war, how the military had targeted their Indigenous community in a horrifically genocidal effort to purify the nation, and why it was so important for Christian solidarity to reach across borders. They spoke from notes, earnestly getting the facts right, and then they thanked those in attendance for their support. They would never have been able to survive the war without the Diocese of New Ulm's Mission, the two of them said, and on this point they were likely correct.[27]

Schaffer's intentions for Justina's stateside trip, however, had little to do with the Mission. Instead, they were almost entirely personal. He wanted a quiet moment to say thank you and goodbye to some of the people whom he loved the most. From April 9 to April 30, 2012, amid the loudest moments of public debate in Minnesota over the Child Victims Act, when Roney's photograph loomed in the background of televised press conferences and the topic of clerical sexual abuse was routinely frontpage news, Justina visited the Diocese of New Ulm for three weeks. Though she did so at Schaffer's request, visiting those parishes on his behalf, she ended up seeing Schaffer only once during her time in the Great Plains. They ate dinner together (just the two of them) at a noisy restaurant, the kind with bright lights, laminated menus, and huge portions. They didn't talk about much of anything, Justina recalls. Schaffer asked her about her studies, which were advancing well, and her search for part-time work, which wasn't really going anywhere. Her hometown, they agreed, is impossibly small. During a lull in the conversation, when Schaffer seemed to be searching for something to say, Justina did mention the inheritance that she had just received from Roney's estate. She thanked him for safeguarding (for so many years) a sum of US$2,000 that she now had in her bank account. "I mentioned the exact amount of money," Justina explained years later, "because I was suspicious. I wanted to see the reaction on his face when I thanked him."

Justina had been waiting on this money for nearly a decade, knowing that it would come to her on her eighteenth birthday. No one had ever told her the exact amount of the gift. Over the years, Justina's thoughts would on occasion drift toward the idea of this inheritance. She wasn't being greedy, she reasoned, just practical. Maybe it would be enough to buy a small house, she would daydream, or pay for a university education. She knew full well that Roney didn't have much family. No one from the United States had attended his funeral in Guatemala, and not a single person had come to the Mission to visit his grave. Justina had never even met anyone close to him. It all made her think that his wealth, such as it was, would not have been divided too many ways upon his death. She knew that Roney had not been a rich man, but she also knew that his capacity to earn money in the United States, even as a parish priest, had far outpaced whatever would have been possible in Guatemala. "$2,000 surprised me," she later admitted. "That's not a lot of money. I wondered whether someone had taken some of it." Schaffer's reaction did not ease her suspicions. "He flinched when I mentioned the money," Justina remembered. "I could see it in his face. He was hiding something."

Justina was right, of course. Schaffer knew more than he was letting on. He knew full well that Roney had set up a financial trust for Justina worth $10,000, not $2,000.[28] The original amount would have given Justina more than enough money to buy a small house and to pursue a university education, effectively setting her up for a lifetime of success in Guatemala. But Schaffer likely had no idea where the rest of Justina's inheritance had gone. A stateside lawyer had managed the financial trust, and Schaffer had never been in contact with him. He was also notoriously absent-minded when it came to money. The more likely reason why Schaffer had twitched at Justina's comment was that her inheritance was the least of the secrets that he was shouldering. If not immediately on his mind during their dinner, then certainly banging around his subconscious was a mountain of information about Roney that Schaffer had never disclosed to Justina. It included the following facts:

Schaffer knew in 1987 about the letters that Bishop Lucker had received from some of Roney's survivors, taking note of one that reads, "My concern extends, of course, to the children of our mission."[29]

Schaffer knew in 1990 about Roney's years of therapy to resolve his sexual disorders and about a report from Roney's therapist that confessed, "Dave did have one incident while he was in therapy with me. He did touch a woman in Guatemala in an inappropriate way."[30]

Schaffer knew in 1993 about the report that the Diocese's Review Board for Sexual Misconduct had written about Roney. Having been interviewed for the report, Schaffer is quoted as saying that Roney in Guatemala "likes to have children around him, that he prefers younger girls to boys" and that "[the children] gather around him, hug him, sit on his lap etc." It also mentioned that "his focus has been on children of the poor and widowed."[31]

Schaffer knew in 1995 that Bishop Raymond Lucker, in a meeting with the Review Board for Sexual Misconduct, had registered his worries regarding Roney's care of Justina. Lucker had scribbled on a notepad that "this new report of Roney 'raising' this little girl is a concern to me."[32]

Schaffer also knew in 1995 that Roney had a novelty t-shirt made with Justina's face on it, had commissioned a life-sized statue in her likeness, and had spent the weekend with her at a hotel to celebrate her fifth birthday.

Schaffer knew in 1997 about a lawsuit against Roney whose documents clearly state that "Father Roney has admitted to the Diocese that he had sexually abused young girls." Schaffer also knew that this was not the first lawsuit against Roney.[33]

Schaffer knew in 2002 that the Diocese's Review Board for Sexual Misconduct had unanimously decided to terminate Roney's pastoral duties and had also requested that Roney return to Minnesota "to discuss what limited options are available for the future."[34]

Schaffer also knew in 2002 that the stateside lawyer Jeff Anderson had written to Bishop John Nienstedt about the whereabouts of Roney: "I have reason to believe," Anderson wrote, "that he may be currently assigned in Guatemala."[35]

Schaffer knew in 2007 that he had been named in an affidavit. "I told [a nun]," a North American missionary in Guatemala testified, "about Father Roney's plans to adopt the child and she was also very upset. She reported Father Roney's activities to Father Schaffer."[36]

Schaffer knew in 2008 about Jane Doe 43A, Jane Doe 43B, Jane Doe 43C, Jane Doe 43D, Jane Doe 43E, Jane Doe 43F, and Jane

Doe 43G. Schaffer also knew that there were dozens of others who had stepped forward after Roney's death.[37]

Schaffer knew in 2012 that Minnesota's Child Victims Act was all but a done deal, with legislators fine-tuning the law's language while attorneys such as Anderson gathered their claims.

Why did Schaffer not tell any of this to Justina, neither in Guatemala, where they both lived, nor at that chain restaurant in rural Minnesota? The most obvious interpretation of Schaffer's silence is that he wanted to protect the Mission and safeguard his legacy. Schaffer knew that Anderson and others had already won a series of multimillion-dollar settlements against various dioceses and archdioceses throughout the United States. The numbers seemed unbelievable to him. The Archdiocese of Louisville had paid 243 claimants $25.7 million; the Archdiocese of Boston had paid 550 claimants $85 million; the Diocese of Orange County had paid 90 claimants $100 million; the Diocese of Spokane had paid 150 claimants $48 million; the Archdiocese of Portland had paid 175 claimants $75 million; the Archdiocese of Los Angeles had paid 508 claimants $660 million; the Diocese of San Diego had paid 144 claimants $200 million; and the Diocese of Wilmington had paid 146 claimants $77 million.[38] Schaffer had also noted the number of parishes and schools that had closed as a result of these payments.

A settlement similar in size, Schaffer reasoned, would level not only the Diocese of New Ulm but also its Mission in Guatemala, eviscerating in an instant a lifetime of work at the Mission that had uplifted and transformed a small Indigenous town and its people.[39] In his half century of ministerial work, Schaffer had opened a medical and dental clinic, elementary schools for more than six hundred students a year, a library, various land projects, a women's center, and the coffee program. What would happen if Anderson extended his investigations to Guatemala and found not just Justina but also dozens of other children whom Roney might have abused? Approaching the end of his life at an unanticipated clip, Schaffer likely winced at the idea of Anderson publicly sullying his pastoral reputation with the accusation that he had aided and abetted a sexual predator such as Roney. The people of Guatemala, knowing that Schaffer was not well, had already begun forming a commission to fast-track his case for saint-hood, erecting statues in his likeness and naming entire parts of their town to commemorate not just him but also his mother, father, and sister. They revered Schaffer, treating him like a living saint, and Schaffer basked in their affection.

The problem with this interpretation is that it does not explain why Schaffer would have sent for Justina in the first place, generously flying her from Guatemala to Minnesota amid such public debate over an impending wave of lawsuits. If Schaffer wanted Justina to abide in silence, to be kept completely in the dark, then it would have been better to leave her on the other side of those volcanoes. This is why a different, slightly more sinister (even if also more banal) interpretation of Schaffer's silence is likelier. Why did Schaffer send for Justina in April 2012 and yet mention neither Roney's history of abuse nor the life-altering settlement that, in both moral and legal terms, she had every right to pursue? The likeliest reason is that Schaffer, like so many other North Americans, could not conceive of Justina or any other Indigenous man or woman as a victim of clerical sexual abuse.[40]

In 1990, after learning that Roney had touched a woman in Guatemala in an inappropriate way, his therapist admitted that "because of cultural differences and [Roney's] role in the Guatemalan mission, I was not sure of the seriousness of the incident."[41] Schaffer's silence can be read in similar ways. Victims and survivors of clerical sexual abuse, Schaffer would have come to know by 2012, made public accusations. They compiled evidence in the form of affidavits and depositions. They partnered with personal injury attorneys and underwent a battery of psychological evaluations to establish credibility. They were also white rather than Indigenous, and North American instead of Central American, filling out survivor testimonies, proofs of claim, and damage questionnaires in English rather than Spanish. The photograph that Jane Doe 43A held at that press conference back in 2012, the one of herself as a nine-year-old girl in a blue dress, presents the clearest image of a survivor: young, innocent, and American. Justina at the time did not match this profile; thus, Schaffer excluded her from these identity-defining activities.[42]

Schaffer's obliviousness placed Justina at the margins of victimhood, and this is a shame. Had Schaffer truly wanted to say thank-you and goodbye to those whom he loved the most, he would have made a public statement in Guatemala about David Roney, established an office for the protection of children and young people in Guatemala, and adapted the U.S. Charter for the children of Guatemala. Just as profoundly, he would have set up an appointment for Justina with one of Anderson's Spanish-speaking legal assistants—to begin the arduous process of filing a claim against the Diocese of New Ulm and maybe even against Schaffer himself. It would have been a truly sacrificial act, maybe even evidence of actual sainthood, and it could have begun to redeem Schaffer's soul while also fundamentally transforming Justina's very way of being. Just as Carol had put pen to paper, making some notes and then writing about her abuse, Justina would have been able to make herself up as a victim and then a survivor while also pursuing the possibility of a proper settlement with the Diocese of New Ulm. Other Guatemalans could have done the same.

Instead of facilitating some degree of justice and accountability, Schaffer planted Justina on a remote farm for her entire time in Minnesota, effectively re-creating the cultural isolation that she experienced in the orphanage and in Roney's house back in Guatemala. "From the front door of the house in Minnesota," Justina remembered years later, "I couldn't see another house. There was no one around. I didn't see anyone else for weeks. No one. Not once. Never." One of the only times that Justina left the farm, other than when she spoke at those two churches and had dinner with Schaffer, was to visit a big-box department store several miles away. Schaffer had given Justina a few hundred dollars after their dinner together, in the hopes that she could buy some items in the United States that might allow her to start a small business in Guatemala. Justina had become known in town for her skill in preparing young girls' hair for their quinceañera celebrations, and so Schaffer thought that, with a small investment of cash, Justina could purchase a new hairdryer and a set of hot curlers, setting her fledgling business apart. These few hundred dollars obviously did not add up to her original inheritance; a set of curlers paled in comparison to the small house and university education that $10,000 could have provided Justina. And Schaffer's cash gift certainly did not match the six- or seven-figure settlement that Justina would have had every right to pursue once the Child Victims Act came into law a few months later.[43] But Justina had little idea about the original amount of her inheritance and still less about the Child Victims Act, and so she spent an entire day at the store, a full ten hours, diligently surveying the aisles, studying products, and ever so carefully deciding how she would spend her money. "I wanted to make sure that I bought the right items," she would later remember. All of it so she could become the only kind of person that Schaffer—and Justina, at the time—thought that she could be.

Claimant No. 68

Saint Paul, Minnesota

July 10, 2017

The Diocese of New Ulm declared itself insolvent in spring 2017. Minnesota's Child Victims Act, with its three-year suspension of the state's statute of limitations, had resulted in more than five hundred credible claims of clerical sexual abuse. More than one hundred of them concerned priests from the Diocese of New Ulm, and the projected impact of these claims quickly outpaced the diocese's total assets, ultimately forcing its bishop—John LeVoir, who had succeeded Nienstedt in 2008—to file for bankruptcy. "I have come to the conclusion," announced LeVoir, "that financial reorganization is the fairest way to compensate victims and survivors of sexual abuse."[44]

Bankruptcy consolidated the many lawsuits against the Diocese of New Ulm into a single case, with one judge and one court. The intention was to distribute the diocese's available assets across a pool of claimants. The alternative would have meant a process of divvying the same amount of money spanning years of litigation, with the earliest claimants likely receiving huge settlements and later claimants possibly losing out entirely because of empty coffers. This is why LeVoir could invoke the language of "fairness" in his announcement, but he must have also had on his mind some of the many advantages that bankruptcy offered the Church.[45]

One advantage was that bankruptcy would allow LeVoir to transfer and reclassify many of the Diocese of New Ulm's assets, effectively shielding these assets from litigation and thereby shrinking the amount of money available to claimants. This became standard practice in the United States. By 2017, more than a dozen dioceses had restructured their investments, land holdings, and bank accounts just prior to filing for bankruptcy. In 2007, for example, the Archdiocese of Milwaukee moved nearly $57 million into a shielded trust for the perpetual care of its cemeteries; in 2012, the Archdiocese of Santa Fe protected $91 million in assets from bankruptcy court, in part by moving $34 million of its properties into a protected trust; and in 2015, after filing for bankruptcy, the Archdiocese of Saint Paul and Minneapolis claimed that it didn't own the parishes, schools, or cemeteries within its ecclesiastical territory. "They took a paintbrush," Anderson explained at a press conference, "and painted over the name 'Archdiocese of Saint Paul–Minneapolis.'"[46] LeVoir followed suit in New Ulm, executing what diocesan legal teams since the 2002 scandal in the Archdiocese of Boston have called "the playbook."

The Diocese of New Ulm might not have taken a paintbrush to its Mission in Guatemala, but it achieved nearly the same effect by establishing a stateside nonprofit organization to manage the Mission's finances. Receiving its certificate of incorporation from the state of Minnesota on October 29, 2012, just six months prior to the Child Victims Act, this nonprofit organization effectively cleaved the Mission from the Diocese of New Ulm—in a formal, legal sense—by disaggregating the former's liability from the latter's assets.[47] Given that declarations of bankruptcy release third-party non-debtors such as the Mission from liability, this nonprofit organization shielded the Mission in Guatemala from any lawsuits brought against the Diocese of New Ulm in Minnesota while also lightening the diocese's obligation to inform the Mission of any stateside instances of clerical sexual abuse. Bishop LeVoir now had no legal obligation to inform the Mission of any wrongdoing in Minnesota.

Crucially, bankruptcy also put a hard stop to the possibility of any future claims. This one case would be the only time survivors of clerical sexual abuse could file suit against the Diocese of New Ulm. By design, there would be no more money available for future survivors. The money would be divided in its entirety among those who stepped forward by July 10, 2017. To do so, claimants needed to submit a sexual abuse proof of claim form to the U.S. Bankruptcy Court Clerk of Minnesota, and Carol quickly complied, working with Anderson's legal team to answer a series of court-approved questions. These questions not only allowed Carol, as a creditor, to establish a claim against her debtor, the diocese, but also served to standardize her experience of clerical sexual abuse across a pool of applicants. This standardization would allow the judge to assess the severity of the harm that each claimant had suffered and adjust the value of the award that a claimant would receive accordingly.

<u>Who committed each act of sexual abuse?</u>
Father David Roney

<u>What is the position, title, or relationship to you of the abuser or individual who committed these acts?</u>
Fr. Roney was the parish priest, where Carol was a student and parishioner.

<u>Where did the sexual abuse take place?</u>
The abuse occurred in the rectory of the church.

<u>If you were sexually abused on more than one occasion, please state when the abuse started, when it stopped, and how many times it occurred.</u>
The abuse occurred approximately at least 1 time.

<u>Please also state your age(s) and your grade(s) in school (if applicable) at the time the abuse took place.</u>
Carol was approximately 11 years old and going into approximately 6th grade.

<u>Were there any witnesses? If so, please list their name(s) and any contact information you have, including addresses.</u>
No.[48]

This was not the first time that Carol had written or spoken about her abuse. Back in 1987, when April and others had written letters to Bishop Raymond Lucker about Roney, Carol had confided in her therapist. She then spoke about her experience with several more therapists over the years, eventually adding her husband, sisters, mother, and children to her list of confidants.[49] At one point, Carol even reached out to a local sheriff to complete a background check on Roney, curious to know if the priest had ever been arrested. In the end, no one did anything about Carol's information except console her. It was not until the summer of 2017 that a member of Anderson's legal team encouraged Carol to write the full story of her experience, as something of a primer for the eventual task of completing her proof of claim form. A legal assistant told Carol to include as many details as she could.

An earnest and careful person, with the conceptual diligence of a professional historian, Carol took weeks to reflect on her experience of abuse and its impact on her life, at first collecting pages of notes and observations—glints of memory—and then organizing them into a storyboard. As she listed the events of her abuse chronologically, Carol gained profound perspective on how Roney's grooming and abuse not only preyed on her as an eleven-year-old child but also had effects that persisted through her adult life, generating a lasting distrust of authority and an unshakable dislike of herself. "Once I collected all of my notes, I just started to write," Carol remembered. "And when I wrote, I kind of lost myself in the process. I wasn't even aware of what I was writing. My mind took over, and it just happened." In probably the most hauntingly beautiful passage of her preliminary account, after admitting that Roney had made her feel as if she "had no rights" and "was just a piece of trash," Carol describes her interiority in a cinematically horrifying way.[50] "If someone were to cut me open," she writes, "all there would be is petrification and not decay."[51]

Anderson's legal team congratulated Carol on her exemplary account, circulated the document among other claimants as something of a model to which they should aspire, and then kept it on file as a resource for future survivors. "It was really nice," she later noted, "how much they liked my essay. I felt validated." Carol was thus surprised when Anderson's legal team harvested her essay for facts and sound bites for the proof of claim form. Most strikingly, the new paperwork transformed her first-person testimony into a third-person report. This shift in perspective was part of a larger process of remaking. Through her proof of claim form, Carol became a different kind of person: Claimant No. 68.

Please describe in as much detail as possible the nature of the
sexual abuse.
On several occasions, when Carol visited Fr. Roney at the rectory, he
forced her to sit on his lap. On one occasion, she went to see Fr. Roney
after her grandmother passed away. Fr. Roney took Carol upstairs in
the rectory to a large office where they talked. Fr. Roney grabbed
Carol's arm and pulled her onto his lap, positioning her to sit perpen-
dicular to Fr. Roney. He wrapped his arms around Carol's waist and
clasped them together so that Carol could not move.[52]

Carol's proof of claim form articulated her abuse with what she felt were
someone else's words. They were forensic in tone, purely descriptive in
their character. Gone were her metaphors and analogies, her flights of
imagination, as well as any reference to her dreams or emotions.
Anderson's legal team had replaced her testimony with a voice and ver-
nacular that Carol did not recognize. "I guess I understand the process,"
Carol later reflected. "They were just doing their job, and they know what
they are doing; but the answers in the [proof of claim] form are nothing
like what I wrote in my essay." Hopeful that the process might carry some
consequence in the form of a financial settlement, Carol deferred to
Anderson's expertise but would nonetheless struggle to recognize herself
as Claimant No. 68. It was like Anderson's team was asking Carol to be
herself and someone else at the same time.

What happened? Please describe in as much detail as possible.
Carol felt something on her thigh. When she looked down, she saw Fr.
Roney's cassock open from his waist and next to the outside of her
thigh she saw Fr. Roney's erect penis. Fr. Roney brushed it against her
thigh. Fr. Roney held Carol on his lap for several minutes. As soon as
he loosened his grip, Carol got up and stood in front of a window,
looking into the street for several minutes and then turned back to the
room to face Fr. Roney. His cassock was buttoned up and he was
standing near the couch he was sitting on.[53]

Carol's construction as Claimant No. 68 had a totalizing influence on her.
Anderson's legal team invited Carol to catalogue her physical, emotional,

and psychological struggles, at one point presenting her with a list of injuries commonly suffered by survivors of sexual abuse. Anderson's legal team wanted to make the strongest case possible that Roney's abuse of Carol had a demonstrably negative impact on her life. Carol quickly moved through this menu of ailments, underlining the injuries that resonated with her unquestionably difficult life. She noted feelings of isolation, weight gain, and nightmares. Each one of her pen strokes darkened a line that connected her abuse in the rectory to her identity as Claimant No. 68.

> What injuries have occurred to you because of the act or acts
> of sexual abuse that resulted in the claim?
> Carol has suffered from various physical, emotional and psychological
> injuries as a result of the abuse, including but not limited to: depression,
> anxiety, PTSD, stomach problems, headaches, trust issues, self-blaming,
> feeling uncomfortable in groups, isolation, feeling less worthy than oth-
> ers, feelings of being tainted, loss of sexual desire and activity, relation-
> ship and intimacy issues, sexual dysfunction, dreams, nightmares, flash-
> backs and sleep issues, feelings of having an unfulfilled life, feelings of
> anger, emotional distress, sadness, shame, embarrassment, weight gain,
> feelings of weakness, feelings of being powerless, self esteem issues,
> fearfulness, feelings of guilt, faith, religion and spirituality issues.[54]

However altered and remade Carol might have become through the process, her claim against the Diocese of New Ulm provided her with an astounding sense of clarity and community. At her lowest point, back on the farm in central Minnesota, a young Carol would tend to her siblings and complete her chores in a constant state of terror. She wrote as much in her free-form essay for Anderson's team, exploring in careful prose how Roney's abuse had led her to believe that she "wasn't good enough to be treated like a real human" and that God had rejected her as a "defective animal."[55] Carol writes almost philosophically about a hierarchy of beings that once seemed to govern her moral imagination, with animals inferior to humans and humans inferior to God. She is clear in her essay that she struggled for years to find her place in the world. But none of her profound existential struggle comes through in her proof of claim form. Claimant No. 68 is an entirely different person.

<u>What effects on your education have occurred because of the act or</u>
<u>acts of sexual abuse that resulted in the claim?</u>
Not long after the abuse, Carol learned about pregnancy. Carol
became terrified that she was pregnant as a result of the sexual abuse.
Carol's fear of being pregnant consumed her and she nearly failed the
6th grade due to her preoccupation. After the abuse, Carol began
engaging in self-injurious behavior including cutting her upper arms
with the claw end of a hammer and hitting herself on her upper arms
and face with the flat side of the hammer. This resulted in bruising
and permanent scars.[56]

The practical virtues of being Claimant No. 68 never once escaped Carol.
The completion of her proof of claim form permanently connected her to
a vast community of survivors, and this was unquestionably the most
important new reality that had come into being for her. "When I completed my form," she later explained, "I finally knew that [the abuse] had
really happened and that I wasn't alone." Carol had always doubted her
experience, never completely accepting that Roney could have abused her.
"I thought that if I never told anyone about the abuse," Carol once
explained, "if I never spoke about it, then I thought I could keep the abuse
from becoming real and that I could be the same person that I was before
he touched me." But then Carol began to learn about the experiences of
others whom Roney had abused, and how closely their experiences aligned
with hers. At times, their testimonies sounded nearly identical to hers,
and so did their symptoms. In part, this was because several of these
claimants modeled their testimonies on Carol's essay while also selecting
ailments from the same menu that Anderson's legal team had provided.
The more important reason, though, was because Roney was compulsive
in his perpetration. He almost exclusively groomed very young girls who
existed on the margins of society, each with an absent or unreliable parent.
"My grandmother had just died; my mother had just tried to commit suicide, and my father was never around," she remembered. "I must have
been trying to find someone to take care of me." Years later, it was all so
obvious to her: "He could see that I was alone," Carol noted. "He could tell
that I was totally isolated, and he took advantage of me." Roney noticed
the same in so many other children.

These commonalities comforted Carol, creating an imagined community of claimants. "There were the dozens of people whom Roney had abused," Carol mentioned, "but there were also all those other people who had been abused by priests in the Diocese of New Ulm." Carol kept expanding the frame, with each new scale seeming to affirm her existence as Claimant No. 68. "Then there were the hundreds of claims in the state of Minnesota," she said, "and the thousands of cases across the United States." With this scaling up—from a single rural rectory to an entire nation—came a sense of confidence strong enough to dislodge the perception that priests should be seen as God on earth. "We could all—all of us claimants—know that we were right about what happened to us," Carol said, "and we could be right about this together."[57]

.   .   .   .   .

On June 28, 2019, three years after the proof of claim forms were submitted, the U.S. Bankruptcy Court of Minnesota ordered the Diocese of New Ulm to pay ninety-three survivors of clerical sexual abuse a total of $34 million, with the diocese and its parishes contributing $8 million and insurance carriers providing the rest. Bishop LeVoir took the decision in stride. He had seen it coming for years, having participated in most every step of the negotiations. He stuck to his talking points on the day of the announcement. "The Diocese of New Ulm and the Catholic Church," he said, "must do everything possible to help protect the vulnerable so that this tragedy never happens again."[58] LeVoir appeared gracious at times, even if his insurance providers likely fed him lines: "[The survivors] have advanced the child protection movement and made their communities safer for kids." The details of the settlement, however, surprised Carol. She hadn't anticipated the scale of her eventual award. "I honestly wasn't expecting much," she later mentioned, but an independent panel had assessed the nature of her claim, how long the abuse had lasted, and how the abuse had affected her life. The court then awarded her a sum of money.

The numbers are easy enough to approximate. $34 million divided equally between ninety-three claimants yields an average award of $365,591. Anderson's standard fee is 35 percent of every claim, or in this instance an average of $127,957 out of each award for a total of $11.9 million. This left the average claimant with the untaxable amount of $237,634, and this was roughly the value of Carol's award. "Jeff Anderson called me on the phone," Carol remembered. "It was the first time I had ever spoken with him directly, and he told me the amount of money that I had been awarded." Carol couldn't believe the number. "I had him repeat it." Carol still giggles a little when she tells the story. "And then I had him repeat the number again." Carol's award came at the right time, providing her with a modest nest egg that began to compensate for a lifetime of opportunity costs. Carol had experienced financial precarity throughout her life. "The money didn't make up for everything," she said, "but the money was a huge help." She recalls Anderson chuckling on the phone call, clearly enjoying the fruits of his labor and the possibilities of survival he had helped to create. Lost in all that laughter, however, were those such as Justina who found themselves on the margins of victimhood: left out of settlements deliberately designed to ensure that little to no money would ever be available to them as future claimants.

Assignment Map

Saint Paul, Minneapolis

Spring 2013

There is a map in David Roney's archive. It represents his ministerial assignments in Minnesota from 1945 to 1994.[59] The map marks state borders, county lines, and the state's famed ten thousand lakes. The Mississippi River juts across the map, running from top to bottom. A legal assistant had pulled the image from a now defunct website and then edited it, somewhat inelegantly. The task was not very complicated. The assistant needed to isolate the state of Minnesota by erasing the neighboring states of Iowa, Wisconsin, and both the Dakotas from the picture, and by cutting out any trace of Canada. With a thick green marker, the assistant then traced the ecclesiastical boundaries of the Diocese of Saint Paul and Minneapolis. With a thick blue marker, he then did the same for the Diocese of New Ulm. Within the space of the two ecclesiastical territories, moving east to west, the assistant then planted eight red dots, each of them identifying where Roney had ministered a parish. He then connected these dots with red looping lines, the kind that suggest air travel, even if Roney had driven himself from town to town: Minneapolis to Saint Croix to Faxon Township to Walnut Grove to Benson to Willmar to Lafayette. These were Roney's lines of flight as he perpetrated acts of sexual abuse across central Minnesota.[60]

Roney's assignment map is based on church records. It provides one interpretation of Roney and his superiors' tactics of evasion. As the map suggests, Roney evaded accountability for his crimes by moving from one small-town parish to the next, quietly packing up and leaving once his parishioners began to raise too many questions about why their priest had been taking so many photographs of their children, spending so much time with them at the lake, and sliding others under his cape. Roney's assignment map, however, makes no reference to Guatemala.[61] Conspicuously absent are any red lines that mark out the other connections Roney made over the course of his half-century career: Minneapolis to Guatemala; Saint Croix to Guatemala; Faxon Township to Guatemala; Walnut Grove to Guatemala; Benson to Guatemala; Willmar to Guatemala; Lafayette to Guatemala. Most noticeably of all, the map erases Roney's near-decade-long retirement in Guatemala.[62] This map is uncomfortably limited in its scope.

In 1962, Pope John XXIII called for dioceses in the United States to send ten percent of their clergy to Latin America to address the shortage of priests there. Clerical transfers transformed countries like Guatemala, with U.S. missions providing a range of services, religious and secular, to remote communities. Yet there is also incontrovertible evidence that bishops transferred U.S. priests to Latin America to avoid scandals at home, with Guatemala becoming something of a dumping ground for U.S. priests suspected of sexual abuse. Roney is a case in point, and thus, it is imperative to redraw his assignment map by connecting Minneapolis to Guatemala.[63] It is an effort at what anthropologists and geographers call countermapping, and it could enjoy, at least in theory, the virtues of righteousness, of peeling away layers of secrecy in the spirit of transparency. But in practice, when pursued up close, as I would find out, this kind of work also involves a heart-wrenching level of intrusion. At least in the case of Justina, it began by explaining that the most important person in her life had sexually abused dozens of children in the United States and that he had done the same in Guatemala. It also involved talking to her, over the course of several years, about the possibility that Roney had been her abuser and that she, if willing, could become his victim and then a survivor. This effort would be in the service of a precedent-setting, trans-border financial settlement, I offered, but it might also, and more importantly, provide some sense of healing.

Justina agreed to participate, and we worked together.

But sometimes I wish she had said no.

V   The Will to Survive, 2017–2023

A Blank Stare

Sololá, Guatemala

August 18, 2017

I was in a motorboat, barrelling across the lake just as Father David Roney had done so many times before me.[1] It was my first trip to the Mission. The sky was electric blue, a wind pressed at my face, and the three volcanoes, one of them active, towered over me. Watching vultures ride tropical breezes clear across the lake, I suddenly understood, at least for a moment, what Roney and Father Gregory Schaffer and all those other missionaries from Minnesota must have found so appealing about this place: its natural beauty, for sure, and its promise of adventure, of course, but also the felt sense that one could disappear out here. That one could live off the grid, become unreachable and maybe even unknowable.

The young man driving the boat cut the engine a few hundred meters from the dock, to make sure that I paid my fare in full, and as we quietly bobbed atop the water—me pulling some money from my pocket, him sitting stoically behind the wheel—I saw the town for the first time in panorama. I had by then a good grasp of Roney's case. I knew about his history of sexual abuse in Minnesota, his retirement in Guatemala, and the Diocese of New Ulm's bankruptcy proceedings earlier that year. I had also heard about—though never had any direct contact with—Justina, but I'd never visited the Mission until that afternoon.

From the vantage of the boat, I spent a moment taking in the full view. I saw the weathered dock where children had greeted Roney on his arrival in 1994, the cinderblock house where he had raised Justina for the next decade, and the bell tower of the church that anchored the Mission and its many programs. I also saw a town bustling with mid-morning activity. There was a main street and a market as well as a handful of hotels that made most of their money on missionaries from Minnesota, and now an anthropologist.

A few hours early for my scheduled meeting with the Mission's main office, I toured the town on foot, immediately finding myself absorbed by Roney's apparent proximity to temptation. This lonely parish priest from central Minnesota, a man who often preached about the occasions of sin, had so clearly structured his remaining years around being as close as possible to children. The distance from Roney's front door to the Mission's playground? Fifteen paces. The distance from his house to the elementary school? Twenty-six paces. To the orphanage? Three blocks, though he could have saved himself a few steps by taking a shortcut. I could also still see Roney in the streets of this small town almost fifteen years after his passing. There is a plaque in the church that honors him by name. His tomb in the cemetery is off to the side but easily found. And that statue of Justina in the Mission's courtyard? It's still there. Another haunting arti-fact caught my eye. On the front door of his former house, Roney had affixed a small handle at just the right height so that a toddler could enter his home without the assistance of an adult. That too was still there.[2]

After only an hour or two in town, I got the strong sense that Roney hadn't really left, that he was in some sense still alive and well in the high-lands of Guatemala. Traces of his life could be spotted most everywhere. However, when I took my meeting at the Mission, I was told—confusingly—that he had never actually spent much time in town in the first place. It was an observably anxious exchange for the administrator who had agreed to meet with me.

"My records show that David Roney lived here for almost ten years," I began, "from 1994 until he died here in 2003." A desk cluttered with paperwork stood between me and the administrator, a Guatemalan woman who had worked at the Mission for decades. This included the years during which Roney lived in town.

"Father David was here only a little bit," she shrugged. "He was not here very long."

I was surprised. "But I understand that David Roney first traveled here in 1973," I countered. Roney's account of that first trip was still fresh in my mind. "We painted houses," he wrote in his diocese's newspaper, "varnished chairs, sewed curtains and helped in the kitchen and orphanage. We hiked up a mountain to a remote village for Mass in a corn-stalk church."[3] I wanted her to know that I did indeed have the facts straight. None of this was in dispute by anyone, not even his bishop back in Minnesota. "Father Roney traveled here at least once a year until 1994," I continued. "Then he moved to town permanently." Nothing I said seemed to stick.

"He only came a few times," she said, avoiding eye contact. "Not very much. Not very much."

Had I somehow misunderstood the facts? Traveled all the way here based on a misapprehension? "I understand that David Roney lived across the street, in that house over there." I pointed out the window. "I understand that he also lived for a time here at the Mission, in that room right over there." I pointed toward the courtyard, but her eyes did not follow my finger. She kept her folded hands atop the desk.

"Father David visited the Mission," the administrator conceded. "Yes, he visited the Mission." Then she tried to shift the conversation onto more generic territory. "People from Minnesota visit the Mission. Many people from Minnesota visit the Mission."

The conversation stunned me. There had already been fifteen years of stateside press releases, newspaper articles, lawsuits, declarations of bankruptcy, press conferences, constitutional amendments, and troves of documents gathered through the legal process of discovery, all related either to Roney specifically or to the broader phenomenon of clerical sexual abuse. Roney himself had written more than 150 articles about his trips to Guatemala for the Diocese of New Ulm's journal of record, *The Prairie Catholic*. "I began with the simple idea of seeing a strange country," he wrote back in 1974. "It has developed into much more than this."[4] The bishop of New Ulm had also released a statement on August 1, 2003, detailing most everything about Roney: the credible accusations in 1987, his stint with the Servants of the Paraclete that same year, and his retirement to Guatemala in 1994.[5] But during that first meeting with the administrator at the Mission, my mind flashed to another article from *The Prairie Catholic*.[6] In October 1995, not long after Roney had moved to the Mission, Schaffer published a puff piece celebrating Roney's fifty years of priesthood. It is a fawning bit of journalism, neither rigorous nor substantial, but it lays claim to the quality of Roney's time in the highlands. Schaffer writes that for twenty years Roney "blessed us here" by organizing and directing the Mission Office in New Ulm. He also made multiple trips to Guatemala "to show care and concern for the people." Schaffer notes that Roney "now lives" in the town, that he has settled there after ceasing his ministry in Minnesota—"even though," Schaffer stresses, "we won't let him retire!" Schaffer also reports that on the anniversary of Roney's ordination people gathered "from all twenty-two communities that make up the parish" to thank him for all that he had done over the years, carving statues in Roney's likeness, filling the church with flowers, and mounting that plaque in his honor. *The Prairie Catholic* also published a photograph of what appears to be a procession celebrating Roney.

"Is there anyone here at the Mission who can tell me about David Roney?" I asked with what I am sure was an observable degree of impatience.

"Father Gregory Schaffer dedicated his life to the Mission and to the people here in Guatemala," she answered. "There are many people here who can talk to you about Father Gregory." Again, she tried to change the topic of conversation, as if she had been coached at some point to exercise caution when discussing the topic of Roney.

"Yes," I said, "I understand that Father Gregory lived here for many years." A towering statue of the man stood just outside the office.[7] "But I would like to speak with someone about Father David Roney." Again, she dodged my request.

"He only came to the Mission a few times, I think," she answered. "Not very much."

Wanting to be clear as to what I knew, I then asked a question that I had planned to save until after I had established a rapport with someone at the Mission. But I had the strong sense that no one at the Mission would be willing to talk, so I went for it. "Are you familiar," I asked, "with an orphan whom Roney adopted? I understand that he cared for a very young girl. She must be twenty-five years old now."

The administrator's eyes widened and then narrowed. "No," she said.

I excused myself from the meeting, dumbfounded by what seemed like such an outdated effort at evasion, an uncanny return to the very tactics that Church administrators had deployed half a century earlier in the comparatively small town of Willmar, Minnesota: silence, denial, and then redirection. It just didn't seem sustainable. As it turns out, it wasn't. Just outside the Mission's main office, only a few moments after that first meeting and less than a few paces from Roney's onetime home, a friend of a friend who lived in town asked me how the meeting had just gone. Equally confused by what had just happened, he told me that the young woman whom Roney had raised was at work. "I'll take you to her," he said.

I climbed into the backseat of his open-air vehicle, and as we puttered across town, at a pace no faster than a brisk walk, it suddenly dawned on me that my first meeting with Justina would happen far sooner than I had ever expected. I had imagined preliminary conversations with the Mission concerning the bureaucratic implications of the Diocese of New Ulm's bankruptcy, its impact on the Mission's operations, and the future of their social outreach in the area. I had also anticipated that the Mission would broker an introduction between me and Justina, carefully defining the terms of the conversation. Instead, the jarring combination of the Mission's near denial of Roney and the community's living memory of the man had created the possibility for an unplanned visit. Before I felt completely prepared to present myself to this young woman, whose life I then knew at only the most superficial level and whose story it would take me years to chronicle, I arrived at the doorstep of her workplace, during her lunch break. I introduced myself as an anthropologist from North America.

Confident and articulate, with a warm smile and a quiet charisma, Justina was indeed in her mid-twenties. She was working for a community-based organization that coincidentally partnered with anthropologists. This bit of serendipity simplified my introduction, saving me from delivering the usual sidebar about fieldwork. Essentially, I tend to tell people that ethnography as a form of research is an extended conversation, one that is iterative as well as anonymous. Justina already knew all of this. Casually eating her lunch at her desk, in an office only a few paces from the lake itself, she asked about the subject of my research. I told her that it was the Mission, but quickly corrected myself by specifying that I was studying the movement of priests from the United States to the

Mission. Nervous, I then qualified my answer a second time, blurting out that the focus of my research was, in fact, Father David Roney.

Justina smiled broadly, explaining that Roney had raised her as his own, that he was like a father to her, and that he was the only one in her life who really cared about her. She mentioned that her birth mother had died young and that her biological father was not fit to care for her. She then recalled the presents that Roney gave her, the Disney movies that he collected, and all the cookies and candies that filled his home. "All the other kids were jealous of me," she mentioned.[8]

"Can I ask you about Father David Roney's history in the United States?" I asked Justina. Directly broaching the topic of clerical sexual abuse felt impossible and inadvisable at that point, and so I found myself alluding to Roney's history only in the vaguest of terms.[9]

Justina looked back at me, her warm smile slowly flattening. She did not frown at the question or even grimace. She was not angry, Justina would later tell me, but pensive, her face forming a somewhat blank expression as she considered my question. It was a face I would soon come to know well. It is the same face that she adopts in the photograph that Roney printed onto his white t-shirt, the same expression she wears in that life-sized statue of her that Roney had commissioned, and the same one that she would eventually strike when deciding whether she should pursue a settlement with the Diocese of New Ulm for putting her in the care of a sexual predator.

"Can we talk somewhere else?" she asked.

Three Boxes

Sololá—Toronto

June 13, 2021

For years, I traveled from Toronto to the Mission to speak with Justina, most times crossing the vast lake near the village by boat and then taking a taxi to Justina's place of work. We always spoke in public places—in cafes, restaurants, or the town square—for fear that private meetings might get people talking, and we were always joined by a research assistant of mine. She is an anthropologist from the area, a Guatemalan woman roughly the same age as Justina. We would carefully and patiently collect Justina's life history, committed to the idea that this extended conversation could only happen on Justina's terms, but we could never seem to establish the kind of rapport that would have made it possible to fully discuss Roney. Justina would drop hints about him from time to time and occasionally intimate that she had more to share with a sidelong glance or a pregnant pause. Still, our conversations never amounted to much.[10] All I could gather from our time together was that Justina was not yet ready to talk about Roney, which I understood, and that she seemed to know next to nothing about the credible accusations, lawsuits, and bankruptcy in Minnesota. None of this news had apparently made it to Guatemala, at least not beyond the guarded walls of the Mission.

Global events in March 2020 finally broke this stasis. The pandemic shut down international travel, threw the world into quarantine, and forced most everyone online, including the three of us. With each of us huddled in our respective rooms, on different ends of a continent, our thirty-minute meetings in a crowded town square suddenly developed into three-hour conversations online, with video conferencing opening an unexpectedly intimate space that felt at times confessional and at other moments therapeutic. We were just three boxes on a screen, but we could suddenly talk to each other.[11]

Justina participated from her bedroom, a sun-filled space that she rented from the woman who had cared for her after Roney died some fifteen years earlier. From the limited view that Justina's camera provided, the room seemed spacious, with big windows, a bed, and a desk, and the objects that appeared at the edge of the frame became natural topics of conversation. The Spanish-to-English flashcards taped to her walls opened onto long talks about her future, while a stack of binders on her desk prompted Justina to discuss the immediate demands of her job. Once, a balloon floated into frame, tipping us off to her birthday. There were also several stuffed animals. "Those are from Papá," she explained. "I've kept most of them." She had also held onto the children's books, Disney movies, and dolls Roney had given her as a child, and she had in her possession more of the photographs that Roney had taken than anyone else in town. These childhood objects clearly helped to anchor Justina's adult life, their materiality reminding her that someone had once chosen to support her rather than abandon her.[12] They were elements of her past that Justina was understandably hesitant to question. At one point, as our discussion began to lean toward the topic of abuse, she stopped short. "When I die," she said, seemingly out of nowhere, "I want to be buried next to Papá," her tomb stacked atop his in the public cemetery.[13]

An ambivalence structured our time together. Justina was wary of discussing Roney directly but was nonetheless eager to tell us the story of her life, which necessarily involved this man. She would sometimes end conversations abruptly, as if offended by something that had been said, yet she would then eagerly set an appointment to speak again, often naming the day and time. Justina seemed not to want to discuss what she may have always already known about Roney, but she nevertheless inched herself ever closer to a more open conversation about him. After months of calls, in which she would carefully approach and then quickly retreat from the edge of what I had come to understand as her willful unknowing, there eventually came a day—on June 13, 2021—when Justina made the decision to step right over that line.[14]

Maybe she had lost her patience. The first hour of our conversation covered some rather delicate topics. She talked about the gold chain that Roney had bought for her just before his death and how Father Gregory Schaffer had safeguarded the gift for years, eventually handing it to her with great ceremony on her fifteenth birthday. She then explained to us that someone had since stolen the chain, an act of betrayal that brought tears to her eyes as she spoke to us. "For me," she said while wiping her face, "this chain was everything. Not because it was made of gold but because Papá bought it for me before he died and blessed it on top of the altar." Justina then talked about being bullied as a child. She held up a photo—taken, of course, by Roney—of five young children, all of them sitting in a row inside Roney's home. It was Justina's seventh birthday, and a pink balloon hovered in the background. Justina then pointed at a young girl sitting next to her in the photograph, explaining that "people always said that she was prettier than me and that I was darker than her." Justina teared up again. She then raised the subject of her inheritance, noting that she had received from Roney the equivalent of US$2,000 when she turned eighteen, but she had also heard from this priest's former housekeeper that Roney had in fact left her as much as US$22,000. "It's really painful to think about who might have taken that money," she said through a new set of tears.[15]

I asked Justina if she wanted to end the call. She seemed a bit weary, and our exchange felt slow and heavy.

"No," she said, "I want to keep talking."

Our conversation then shifted—at once and for always. Justina recalled how the woman who had raised her after Roney died had asked her a few days earlier about our many meetings. She had heard some of our conversations and was concerned, but Justina had assured her that I was just an anthropologist with a research project about the Mission. After asking whether I was interested in Roney, which Justina admitted, she then told Justina for the first time that there had been some talk at the Mission years ago about Roney having touched children. "And that reminded me," Justina added, "of at least three times in the past when she asked me whether Papá had ever touched me or tried to touch me." Justina's face flattened.

"Do you know anything about this?" she asked me. "Because I would like to know." Her voice quickened as she moved from her bed to the desk, her camera jostling wildly along the way as if she were being chased. Then, leaning toward her camera while lowering her voice to a whisper, she admitted to us that she knew nothing. "No one has ever told me anything about this. Never. Not anything." She was upset.

Justina then asked me again, this time with a sense of urgency, "Can you tell me everything that you know?"

My heart rate quickened. I couldn't tell whether Justina was ready for the full story, since video conferencing is such a two-dimensional medium. Then I quickly checked myself. Who was I to keep this information from her? I had trodden lightly for years, allowing Justina to set the pace of our conversations, but along the way, I had also experienced flashes of right-eousness. She should know everything that I know, I would think to myself. The information that I had in my possession is public (albeit in English) and readily accessible online. She deserved to know everything, even if the Diocese of New Ulm didn't agree. But when I would press in our meetings, Justina would return the exchange to a pace that she could handle, as if to remind me that this conversation would indeed only happen on her terms.

"Tell me," she said. "Please."

Clearing my throat and sitting up in my chair, I conceded that I knew very little about Roney's time in Guatemala, but told her that there was a generally agreed upon history of his sexual abuse in the United States. I stated as plainly as possible that Roney had sexually abused dozens of children in Minnesota, both boys and girls. They had been between the ages of six and twelve years old but were now adults. I added that the actual number of children he had sexually abused had continued to grow as more survivors came forward, and was likely much higher still, as victims of sexual abuse rarely report this crime.[16]

"Did he ever go to jail?" Justina asked. Her question might have been a surprising one in a U.S. context, where statutes of limitations have generally kept cases of clerical sexual abuse from entering the criminal court system, leaving most survivors to pursue some form of accountability through the civil courts. But it made perfect sense in postwar Guatemala, where sexual abuse tends to refer almost exclusively to wartime rape and domestic violence.[17] As I explained why clerical sexual abuse rarely ended in prison sentences in the United States, Justina asked about the difference between criminal and civil courts. Before I could answer, though, she asked whether I was talking about David Arthur Roney of Minnesota. Having slipped into a temporary state of disbelief, she wanted me to confirm that we were indeed talking about the same person.

"Yes," I told Justina. "There is no doubt in my mind about the history of David Roney's sexual abuse of children in the United States. His bishop in Minnesota knew that he abused children. A judge in Minnesota has said that he abused children. Father Gregory knew that he abused children."

Justina fell silent. I did too, only mentioning something about how I wished that this conversation could have happened in person. I felt my stomach begin to twist.

"No one ever told me about this," she repeated. "No one at the Mission. Not Father Gregory. No one from Minnesota. No one even told me when I was in Minnesota." Justina remembered her stateside visit back in 2012.

Justina then turned toward someone off camera. It was the woman who had raised her after Roney's death. She had been eavesdropping again, and Justina now wanted to end the call, which we did, but not before Justina asked me for some more information about Roney. "I want to know more," she said. "Can you send me newspaper articles? Court records?"

I promised to send them to her in Spanish.

Before the call ended, Justina also asked about the possibility of speaking with a therapist. "I've heard that there are forms of therapy," she said, "where a psychologist can put someone into a dream so that they can remember the things that they don't want to know."[18]

"Of course," I said, "I will email you tomorrow with more information." I promised to connect her with a therapist immediately.

After our three boxes became a blank screen, I stood up from my desk in distant Toronto, stepped outside for some fresh air, and walked the streets. It was dark, and only a sliver of moon hung in the sky. My mind raced as my stomach continued to turn. I worried about everything that Justina now knew and how much more she would come to know. I also kicked myself for having waited so long to tell her these basic facts about Roney but reminded myself of my steadfast commitment to Justina's well-being. She could have asked me sooner, I reasoned. The timeline of this disclosure was not for me to determine. Placing my hand against a building, its concrete surface cooling my sweaty palm, I suddenly and unexpectedly threw up, overwhelmed at the thought of what might lie ahead for Justina.

Dear Justina,

I hope you are ok after last night's conversation. Please take good care of yourself. I understand that the news is difficult, but I know that you are a very strong person. If possible, I would like to clarify that the information here about Father David is public. It is available on the internet (in English) and some of it has been published by the Catholic Church. The Diocese of New Ulm has had significant problems with the sexual abuse of minors, with 93 cases against 16 priests. The latest news is that the 93 survivors won their court case against the Church in March 2020. One of the articles that I have pasted below states that "A portion of the funds is also being set aside for victims of sexual abuse who may come after the settlement is complete." We can talk about your options when you are ready. I also have information about a therapist located near you, on the other side of the lake.

Best,

Kevin

Justina wrote me back the very next day:

Hi Kevin,

Thank you for forwarding this information to me. It is very useful, since for me all of this is hard to believe. As for my emotional state, I think I'm a little scared. Thank you for worrying about me. On Sunday night, I had a hard time sleeping because I was thinking about Father David. I also searched for information about Father David on the internet, and I found an article [in English]. It was very hard for me to read that he abused so many girls and boys. . . . What I do understand, and it is very clear to me now, is that I was at great risk and many children in Guatemala were too.

On Sunday I couldn't sleep well because of this information and on Monday I woke up feeling down and a little upset with [the woman who raised me]. I don't understand why but that's what I felt. When I was sleeping, I felt that someone was hugging me very tightly and someone's presence was very strong and when I woke up it crossed my mind that perhaps it was Father David hugging me but with great force until I thought that he was doing it so that I would not leave him even though I wanted to, but that hug scared me because I felt like I couldn't breathe and I wanted to wake up and it was very difficult for me to open my eyes.

Yesterday you sent me the information about him, and I didn't want to read or see anything, but today I want to learn more. Please send me more information. I feel that my story might never end as there are more and more things to discover.

Best.

Justina

Not wanting to overwhelm Justina with too many documents, I sent her a Spanish translation of the public statement that the Diocese of New Ulm released a few months after Roney's passing, on August 1, 2003. I also included a Spanish translation of April's letter to Bishop Raymond Lucker, the first note that the bishop received in 1987. I thought that the letter might allow Justina to begin to appreciate what counts as sexual abuse in Minnesota, as this category of experience was not meaningless in the Guatemalan context so much as narrow and specific. Justina could not yet understand her own experience as part of that phenomenon within the framework of the postwar Guatemalan definition of sexual abuse, but April's letter seemed to help. "[Father Roney] would tell us he had candy or a quarter in his pocket," April writes, "and to reach in and get it. There was always a very large hole in his pocket, no underwear. Shocking. He also loved to tickle children, which could lead to touching other areas."[19] April's letter connected squarely with Justina.

Dear Kevin,

This letter really awakens a lot of memories in my life and what it says in the letter is really true. I remember that he took me alone to a pool, and I even have a photo of when we were on the boat and he changed me to get into the pool. He also took me to the lake to go swimming with other girls. He asked me to take money out of his pants pocket too. It happened every day. I think letters like these help me remember things he did to me or asked me to do. Like tickling too, I remember he tickled me too and he did it constantly.

Best,

Justina

We exchanged emails and spoke online for months. Justina also began to meet with a therapist, both in person as well as online. At times, it was an overwhelming process for her, involving both an implosion of personal history and an education in the subtle contours of sexual abuse. Justina apparently spent most of her time with the therapist recuperating repressed memories; these were traumatic events that Justina had blocked from her consciousness in an effort at self-preservation. Justina explained this theory to me several times, and it seemed to make good sense given the context. Why wouldn't her mind block these horrible experiences? Roney was the only person in her life who seemed to have truly cared for her, and these events threatened her otherwise loving memory of him. I understood the idea at an intuitive level.

Yet the more I spoke with Justina, and the more (and ever more troubling) memories she recuperated, I couldn't help but wonder if the process of recovering these repressed memories wasn't also a process of applying new forms of understanding to past experiences. Moments after learning about Roney's history of sexual abuse in the United States, for example, Justina insisted that she had been spared because she could not immediately remember Roney ever raping her. It was an eminently reasonable response as Justina continued to navigate the gaps between two overlapping but fundamentally different frameworks for understanding sexual abuse. Against the backdrop of postwar Guatemala, and its violence against women, Justina slowly came to learn through therapy that codes of conduct for clerics in the United States forbade the most common ways in which Roney had interacted with her: kissing her on the mouth; holding her on his lap, touching her buttocks, genital areas, and breasts; doing all of this in bedrooms, closets, and private rooms; sleeping in the same bed with her; bathing her; wrestling with her; and tickling her. Therapy transformed a once uncoordinated constellation of behaviors into a legible series of transgressions, and then a series of transgressions into a more expansive phenomenon that Justina began to understand as clerical sexual abuse.[20]

"Roney sometimes didn't even touch children," I mentioned to her at one point, at first apologizing for the explicit nature of the conversation. "Many times, he would expose himself to children or masturbate himself in front of children." A person could sexually abuse children without touching them.

"I did not know that this was sexual abuse," Justina replied, not with any kind of naïveté but rather with a studied appreciation for categories. She knew that these kinds of acts were wrong, but she hadn't yet had the opportunity to consider them as acts of sexual abuse. This realization, which came like a bolt of lightning, prompted Justina to remember a time when Roney was bathing her. She was very young, and Roney apparently slapped her because Justina would not turn around and get on her knees as she had been told.

Had Justina repressed her memory of this event? It is certainly possible. But perhaps the most important development for Justina in this period wasn't so much the recollection of individual memories but rather the reframing of these memories under a new framework—and, even more significantly, the consequent shift in her self-understanding. This new perspective was what allowed her to begin to understand these past experiences as acts of clerical sexual abuse, to understand herself as a victim and a survivor of this abuse, and eventually, emporeringly, to apprehend new possibilities for action.

It was this new self-understanding that ultimately made the possibility of taking legal action thinkable. Uninterested, at first, in speaking with a lawyer in the United States—at times even afraid of the idea—she eventually requested a meeting with someone I knew through the offices of Jeff Anderson & Associates. Justina wanted to meet with a lawyer to have a preliminary and completely anonymous conversation, asking that all four of us meet online but insisting that she would keep her video and microphone muted the entire time.

Four Boxes

Sololá—Toronto—Minneapolis

October 16, 2021

A computer screen. Four boxes.

One of them muted, with camera off.

The personal injury attorney from Minneapolis spoke reverently about Justina. Through short, simple sentences in English, which my research assistant and I translated into Spanish, he explained to us (but really to Justina) that various versions of her story had circulated among lawyers and journalists tracking clerical sexual abuse in Minnesota at least since Father David Roney's death in 2003. Roney had adopted an orphan in Guatemala, it had been said; she was very young, others added. No one knew much else. The rest of the rumors were based on pure speculation as to what had likely happened to this little girl.

It was an honor, the lawyer added, to have the chance to speak with her.

Justina sent me a private message to relay to the lawyer, thanking him for his time.

"She would also like to know more about her legal options in the United States," I added. "The facts of her case, at least to our understanding, are straightforward: Roney had a history of sexual abuse in Minnesota; the Diocese of New Ulm and the Mission in Guatemala knew about his history of sexual abuse, but they allowed Roney to care for this woman for many years. Roney cared for her for nearly a decade."

"Allow me to explain the legal terrain," the lawyer replied. He then stitched together a history of clerical sexual abuse in Minnesota, focusing on the two ecclesiastical territories where Roney had worked: the Archdiocese of Saint Paul and Minneapolis and the Diocese of New Ulm. Both dioceses had filed for bankruptcy, the lawyer explained, in large part because of how the Child Victims Act in 2013 had suspended the state's statutes of limitations for three years, allowing survivors of sexual abuse to file civil action against parishes and dioceses regardless of when the abuse took place. "The Archdiocese of Saint Paul and Minneapolis and the Diocese of New Ulm got pummeled by claims," the lawyer added.

My research assistant and I diligently translated for Justina, taking some additional time to clarify for her that Roney had first served the Archdiocese of Saint Paul and Minneapolis from his ordination in 1945 until the creation of the Diocese of New Ulm in 1955, after which he served parishes in the Diocese of New Ulm until his move to Guatemala. We also explained that the Diocese of New Ulm inaugurated, funded, and managed the Mission in Guatemala, and that it was under the control of Bishop Raymond Lucker when Roney arrived in 1994.

Justina then sent me another private message. She wanted me to tell the lawyer that she had visited Minnesota in 2012, for three weeks, but no one had told her about the lawsuits or the Child Victims Act, which, though not passed until 2013, had been the subject of widespread public advocacy at the time of her visit. No one had mentioned anything to her about clerical sexual abuse.

The lawyer winced, his eyes squinting and cheeks scrunching. "That likely cost her hundreds of thousands of dollars. Maybe even millions of dollars," he said, slowly exhaling.

I paused, not wanting to translate his response, but then I did, out of fidelity to the process. I also did not want to keep secrets from Justina. I immediately regretted it, though, and I still do—not simply because the lawyer's comment was painful to hear, but also because I had begun to realize that it might not have mattered if someone *had* spoken to Justina about Roney's history of abuse in 2012. It was true that Justina had missed an opportunity to file suit against the Diocese of New Ulm. It was also true that she likely would have been awarded hundreds of thousands of dollars if she had filed suit before the deadline. This is a brutal, painful fact. But even if someone had pulled Justina aside during her trip to Minnesota in 2012, what would Justina have been able to do? She likely would not have had the capacity to recognize herself as a victim at that point. In April 2012, unlike in October 2021, she did not have access to a therapist, a pair of anthropologists, or a personal injury attorney. She was not privy, in 2012, to the United States' accelerating conversation about clerical sexual abuse. In Guatemala at that time, the phenomenon was completely illegible. There had not yet been a single reported case of clerical sexual abuse in the country—a situation that those leading the Diocese of New Ulm were happy to see persist, even if that meant protecting abusive priests they had transferred to Guatemala. While continuing to send short-term missionaries from Minnesota to the Mission to build cinderblock houses and read the gospel by candlelight, the Bishop of New Ulm never once released a statement to the Mission, never once held a town hall on the topic, and never once reached out to those in Guatemala who might have been abused by David Roney. Amid a flurry of activity in Minnesota—managing public relations and assessing legal liability as waves of lawsuits rolled in—the Bishop of New Ulm did nothing for the Mission. There were no public relations to manage, no liability to assess.

"Built into these settlements are what is known as 'future survivor funds,'" the lawyer continued. "This is a limited amount of money set aside for those who missed the process but who have a legitimate claim to the settlement. The money for these claimants is capped."

"How much could she be awarded?" I pressed, excited to hear that Justina might have some chance at holding these dioceses accountable.

"The Archdiocese of Saint Paul and Minneapolis has capped the awards that come from their fund at $50,000 per survivor," the lawyer answered, adding that he worried a bit about the challenge of creating a direct line between Justina and the Archdiocese of Saint Paul and Minneapolis. Roney had left the Archdiocese nearly two decades before he ever set foot in Guatemala and four decades before he ever met Justina. "But it's possible," he concluded optimistically.[21]

I later explained to Justina, because she had asked, that those who filed their claims on time received an average award from the Archdiocese of Saint Paul and Minneapolis of more than $450,000.

"And the Diocese of New Ulm?" I inquired.

"It should be very straightforward to prove that the Diocese of New Ulm placed this woman in harm's way and that she has a right to their fund," he said.

"Has the Diocese of New Ulm capped these awards?" I asked.

"Yes," he said.

"How much?"

"It's a really small amount," he said.

"How much?"

"It's actually embarrassing to say," the lawyer hemmed.

"How much?"

"Two thousand dollars," he said.

The number hit me square in the chest. I could feel my face turning red. Two thousand dollars? I later explained to Justina, because she had asked, that those who filed their claims on time received an average award from the Diocese of New Ulm of more than $365,000.

Justina messaged me privately. She had some questions for the lawyer, most of them prepared in advance of our meeting.

"Do I need to be present in the United States to file a petition?" she asked via a private message to me.

"No," the lawyer answered, now addressing the blank box on his screen directly. "It is not a problem that you are in Guatemala."

"Will I be able to enter the United States after filing a petition," Justina asked next, "knowing that the Catholic Church has a lot of power worldwide?"

"The Church has no control over your movement," the lawyer answered with a slight lilt of confusion. I could see him trying to calibrate the difference of context.

I mentioned to the lawyer that the Roman Catholic Church is arguably the most powerful institution in Guatemala, more so than even the military. It made sense that Justina would be wary of petitioning the Church.

"She has to understand," the lawyer interjected, "that her petition to these two survivor funds in Minnesota would have no relationship to any parish or diocese in Guatemala." These were distinct corporate entities: different leadership, different land holdings, different bank accounts. "I'm not even sure how anyone in Guatemala would ever find out about these petitions," he added.

"Will this petition put my life in danger?" Justina then asked. "And will my family be in danger by filing the claim?"

"I have no reason to believe so," the lawyer stuttered. Again, his reaction spoke to the differences between their two worlds. Justina, unlike this lawyer—or any lawyer from Minnesota, for that matter—carried with her the living memory of a genocidal civil war, with all of its lynchings, mass graves, and political disappearances. The woman who raised Justina after Roney died was a constant reminder of this violence: her husband had been taken in the middle of the night by paramilitary operatives during the war. He was never seen again.

Justina's questions continued through private messages and bouts of translation until she asked about next steps.

"What would she need to do to file a petition?" I relayed.

"She would have to sign a retainer fee," the lawyer answered. "For my services, I receive 35 percent of every award. She would then need to complete a Proof of Claim Form. I would then submit a Proof of Claim Form to both the Archdiocese of Saint Paul and Minneapolis and the Diocese of New Ulm."

"How long would she have to wait for a decision?" I asked.

"It depends," he replied. "Sometimes people get an answer in two weeks. Sometimes they get one in two months."

Either way, it didn't sound like an arduous amount of time to wait.

The lawyer then provided some counsel. "These funds are limited," he said, "and eventually they will run out of money. If she wants to submit a petition, I recommend doing it immediately."[22]

The lawyer's attention to timeline immediately reminded me of a theoretical insight that had long organized my research, an insight concerning the historical specificity of clerical sexual abuse: that the category and its corresponding identities exist only at certain times, in certain places, and in certain social settings.[23] I had up until that moment considered this point in somewhat broad comparative terms. Jouy became a sexual deviant in France in 1867, and something similar had happened to Roney in

1987. Michel Foucault dodged deviancy with a move to Tunisia in 1968, while Roney did the same with a one-way flight to Guatemala in 1994. The capacity to become legible as either a sexual deviant or the victim of such a person can vary between places and times. Still, I had not yet appreciated the ways in which victimhood as a category of person had already begun to become less accessible in the United States, in large part because of bankruptcy. The Diocese of New Ulm's headline-grabbing and life-altering settlement with ninety-three survivors in 2019 had the immediate effect of reducing other victims' possibilities for action: even if someone such as Justina filled out a Proof of Claim form and received an award from the future survivors' fund, the award from the Diocese of New Ulm would be paltry. A possible award from the Archdiocese of Saint Paul and Minneapolis seemed more promising, but once these funds ran out of money, there would be no reason to go to the trouble of gaining the law's recognition as a victim at all. For cases related to priests ordained in Minnesota, at least, clerical sexual abuse as a historically contingent phenomenon had already begun to fade from existence.

"She should act fast," the lawyer advised.

I translated this last point for Justina and waited for her reply.

Instead of receiving a private message, though, Justina turned on her video and unmuted her microphone, appearing on screen with bright eyes and a wry smile.

"Hello," she said in Spanish. "My name is Justina."

The lawyer gasped, and I smiled.

It was the bravest thing I had ever seen.[24]

Proof of Claim

Sololá—Toronto—Minneapolis

January 9, 2022

Justina walks to work most days. When she is running late, she hails a three-wheeled taxi to zip her across town, or she hitches a ride on the back of a friend's motorbike. But the cost of taxis adds up, and it's tough to make the timing of motorbike rides work. She leaves home early most days, moving through a maze of unpaved streets as the sun slowly peeks over the volcanoes, warming the mountain air and casting long shadows across town.

Justina sees the same people on her walk most every morning, at the exact same points and doing nearly the exact same things: sweeping a stoop, selling tortillas, or kicking at a stray dog. One of the reasons why Justina tries so hard to leave for work on time is so that she can see these people every morning. They are her community. Another reason, which may be more powerful than the first, is to avoid their judgment. She once took a taxi two days in a row and people started to talk. Her town is incredibly small, and people gossip about anything that seems unusual.[25]

The moment that Justina turned on her camera during our conversation with the lawyer—that is, the moment she irrevocably declared herself a survivor—was also the moment she began to live a double life. Online, whether as one of two, three, or four boxes on a screen, Justina could speak with her therapist, engage a pair of earnest anthropologists, and explore her rights with a personal injury attorney, all within the privacy of her bedroom. Technology allowed her to tunnel into contexts where her identity as a survivor was perfectly legible, and this allowed Justina to see herself as a survivor of clerical sexual abuse with increasing clarity. Offline, though, her life remained to all observers the same: the same walk to work, the same friends and neighbors, the same Justina.

The attorney in Minnesota required Justina to sign a retainer agreement. This was a one-page, bare-bones service contract that stipulated his fees ("A sum equivalent to 35% of any amount recovered") and his conditions of payment ("In the event of no recovery, no attorney's fees shall be payable"). If awarded money, Justina would also be on the line for any out-of-pocket expenses, which could include court costs, investigation fees, witness expenditures, discovery costs, and photographs. Even the costs of printing documents would be drawn from her hypothetical future award. My research assistant and I translated the agreement and spoke with Justina about any concerns that she might have, and then we directed her to the attorney, who answered them. It was an intimidating document, especially for someone living far outside the United States, with its long history of litigiousness, but Justina saw its virtues and understood its advantages. She just couldn't figure out how to sign the agreement.[26]

In between Justina's home and her place of work exists a modest storefront. It has a concrete floor and walls made of wooden planks. There are no windows, but midmorning sun often pierces through the beams. The place sells pens, pencils, and paper as well as long-distance phone cards and wrapping paper. It also has a second-hand copy machine: a behemoth, once lugged from the capital city in the bed of a pickup truck so as to profit from an obvious need in the local economy. Run by a young couple, with their school-aged kids often darting in and out of the premises, the store is where people in town print, sign, and scan documents—by handing them over to whoever is behind the counter and then waiting for this person to feed them into the copy machine, maybe collate them, and perhaps, out of curiosity, read them. The contract that Justina would print, sign, and scan was in English and written in a legalese that was almost impenetrable even to the average anglophone. Although Justina knew that the store owner would never be able to understand the intricacies of the agreement, or even what it might be, she also knew full well that the contract's illegibility would only add to the mystery. People would talk, if only because the document would seem unusual.

Eager to proceed with the Proof of Claim form—the same document that Carol had completed years earlier in Minnesota—Justina formed a plan. She gathered a pile of equally illegible documents, some of them from her place of work and others pulled from the internet. Many of them were in English, some of them in Spanish. A dozen of these documents had her name printed across the top and just as many of them included boxes "requiring" her signature. It was an illogical heap of materials meant to distract whoever was manning the copy machine that day. With any luck, aided by a steady stream of small talk, Justina's contract with the lawyer would get lost in this storm of paper.

It did, thankfully.

And we got to work.

The three of us tackled the Proof of Claim form first, dividing its prompts into two groups. The first included those that seemed straightforward. For example, the form asked for Justina's full name: we could answer that on our own. The second group of prompts demanded substantially more expertise to answer: "Please describe in as much detail as possible the nature of the sexual abuse." For those prompts, we concluded, we needed the support of a lawyer to make her experiences as legible as possible to a narrow audience of judges in Minnesota. The hitch, however, was that hardly any of the prompts turned out to be straightforward. Even the questions that appeared the simplest relied on a set of specifically North American assumptions—about clerical sexual abuse to be sure, but also about what it means to be a person with legal standing. Little of it seemed to apply to Justina's life, and thus, her legibility as a victim seemed far from assured.

"Let's begin with your mailing address," I suggested to Justina. Each of us appeared on screen, framed by our respective boxes. The Proof of Claim form provides the usual categories: city, state, postal code, and country. It was the first of fifteen questions that the three of us had planned to answer before our first full meeting with the lawyer. I had scheduled an hour for the task, which seemed like more than enough time.

"My address?" Justina asked, somewhat quizzically.

"Yes," I answered as I organized some materials on my desk. I was still settling into the conversation. "What is the number of your house?"

"I do not know," she said as if I had asked her for the exact weight of her home in pounds. "I don't think the house has a number."

"Can you go outside to check?" I asked, imagining a two- or three-digit code painted across the top of the front door.

Justina walked away from her computer to scour the front of her house, chatting along the way with a neighbor about whether the house in which he lived had a number (it did not). She then spoke to a few more people, eventually returning to her computer and reappearing on camera.

"There is no number," she reported.

"What is the name of the street?" I then asked.

"The street doesn't have a name," she said with real certainty.

"Maybe it is called Tenth Street," I offered, "or maybe it's named after someone." I mentioned that some of the major streets in town had been named after Father Gregory Schaffer. While these naming ceremonies had brought out the entire community, with music and food, it had never occurred to me that what was now an avenue named after Schaffer might not previously have had any name at all. In fact, it began to occur to me that no one had ever given me an address during my many trips to the Mission. When I needed to meet someone or to travel somewhere for an appointment, people would offer me what are best described as relational directions. And when I asked Justina what she told people when they wanted to visit her home for the first time, she too offered relational directions.

"I ask them if they know where the Mormon church is," she answered with some confidence. "It's easy to find because everyone knows where it is. And then I tell them that they'll see a green house."

"You live in the green house?" I asked.

"No," she replied, somewhat annoyed that I had cut her off. "I tell them to walk three blocks west from the green house, until they reach the place where they sell the tortillas. If they don't know which way is west, then I just tell them to ask someone where the tortillas are." Justina began to lose focus. "West is pretty easy to figure out if you know the volcanoes." She started mapping cardinal directions in relationship to volcano peaks, but

I pulled her back to the matter of her home address. "I live five houses down from the place where they sell the tortillas."

Her home address was no longer a purely empirical concept. This question, like so many others on the form, was shaped by a standard of normalcy that those in North America, me included, largely take for granted. In North America, the home address locates a person, in terms of their geographical whereabouts and even in terms of their social standing, but it also connects the individual to vast regimes of government bureaucracy and public infrastructure, from the postal service and federal tax system to gas lines and electrical grids. It is a requisite piece of information for an identification card. The home address also helps to incorporate a person into the very system of accountability that Justina now wanted to access in the United States. In the highlands of Guatemala, however, where few people pay federal taxes and most live off the electrical grid, a home address is not necessary, and the concept can be literally meaningless. It all brought to the fore the observation that the idea of what a survivor of clerical sexual abuse *is* was formed in the United States in the context of a historically specific set of developments about personhood. Therefore, this idea's prerequisites include the relatively recent invention of the home address.[27] People with standing have one.

We left her home address blank.

Our conversation with Justina's lawyer a few weeks later proved no less fraught, as the four of us completed a section of the form titled "Nature of Abuse." It too began with a set of short questions that initially appeared simple, such as the name of the perpetrator and the years of abuse, but the form quickly moved onto far less stable ground. To negotiate the challenge, the lawyer began by asking Justina a series of preliminary questions. He wanted to establish that Roney cared for Justina, and then he wanted to show that Roney's care for Justina mirrored his already well-established history of abuse.

"We don't need to prove that Roney was a perpetrator," the lawyer assured Justina. "We know that Roney abused children in the United States. We need to establish that Roney had access to you, and then we need to demonstrate that Roney took advantage of this access."

The lawyer began by asking Justina how she came to live at the Mission, and how she fell under the care of Roney. Justina dutifully responded, recounting the major plot points of her childhood: the trauma of losing her mother as an infant and then being raised by an alcoholic father until he left her at the steps of the Mission. It was a courageous disclosure of life history that echoed both the Latin American tradition of *testimonio* (first-person narratives marked by the urgency of injustice) and the personal essay that Carol had written at her lawyer's behest a few years earlier.[28] As with Carol's account, however, the lawyer's statement jarringly reframed Justina's testimony, putting it in the third person and compressing it: "Justina was brought to the Church at about nine months old. Her mother had passed away and her father was unable to care for her. Justina was left in the care of the Church because she was too young to go to the orphanage. . . . Fr. Roney came to live and work within the mission held there at the Church."[29]

Yet Justina faced additional challenges in making her experience legible. At one point, the lawyer asked if Roney had ever prepared food for Justina. The lawyer wanted to present an image of domesticity that might resonate with a North American audience: scenes of a sinisterly doting man making peanut butter and jelly sandwiches for a young child.

"No," Justina answered, "he never prepared my food."

"Never?" the lawyer clarified with some confusion. His understanding had been that Roney had effectively raised Justina as his own, and to his mind, this would have included meal preparation.

"Never," she responded.

I interjected, offering my own expertise on cross-cultural differences relating to parenthood. As an American priest in rural Guatemala, I explained, Roney had a fulltime housekeeper. He would never have prepared his own food, let alone Justina's meals, and he would never have needed to complete any of the daily chores that regularly constitute parenthood in the United States: washing and folding laundry, dusting and sweeping the house, making beds and gathering toys. Other people completed these chores, and yet he was the parent figure.[30]

"He did bathe me," Justina spoke up, quickly deducing the kinds of domestic rituals for which the lawyer seemed to be searching. "He bathed me almost every day."

Justina shared her story with us, pausing for translation, and then continuing with the painful process of connecting her childhood experiences with what she had only recently begun to understand as clerical sexual abuse. The lawyer later transcribed her statement, edited it, and then compressed it again into a block of text:

> Fr. Roney spent a great deal of time with Justina. He would play and read with Justina. Justina remembers going to the patio of the Church to play with Fr. Roney and would nap in his bed and he would give her baths. Justina remembers Fr. Roney bathing her and using his hand to wash her intimate parts and not a washcloth. She remembers one bath that Fr. Roney hit her. He was mad that she didn't turn around and get on her knees. Justina believes this was because Fr. Roney wanted to see her naked.[31]

One of the most painful parts of the process for Justina proved to be the new associations that her victimhood and survivorship invited. Becoming a survivor for Justina meant reinterpreting and then reorganizing her memories along the coordinates of clerical sexual abuse. She had never thought much about how Roney had comported himself at home, but then this new category of experience created the possibility for new interpretations of old memories: "Justina has an early memory of laying on his carpet naked and Fr. Roney was in his underwear and had an erection. She remembers seeing him often without a shirt on or naked. Justina remembers through her childhood asking for money and Fr. Roney would have her grab it from his front pocket."[32]

Justina's memories of the coins in Roney's pockets, the warm baths at his home, and the many naps in his bed had never assembled into anything of substance—until she read the letter that April wrote to Bishop Raymond Lucker in 1987. The press releases from 2003 had also helped, as did her survey of the many legal claims brought against Roney and his diocese. Translated copies of stateside pastoral codes of conduct had also added perspective, allowing Justina to slowly see herself as a member of the same imagined community that Carol had joined by completing her own Proof of Claim form: "Fr. Roney would frequently kiss Justina on the lips. Fr. Roney would encourage Justina to invite her friends over. Fr. Roney would buy Justina toys and the girls would all play with these toys. Justina recalls her and her friends taking baths together at Fr. Roney's. Fr. Roney would tell her to keep secrets and put his finger to his mouth and say, Shhhh."[33]

Justina's imagined fellowship with Carol and the dozens of other men and women whom Roney had abused, however, belied the fact that she

felt increasingly alienated from her local community. For when our conversations with her lawyer ended and after she had had a chance to offer
edits to the completed Proof of Claim form, Justina once again had to
figure out how she would print, sign, and scan the document. She did
what she had done before: walking that short distance from her home to
the storefront, handing over an absolute mess of materials, and then surreptitiously signing and scanning the ones that her lawyer needed. It was
a scheme that ended up leaving Justina feeling rather alone. She had her
lawyer, a pair of anthropologists, and a therapist, but they were all online,
only occasionally present in person. Meanwhile, the people in her life, and
in the community in which she lived, could not even begin to conceive of
the kind of person she had become, or that the priest who raised her had
been an "abuser" and that this made her a "victim" and "survivor." Neither
would anyone in town have understood, at least not immediately, that in
becoming a survivor, Justina had also made herself eligible to be awarded
a financial settlement.

   In signing and submitting her Proof of Claim Form on January 9, 2022,
Justina had become—officially—a survivor of clerical sexual abuse, and
new possibilities for action had opened for her as a result. It was a thrilling
moment, one that we celebrated. But Justina would not hear from the
fund for more than a year. Though the lawyer in Minnesota had told her
that survivors have received decisions in as little as two weeks, waiting two
months at most, Justina waited for nearly a year and a half, for news that
none of us wanted to hear.

Awarded

Sololá—Toronto—Minneapolis

May 22, 2023

Waiting. Alone. For two weeks. Then two months.

We met with the lawyer at three months. Four boxes on the screen again. No news.

We met at four months. No news.

If nothing else, the meetings served to remind us that Justina had indeed completed her Proof of Claim form, but the whole thing was starting to feel like a fading dream whose plot points had begun to scramble.

We met again at five months. No news.

Six months. No news.

We kept busy. Justina and I practiced her English every week. She had a workbook. "Last year I _____ my husband pajamas." Justina gave it a shot, and then I corrected her. "*Gave* my husband pajamas," I said, "not *give*."

I also spoke with Carol every Wednesday.

"How is Justina doing?" she would ask me.

"Still waiting," I would tell her.

At one point, Carol said that she wanted to write a letter to Justina, or maybe I planted the idea in her head. I can't remember, but I did tell her that a letter would be helpful. "Justina feels so alone," I said, and it was true. Justina had cut ties with her therapist, frustrated by how much time they spent talking about her biological father, and Justina's lawyer in Minnesota was busy with other cases. Only a couple of anthropologists knew what she was going through or who she had become. In the end, though, Carol couldn't bring herself to write to Justina.

"It doesn't have to be profound," I encouraged. "It could just be a note, telling Justina that she's not alone." I imagined their correspondence blossoming into some kind of cross-border camaraderie, a community of survivors that knew no bounds, but the pressure seemed to be too much for Carol.

"I wouldn't know what to write," she eventually told me.

Seven months. Eight months. Nine months. No news.

I visited Guatemala, often. At one point, Justina and I visited her biological father. Having moved away from the town, he now lives in the mountains, a good two hours away from the Mission, which is itself a solid four hours from the capital city. We drove slowly around hairpin turns and then up dirt roads that were so steep that it felt like the car might tip backwards. He lives on a few acres, in a one-room house without any windows. In his mid-sixties, he looks much older, with crushing arthritis having deformed his hands and feet. He cannot walk. Instead, his brother scoops him out of bed each morning, plants him in a plastic chair under a tree, and then places him back into bed at night. I'm not sure what he does during the rainy season. We brought him food and a wheelchair and then promised to visit him again in a few months, which we did. After each of our visits, Justina would get quiet, totally lost in her thoughts.

Justina once asked me whether she owes her biological father anything.

"I have no idea," I told her.

"I don't know either," she replied.

Ten months. Eleven months. A full year. Nothing.

Then, in February 2023, the lawyer called an impromptu meeting. A bolt of excitement shot through me. Justina got nervous as we quickly coordinated schedules, found a window of time, and sat expectantly, each of us in our respective box. I remember my right hand shaking with anticipation. The lawyer had even brought his paralegal. There were now five boxes.

"Did I call this meeting or did you?" the lawyer asked.

"You did," I answered as excitement morphed into confusion and then disappointment.

"Oh, OK," he stumbled. "I don't have any updates. My mistake." The lawyer then mentioned that he had been at a professional meeting the month before for personal injury attorneys working with insurance providers. He said that these providers had never anticipated the volume of petitions that these future survivor funds would eventually handle, and this explained why we had been waiting so long.

"Did Justina miss the window?" I asked, remembering how the lawyer had once counselled Justina to submit her petition before the money ran out.

"I don't know," he said, and I believed him. Her recognizability as a survivor, and the possibilities for action that were supposed to come with that new identity, seemed to be shifting beneath our feet.

Thirteen months.

Fourteen months.

Fifteen months.

And then the lawyer requested another meeting. This time he had news.

"The Archdiocese of Saint Paul and Minneapolis has denied Justina's petition," the lawyer began, without any pleasantries or small talk. He just got right to it. Their argument, he said, was exactly the one that he had worried about: that Roney's time with the Archdiocese had ended in 1955, long before he met Justina or even visited Guatemala.

"An argument could be made that the archbishop's inaction at the time facilitated the abuse of every one of Roney's subsequent victims," I responded, but I was preaching to the choir.

News of the decision was painful to hear and even more difficult to communicate to Justina. I used an ecclesiastical map of Minnesota to remind Justina that the Archdiocese of Saint Paul and Minneapolis and the Diocese of New Ulm are distinct entities. They have different bishops, priests, and even bank accounts. The two dioceses operate as separate corporate entities and thus structured their bankruptcies differently, with even their survivor funds managed and capped with different terms of agreement. It was a brutal lesson in accountability, in part because we had placed too much hope on the Archdiocese of Saint Paul and Minneapolis.

With its awards capped at $50,000, a settlement from the Archdiocese, we quietly agreed, could have made a substantive difference in Justina's life.

"I have also learned that the Diocese of New Ulm approved Justina's petition," the lawyer then added.

"How much?" I asked.

"Two thousand dollars," the lawyer answered.

Justina kept quiet, for a long while.

We all did.

Many More

Sololá, Guatemala

August 15, 2023

Justina still walks to work most mornings. While ambling through the streets of her small town, she appears to her community as the exact same person she has always been. Neither the neighbor sweeping the stoop nor the tortilla seller nor the person kicking at the dog sees her differently, and at first, this was reassuring. After she learned about Father David Roney's history of abuse in 2017 and then became a survivor by submitting her Proof of Claim Form in 2022, Justina worried that the truth about her adoptive father would change everything: that it might capsize her community and throw her life into crisis. But none of this happened, and this absence of any public reckoning was probably more devastating to Justina than any kind of scandal would have been. Committed to maintaining her anonymity, not least out of a sense of privacy, she suddenly found herself alone in Guatemala: steadfastly guarding not just the secret of Roney's abuse but also the story of her victimhood. It was one of the most painful consequences of Roney's time in the highlands. Justina—unlike Carol— confronted her history of abuse without a community of survivors. She had her small team of North American experts to consult, but her meetings with us were almost always virtual. The people in her life and in the community in which she lived, whom she saw every day, could not conceive of the kind of person she had become, as both a "victim" and "survivor." They also had no idea that this new identity made Justina eligible to be awarded a financial settlement. Over the course of a few years, through therapy, open-ended interviews, and legal action, she had become a survivor of clerical sexual abuse, and new possibilities for action had indeed opened for her as a result—but only in the United States and not in Guatemala.

Between the winter of 2017 and the summer of 2023, Justina came to learn what Roney and his bishops in Minnesota had always known: the conceptual and administrative tools necessary to recognize clerical sexual abuse are not equally available everywhere in the world. She already knew that her country was not as privileged as the United States, especially when it came to the rule of law, a free press, and psychological expertise, but never had these deficits so intimately structured her way of being, effectively foreclosing what she could say, feel, and do about the person who raised her. When framed by a box on a screen and in the company of stateside experts, Justina could see clearly that a diagnosis of sexual deviancy in the United States had consequences, and that the identities of "abuser," "victim," and "survivor" meant something. She could see from afar that a historically contingent assemblage of experts in the United States held priests and their dioceses accountable for the sexual abuse that they perpetrated, with survivors like Carol being awarded hundreds of thousands of dollars as a result. But she could also see that this wasn't the case in Guatemala.

"I understand why they sent him here," Justina told me once, referring to Roney. We were in the mountains near his home and a bank of clouds had just begun to roll in on us. Having been raised in the United States, amid a stretch of impossibly flat country, I probably too easily revel in the alterity of such moments, in how a mountain and a little mist can make me feel a million miles from home, but Justina also seemed aware of the vast distance between where we were standing now and the American Midwest where David Roney had come from.

"He answered to no one out here," she said. "And no one knew him for what he was."

"No one here could have known him for what he was," I responded. "Because in Guatemala he never *was* and could never have been."

"I see that," she sighed.

Roney's bishops in the United States also saw the historical contingency of clerical sexual abuse, and they leveraged it to safeguard priests, mitigate liability, and evade accountability. This strategy meant seeing the world not as one contiguous territory subject to the same universal rules, but rather as a patchwork of differentiated and sometimes disconnected conditions of possibility. Bishops understood the United States in the late twentieth and early twenty-first centuries as a time, place, and social setting that could sustain the existence of clerical sexual abuse and its corresponding identities. They also, adroitly, spotted patches of Latin America where clerical sexual abuse did not yet exist in any consequential sense. And so they moved sexually abusive priests to places like the highlands of Guatemala, where their sexual deviancy also did not exist. It was a diabolical tactic with material effects. While an assemblage of expertise in the United States has thus far cost dioceses nearly $4 billion in awards and settlements, with some individual survivors receiving more than $1 million, the Diocese of New Ulm in the summer of 2023 cut a check for Justina in the amount of $2,000 as compensation for allowing her to be raised for nearly a decade by a sexual predator.

Justina did the math.

"I read the news on the internet about the ninety-three survivors from the Diocese of New Ulm and their $34 million," Justina wrote me soon after receiving her award. She was upset.

"I would like to mention how sad it is," she wrote, "that people like me, who live in the background, do not receive the same amount of money as those who live in the United States." I found Justina's use of the word "background" poignant. It was an apt shorthand for her experience of having been kept out of sight and completely unrecognizable for so many years.

"There is no equality between these amounts," she wrote. "There is no justice."

She was right, of course.

"And I wonder," she finished, "maybe it is because I am a woman, Indigenous and from a Third World country. Maybe they think that I should receive less money."

I told Justina that this was and remains the Church's exact strategy, with her paltry settlement not only saving the Diocese of New Ulm hundreds of thousands, if not millions, of dollars, but also serving to maintain a silence that has been central to the Roman Catholic Church's worldwide perpetration of sexual abuse. Two thousand dollars was the perfect amount not only to maintain silence at the Mission but also to forestall clerical sexual abuse's emergence in the highlands of Guatemala. Two thousand dollars was not enough money to encourage Justina to tell her story outside the conditions of strict anonymity. Twenty thousand dollars might have given her a more stable platform from which to make demands on the diocese and its mission, maybe even to approach the press and the Vatican, and $200,000 would have provided her with complete financial freedom to do and say whatever she wanted. But $2,000 made her question whether the entire process was even worth it.

"Two thousand dollars for me is a lot of money," Justina later explained, "and I am very grateful for it, but it really does not make up for the years of abuse."

Two thousand dollars was also not enough money to encourage others living near the Mission to step forward with their own experiences of clerical abuse. Roney's many godchildren and the hundreds of other children (now adults) who appear in his photographs also have the right to file a petition with the Diocese of New Ulm's future survivor fund. They too could become victims and survivors, but who would take such an extraordinary risk for such a meager reward? Justina's personal history imploded through this process. She stitched it back together over several years with a team of stateside experts, and yet she ended up with only a pair of imperceptible identities (victim and survivor) and a couple of thousand dollars. There were times when Justina had doubts about our work together.

"You have to remember that your story is important," I would tell Justina. "And not just here in Guatemala. It is important for people around the world."

"I see that," she would admit.

David Roney was not an outlier, and Bishop Raymond Lucker and Father Gregory Schaffer were not evil geniuses. They were simple, albeit troubled, men who manipulated a variegated world to protect themselves at the expense of others. They were weak, selfish, and immoral. Their actions decimated childhoods, faiths, and entire families, but they were not extraordinary men. There have been a tragic number of Roneys,

Luckers, and Schaffers in the history of the Roman Catholic Church, as well as a heart-piercing number of Justinas.

For now, it remains true that clerical sexual abuse is scarcely legible in Guatemala, and it may never be fully comprehensible there. The Diocese of New Ulm's negligible $2,000 settlement to Justina will likely play a small but consequential role in keeping it that way, and for as long as this is the case, the conditions exist for more stories like Roney's and Justina's.

There are already so many.

Ordained in the Diocese of Natchez-Jackson, Mississippi, in 1970 and then credibly accused in 2002 of sexually abusing a young boy on a trip to Ireland, Paul Madden transferred to the Diocese of Chimbote, Peru, in 2003.[34]

Ordained in the Archdiocese of Los Angeles, California, in 1990 and credibly accused of sexually abusing a young boy in 1991, Jeffrey David Newell sought treatment in Maryland and then left for Mexico, where he has since worked as a priest in the Archdiocese of Tijuana.[35]

Ordained in the Diocese of Sacramento, California, in 1979, Jose Luis Urbina pleaded guilty in 1989 to committing lewd acts with a child under fourteen years of age, but then skipped bail and fled to Mexico, where he has worked as a priest in Navjojoa, Mexico.[36]

Ordained in the Diocese of Worcester, Massachusetts, in 1969 and accused in 1993 of sexually abusing a nine-year-old boy, Thomas A. Kane founded the House of Affirmation, a treatment center for clergy in Whitinsville, Massachusetts, before moving to Guadalajara, Mexico, in 2002.[37]

Ordained in the Diocese of Scranton, Pennsylvania, in 1995 and accused in 2001 of sexual misconduct with a sixteen-year-old boy, Eric Ensey moved in 2006 to Paraguay, where he served as a priest of the Society of Saint James in the Diocese of Ciudad del Este.[38]

Ordained in the Diocese of Scranton, Pennsylvania, in 1995 and accused in 2001 of sexual misconduct with a sixteen-year-old boy,

Carlos Urrutigoity moved in 2006 to Paraguay, where he served as a priest in the Diocese of Ciudad del Este and was named its Vicar General in 2012.[39]

Ordained in the Archdiocese of San Francisco in 1962 and credibly accused of sexually abusing at least eight children, Austin Peter Keegan fled to Baja, Mexico, in 1981, where he worked as a parish priest and also worked for a time in an orphanage.[40]

Ordained in the Diocese of Sacramento, California, in 1980 and accused in 1989 of sodomizing a fourteen-year-old boy on a trip to Mexico, Jose Antonio Pinal moved to the Diocese of Cuernavaca, Mexico, in 1989, where he has since worked as a parish priest.[41]

Ordained in the Diocese of Los Angeles, California, in 1991 and then credibly accused of sexually abusing a teenage boy a few years later, Carl Tresler denied the allegations and moved to Huancavelica, Peru, where he works as a pastor and a seminary and diocesan administrator.[42]

Ordained in the Archdiocese of Milwaukee, Wisconsin, in 1967 and later transferred to the Diocese of Orange, California, in 1973, Siegfried F. Widera sought treatment with the Servants of the Paraclete in 1985 and then fled to Mazatlán, Mexico, in 2002.[43]

Ordained in the Diocese of Spokane, Washington, in 1949 and then assigned to the diocese's mission in Sololá, Guatemala, from 1961 to 1977, Arthur C. Mertens sexually abused children in Guatemala before returning to Spokane to serve as a parish priest.[44]

Ordained in the Diocese of Lafayette, Indiana, in 1967, where he was accused of sexually abusing teenage boys, Ronald J. Voss moved to Port au Prince, Haiti, in 1993, where he served as a parish priest, and then to the town of Abaco in the Bahamas.[45]

Ordained by the Salesians of Don Bosco in 1989 and credibly accused of sexually abusing children in Peru, Guatemala, and Argentina, Carlos Enrique Peralta joined the Archdiocese of Chicago, Illinois, in 1998, where he was again accused of abusing children. Peralta then moved to Mexico City in 2001.[46]

Ordained in the Diocese of Fall River, Massachusetts, in 1964 and credibly accused in 1992 of sexually abusing a nine-year-old girl, Donald J. Bowen served as a missionary priest in Bolivia with the Society of Saint James for twenty-eight years.[47]

Ordained by the Theatine Fathers in 1980 and convicted in 1989 of sexually abusing a minor in the Diocese of Pueblo, Colorado, Lucas A. Galvan sought treatment with the Servants of the Paraclete before moving to Argentina and then Mexico, where he is the pastor of a small parish in Mexico City.[48]

Ordained in the Archdiocese of Saint Louis, Missouri, in 1975 and credibly accused of sexually abusing a high-school student in 1993, Kevin Hederman moved to Belize in 1999 to serve as a priest in the Archdiocese of Guadalupe.[49]

Ordained in the Diocese of Bridgeport, Connecticut, in 1962 and accused of abusing over two dozen boys between the ages of ten and eighteen, Laurence F. X. Brett sought treatment with the Servants of the Paraclete in 1993 and then fled to Sint Maarten in the Caribbean the same year.[50]

Ordained in the Archdiocese of Saint Paul and Minneapolis, Minnesota, and accused of molesting a four-year-old girl, Freddy Montero fled to his native country of Ecuador to serve as a priest in the remote parishes of the Diocese of Guaranda.[51]

Ordained by the Society of Mary in 1988, John Velez served the Diocese of El Paso, Texas, and then the Diocese of Salinas, California, before admitting in 1991 to sexually abusing an altar boy in California. He moved to Mexico and then Colombia, where he serves as a priest.[52]

Ordained in the Archdiocese of Dubuque, Iowa, in 1955 and accused of abusing boys in the 1970s, Robert J. Reiss had his ministerial activities restricted in 1990. He then moved to Mexico and was eventually murdered in 2005 in Chilpancingo in the state of Guerrero, Mexico.[53]

Ordained in the Diocese of Phoenix, Arizona, in 1981, Joseph Cervantez Briceno was placed on leave in 1992 for allegedly abusing a pair of siblings. He then fled to Mexico, where Briceno served the Diocese of Mexicali until captured by U.S. authorities in 2005.[54]

Ordained in the Diocese of Brooklyn, New York, in 2003, Augusto Cortez faced multiple charges of sexually abusing minors. One case involved a six-year-old who contracted an STD. Cortez fled the United States for South America; he was found years later by Interpol in Guatemala.[55]

Ordained in the Diocese of Bridgeport, Connecticut, in 1970 and accused of sexually assaulting a former altar boy in 1985, Stanley F. Banaszek served Maryknoll Missions in Guatemala and Nicaragua for several years, including the time immediately following the accusations of abuse.[56]

A Brother of the Franciscans' Province of the Immaculate Conception, Brother Fidelis DeBerardinis was convicted in 2003 of sexually abusing eight altar boys in an East Boston parish after having been moved to parishes around the world, including a decade spent in Central America.[57]

Ordained in the Archdiocese of Boston, Massachusetts, in 1959, Father Mario Pezzotti was accused of molesting students in a private high school in New York in the 1960s and 1970s. Pezzotti then fled to Brazil, where he worked in ministry for decades.[58]

Postscript

Vatican City

January 5, 2024

Over the years, while researching and writing this book, I spent months in Rome trying to gauge the frequency with which bishops transferred priests from North America to Latin America. Sometimes, when the research would get to be too much for me, when the number of sexually abusive priests moving across borders suggested that I was dealing with a transnational criminal organization rather than a worldwide religious community, I would climb to the top of Saint Peter's Basilica to clear my head. It's a slow walk up a narrow, relentlessly corkscrewing staircase. At one point, near the end of the ascent, there are no handrails to steady yourself, only tiled walls and a thick rope dangling from a distant ceiling. The corridor also tightens, and the steps tilt inwards. This would always deliver, at least to me, a punch of anxiety, something like claustrophobia. But then the world would suddenly open up again. At the top of the dome, in the fresh air, the basilica's cupola offers unrivaled views of Vatican City and Rome, lending me an almost godlike perspective on the Papal Gardens, the Vatican Museum, and Saint Peter's Square. On a clear day, I could see as far as the Alban Hills.

From this privileged perch, far above the confused bustle of clerics and tourists, I would think about what I wanted readers to learn from the story of Father David Roney. Then I would scribble some ideas in a note-book, always putting what I considered to be the most important points at the top of the page. For the last few years of this project, even up until the moment of handing my manuscript over to the publisher, I would sum-marize the two most central of these ideas with a pair of words: "global" and "uneven." Sometimes I would write them in all caps and then slowly trace and retrace their letters with my pen until they thickened into chunky blobs of ink. I would especially linger on the word "global," because for me the story of David Roney demonstrates that the phenomenon of clerical sexual abuse is as global as the Roman Catholic Church. We have known for decades that, bishops across the United States moved—and continue to move—sexually abusive priests between parishes to evade accountability. This is a well documented and indisputable phenomenon. Less widely discussed is the fact that the Church has also moved these men across international borders, effectively disappearing them. This means that the true geographical coordinates of clerical sexual abuse are not limited to either the parish or the diocese, as earlier accounts assume; rather, they encompass the world.

Glancing again at my notebook, the word "uneven" would then remind me that the world appears to Roman Catholic bishops in very specific ways. Church leadership would likely be the first to acknowledge that cer-tain countries, such as the United States, enjoy the rule of law, a free press, and a wealth of psychological expertise. These are political and legal con-texts in which sexually abusive priests can be held accountable for their crimes. Yet, as the cross-border transfer of priests amply demonstrates, the world is not made up simply of relatively privileged countries. There also exist vast stretches of unevenly governed terrain, replete with safe harbors and soft landings, where the promise of accountability is attenu-ated at best and nonexistent at worst. Bishop Raymond Lucker, for exam-ple, did not just move Roney to Central America because the Mission is far away from Minnesota. Lucker also stashed Roney there because he knew that the highlands of Guatemala lacked the administrative and conceptual tools necessary to recognize, and thus prosecute, clerical sexual abuse as a crime. The very kind of person whom Roney had become in New Mexico and then Minnesota did not even exist in Guatemala at the time of his retirement. In a very practical sense, this unevenness must have assured

Lucker that Roney could never have been convicted or even accused of clerical sexual abuse in Guatemala, no matter what he did.

Other words also came to mind as I would stare down Via della Conciliazione, that elegant stretch of avenue connecting Saint Peter's Square to the western bank of the Tiber River. Further down the page, I would scribble "business model" into my notebook, and on more than one occasion, I framed this phrase with exclamation points and then underlined it for effect. In those moments of quiet reflection at the very top of Vatican City, I would worry that people might misread the story of David Roney as evidence of some grand conspiracy, of wicked Church leaders plotting against vulnerable parishioners on behalf of their pedophilic priests. While it is true that Roney did not move to Guatemala by chance, and that Lucker seemed to know full well what he was doing, the movement of these men from North America to Latin America is no conspiracy. It's a business model: a clever and deeply calculated plan to protect assets, mitigate liability, and avoid scandal by shifting risk from North America to Latin America. Roney's sexual abuse of children in Minnesota cost the Diocese of New Ulm millions of dollars, but his abuse in Guatemala only cost the diocese $2,000. This settlement was so meager that it effectively silenced Justina, while also foreclosing the possibility that anyone else from Guatemala might ever file a petition against the diocese.

The last two words that would always end up in my notebook were "tree" and "time." The former was shorthand for a mashup of clichés that, tired though they may seem, have always guided my research and writing about Roney. They are my way of responding to apologists who defend the Church by saying that the problem of clerical sexual abuse is the result of a "few bad apples," meaning a handful of corrupt outliers. In contrast, I have always maintained that it is not just the apples that are rotten but, more importantly, the tree itself. The full story of David Roney lays bare the fact that he never acted alone. The Church in its entirety facilitated his perpetration of sexual abuse: from nuns to lawyers to missionaries to therapists to law enforcement officials to theologians to priests to bishops to the pope himself. The rot began to surface centuries ago when Augustine shouted down the Donatists to say that priests are priests forever. It later spread rapidly when Pope Pius XI (1922–1939) and then Pope John XXIII (1958–1963) transferred priests en masse from the United States to Latin America, never bothering to check why bishops were shipping certain priests south. The decay was also present in the quietest, most banal moments of complicity. Father Gregory Schaffer and David Roney ate dinner together almost every night at the Mission. They would sit across a small table from each other as women from the community prepared and served their meals. They were often the only two in the room who spoke English, and it pains me to think about their small talk, both what might have been said and what might have been left unsaid. "So David," Schaffer must have asked Roney hundreds of times, "what did you do today?"

"Time" was always the last word on the page and probably the one that haunted me the most. While much of my research and writing about Roney focused on space, and on the movement of this man from one end of a continent to the other, the Church's full strategy for evading accountability also included a keen awareness of time. Bishop Raymond Lucker got Roney out of Minnesota just in the nick of time, before his past could really catch up with him. Meanwhile, lawyers in Minnesota battled fearlessly against the Church to suspend the state's statutes of limitations so that survivors could make claims against dioceses. Even when the time-bound restrictions imposed by these statutes were successfully overcome, Church leaders and their legal teams proved to be incredibly effective at dragging their feet. Justina's petition to the Diocese of New Ulm, which was supposed to take as little as two weeks to resolve, stretched well beyond a year. The anthropologist in me could not help reading this exaggerated delay as a message of indifference, acknowledging that although Justina would eventually receive a reply from the Diocese of New Ulm, she would have to wait for that response in ways that accentuated the very vulnerabilities that had rendered her susceptible to Roney in the first place. After working on the case of David Roney for so many years, I also got the sense that the Church is more than willing to weather these scandals, however many more there may be, by working from the assumption that this too will pass. From the top of Saint Peter's Basilica, overlooking what some have come to call the Eternal City, I realized that in writing a book about the Church's manipulation of space I had also written a book about the Church's weaponization of time. I became increasingly aware that although everyone connected to the case of David Roney would one day pass from the earth, Justina and I included, the Roman Catholic Church would likely remain as powerful as ever.

Standing at the top of St. Peter's, reflecting on the words in my notebook and looking out at the scattered people and winding avenues below, I would ultimately be reminded of the limits of inhabiting such a godlike perspective. There are things that can't be seen from so high up, including the toll that the Church's worldwide movement of sexually abusive priests has taken on individual survivors, as well as the courage and resilience it has taken for these survivors to try to hold the Church accountable. In the end, I had the words in my notebook—words like "global" and "uneven," words like "tree" and "time"—and each told a crucial part of the story, but the words that matter most have always belonged to survivors such as Justina.

Acknowledgments

Justina read a Spanish translation of this manuscript before it went into production, and this allowed her to make some notes and offer corrections. One of them changed the entire tenor of this book for the better. I wanted the reader to understand Father David Roney, the priest whom I had come to know through the course of my research, including the specifics of his violence and cruelty. But Justina helped me to see that it was not necessary to detail the extent to which she and so many others suffered. Instead, she suggested that the book more firmly establish how Church leadership in and beyond the United States had placed them all in the position of suffering. "I hope we can achieve something with this book," she told me a few days before I handed the manuscript over to the press. "Me too," I replied. For your courage and insight, wisdom and generosity, thank you, Justina.

I can still remember my first phone call with Carol. "Well?" she asked me, with that quintessential Minnesota accent. "How can I help?" Her enthusiasm and warmth carried a conversation that lasted for years. We spoke every Wednesday, at first about David Roney and then increasingly about life in rural Minnesota. Her willingness to reminisce with me about snowdrifts and pagan babies as well as life on the farm gave me just enough cultural proficiency to interview a cohort of survivors from Minnesota to whom I owe a debt of gratitude. My weekly conversations with Carol also allowed me to better understand the kind of children whom Roney so clearly targeted. The more I got to know Carol, the more I seemed to understand Justina, and through me, the two got to know each other. "How is

Justina doing?" Carol would always ask near the end of our calls. My answers would vary week to week, but Carol's concern allowed me to twine their lives together through the pages of this book. For your willingness to contribute so much of yourself to this book, thank you, Carol.

Lawyers, journalists, archivists, and activists in the United States provided me with the information that I needed to pursue original research in Guatemala. BishopAccountability.org is an invaluable resource. The Survivors Network of those Abused by Priests (SNAP) was always generous to me, and the reporting of Madeleine Baran's team for Minnesota Public Radio proved essential. Jeff Anderson & Associates P.A. in Saint Paul, Minnesota, was also vital. Thank you, Jeff Anderson, Patrick Wall, Mike Finnegan, and Molly Burke. My deepest gratitude to Michael Bryant and Cheryl Pojanowski. I will never forget what you two did for Justina. Thomas Doyle is a wise man who offered much-needed advice on how to navigate an ever-growing number of stateside cases and reports, while John Bellocchio proved to be the right kind of persistent. Thank you all.

I sharpened my thoughts for this book by writing articles and giving invited talks. My published essays include those that appear in the journals *Comparative Studies in Society and History*, *Representations*, and the *Journal of the American Academy of Religion*. I appreciate the anonymous reviewers and editorial collectives who pushed me along the way. Thank you also to those colleagues who hosted me for talks at the University of Cambridge, Cornell University, University of Michigan, University of Leiden, Indiana University, McMaster University, University of California San Diego, Washington University in St. Louis, University of Victoria, and University of Toronto. Those articles and talks, and this book, draw on research supported by a suite of grants from the Social Sciences and Humanities Research Council of Canada—a Connections Grant, Insight Development Grant, Insight Grant, and Partnership Development Grant. I also benefited immensely from a John Simon Guggenheim Fellowship, Mellon Foundation Sawyer Seminar, and grant support from the University of Toronto Faculty of Arts and Sciences as well as the University of Toronto Faculty of Law.

Three milieus have shaped my thoughts about this book. The first is the University of Toronto Centre for Diaspora and Transnational Studies, which I had the honor to direct from the fall of 2017 to the summer of 2024. Its inaugural director, Ato Quayson, has always been a model of ambition and excellence for me, while the Centre's associate director, Antonela Arhin, has been something of a north star for a unit constantly in search of its true potential. Thank you also to my longtime colleagues at the Centre, Anna Shternshis and Ken MacDonald. They have provided perspective and insight along the way. From 2018 to 2024, the Centre grew quickly, with this rather small unit doubling, tripling, and then quadrupling in size. Every hire brought new lines of thought and debate, each of which shaped this book in unexpected ways. Thank you, Andrea Allen, Kamari

Clarke, Alejandra González Jiménez, Sumayya Kassamali, Tracy Lemos, Ted Sammons, Padraic X. Scanlan, Naomi Seidman, and Angelica Pesarini.

The second milieu is a book series that I edit with the University of California Press. From its writing groups and book workshops to its happy hours and week-end retreats, the opportunity to edit Atelier has given me far more than I have ever been able to give its authors. Thank you, Peter Benson, Sarah Besky, Amiel Bize, Alessandro Angelini, Tracie Canada, Lauren Coyle Rosen, Emma Crane Shaw, Darcie DeAngelo, Laurie Denyer Willis, Jacob Doherty, Jatin Dua, Michael Edwards, Anthony W. Fontes, Duana Fullwiley, Sahana Ghosh, Erica C. James, Alix Johnson, Keisha-Khan Perry, Charline Kopf, Kathryn Mariner, Samuel Shearer, Nestór Silva Sharika, Nomi Stone, Sharika Thiranagama, Christien Tompkins, Namita Vijay Dharia, Marina Welker, Kaya Williams, and Emrah Yildiz. Even if the conversations have always ostensibly been about these authors' books, they have also always been about my own work. Thank you for helping me think through such aesthetic challenges as tone, atmosphere, and even endnotes.

The third is the Evasion Lab, which I inaugurated out of necessity. To really understand the Church's techniques of evasion, I needed to put myself in conver-sation with those studying other transnational criminal organizations, such as Mafia and drug cartels, as well as multinational corporations. From graduate and postdoctoral fellows to faculty collaborators and invited guests, this extended thought experiment about evasion as a broad analytic drove this book at a con-ceptual level. My many thanks to Jatin Dua, Kamari Clarke, Ananya Roy, Clau-dio Lomnitz, Laurence Ralph, Naor Ben Yehoyada, Austin Zeiderman, Sergio Montero, and Graham Denyer Willis, as well as Laura Acosta-Zarate, Sadaf Ahmed, Lisa Ariemma, Niyousha Bastani, Daniel Bergman, Jacob Bessen, Jes-sica Cook, Wumi Asubiaro Dada, Jaime Duncan, Noah Khan, Kanika Lawton, Yang Liu, Laura Lorena De Souza Carvalho, Alaa Mitwaly, Louis Plottel, Ryan Smyth, Chiho Tokita, Jorge Vargas Gonzalez, Aamer Ibraheem, Heba Ghannam, Dalia Gebrial, Huibin Lin, Navjit Kaur, Dan Li, Nikhil Pandhi, Greg Odum, Swa-gat Pani, Adina Radosh, Victoria Tran, Henry Osman, Christopher Giamarino, Amber Fatima Rahman, and Samuel Nossa Aguero. The Evasion Lab is an initia-tive that has been funded by the Social Sciences and Humanities Research Coun-cil of Canada, Mellon Foundation, and University of Toronto Faculty of Arts and Sciences. Dean Melanie Woodin and my chair in the Department for the Study of Religion, Pamela Klassen, deserve great credit for championing the Evasion Lab. Thank you.

This book progressed faster than expected because of a dedicated team of research assistants. Jessica Loudis generously guided me through conversations about narrative arc while Philip Sayers supported me with everything else, from this book's conceptual insights to the structure of its sentences. Daniel Bergman then picked up where Philip left off. I'm not sure what this book would have looked like without them. Clara Secaira made the fieldwork possible while also providing a constant sounding board for how the work itself might be progressing. I couldn't have completed this book without her. Thank you. Jacob Bessen thought through the footnotes with me, Katie Jones and Nathaly Sanchez Vasquez scoured the archives, Thien Thuong Hoang tackled the legal records, and Juan Bautista often got me from one end of Guatemala to the other. Thank you all.

The support I received at the University of California Press was unparalleled, with special thanks to Kate Marshall and Chad Attenborough. I handed an early draft of the manuscript to Kate sometime in mid-December, near the holidays, and I suggested that maybe she should wait until the new year to read it. "It's not really meant to be a 'stocking stuffer' of a story," I mentioned. She shrugged and then got to work, sending me comments that would elevate this book beyond what I could have done on my own. Thank you.

My parents, Bruce and Mary O'Neill, raised me to question authority, while my in-laws, Mojundar and Usha Sridhar, have supported so much of this life-long questioning by being a part of my home life throughout this book's creation. Thank you. My wife's uncle and aunt, Dr. YKS Murthy and Sudha Murthy, have lived in Rome for nearly half a century and have now hosted me too many times to count, helping me with everything from wi-fi to local bus routes. It has been an absolute pleasure getting to know them and their city. My brother, Bruce O'Neill, is also an anthropologist. He works in a different part of the world on entirely different themes, but our conversations are always invaluable. Finally, my wife, Archana Sridhar, has been my greatest supporter, encouraging me to turn life's questions into research. We are both grateful to see our son, Ignatius, become such an impressive young man. It would have been nice to have had the Church contribute to his formation, but I now know too much about how unforgivable this institution can be. And my son's gentle charisma is radiant proof enough that the Church needs him far more than he needs it.

Reading Group Guide

1. In the preface, author Kevin Lewis O'Neill argues that clerical sexual abuse did not exist in Guatemala at the time of Father David Roney's retirement. How did you respond to this argument that clerical sexual abuse is a phenomenon that can only exist when people are able to recognize it?

2. The book focuses on just one abusive priest, though it mentions many more. How did the decision to focus on a single figure affect your reading of the book?

3. Part 1 of the book discusses the difference between a conventional secret and a public secret. What is the difference between the two?

4. One of David Roney's early sermons concerned the "occasions of sin," and the idea that Adam and Eve first sinned not by eating the apple but by moving closer to the tree. Do you find this a useful way of thinking about sin? Do you find it a useful way of thinking about David Roney?

5. Much discussion of clerical sexual abuse has focused on the idea that it is not an individual problem with specific priests, but rather a systemic problem sustained by the Roman Catholic Church as an institution: the issue is not just with "bad apples" but with the roots of the tree itself. How do you think about the question of accountability and responsibility when it comes to clerical sexual abuse?

6. The book frequently discusses the bravery of survivors in speaking out about their experiences. What makes it so difficult for victims to share their experiences? What could make it easier for them to do so?

7. The book suggests that the Servants of the Paraclete "made" Roney into a sexual deviant through their systematic administration of specific physical and psychological evaluations. Do you think that scientific tests have the capacity to change how people see themselves, or to change how others see them?

8. In part 3, O'Neill discusses the theology behind the idea of "pagan babies." Is this an idea you had encountered before? What does this insensitive phrase say about changing attitudes within the Church?

9. David Roney gave people in Guatemala photos as gifts, but O'Neill suggests that these gifts weren't selfless—that they were ways for Roney to impose obligations on the people he gave them to. Discuss the idea of the gift as a way of manipulating people.

10. The book recounts a June 2002 meeting in Dallas, Texas, in which the Roman Catholic Church expressed its remorse in public for clerical sexual abuse. Was this kind of public reckoning the right strategy? How might Church leadership have acted differently at this key moment?

11. Father Gregory Schaffer didn't tell Justina about Roney's past when she visited Minnesota in 2012. O'Neill suggests that this is because he couldn't have recognized Justina as a victim of clerical sexual abuse, though he also mentions that Schaffer may have wanted to protect the Mission in Guatemala. Do you think this situation reflects a problem of individual perception, a systemic oversight, or something else?

12. Carol finds the act of writing about her abuse a useful way of processing trauma. Why might writing be a helpful strategy for dealing with difficult experiences?

13. In part 5, O'Neill becomes an important character in the story he is telling. How did you experience this shift as a reader? Would it have been possible to tell the story in any other way?

14. The book's first three parts revolve around the ideas, attitudes, and external circumstances that shaped David Roney's life. What sort of explanation for Roney's abusive behavior emerges out of these accounts, if any? Is it possible to try to understand the inner worlds of people who commit acts of clerical sexual abuse without excusing or justifying their crimes?

15. One of the book's central points of focus is the transfer of Catholic priests across international borders. Did the book's discussion of these transfers change the way you think about the Catholic Church's relationship to specific nations, or the way you think about the role of national borders more generally?

Notes

The names of public figures, such as clerics, appear throughout this book. Others remain anonymous or are cited by pseudonym. In some cases, certain details (insignificant to the analysis) have been changed to protect the identities of specific people. These changes include the use of composite scenes that contain elements from more than one situation. These scenes accurately reflect actual events but have been rearranged to preserve anonymity. Quotations are from recorded interviews or from detailed notes. All translations from Spanish to English are my own. Some of the archival materials used here are publicly available, often via Bishop Accountability, a public archive of materials related to clerical sexual abuse in the Roman Catholic Church. Others are in the possession of the author: many of these belong to a collection of documents referred to in citations as the Roney Files (RF), attained through the legal process of discovery. Full citations of all archival documents appear in the endnotes. So too do the works of scholarship and literature that orient this book's analysis. I list the most influential of these materials in the bibliography.

PREFACE

1. Roney was preparing for his final retreat, a form of anachoresis. Roland Barthes describes anachoresis as a "separation from the world that's effected by

going back up to some isolated, private, secret, distant place"; *How to Live Together: Novelistic Simulations of Some Everyday Spaces*, trans. Kate Briggs (New York: Columbia University Press, 2013), 24. Barthes writes: "Anachoresis: its foundational act is to break away, the abrupt jolt of departure. The distancing has to be symbolized in some way. Anachoresis = an action, a line, a threshold to be crossed" (25).

2. The brevity of his speech at the gala offers a central example of how Roney repeatedly fell silent when pressed to account for himself. It was a tactic that he deployed to gain some control over his life, and it calls to mind silence as a crucial part of Christian semiosis. Richard Bauman writes that "silence, in its broader sense, demands the suppression of self and of self-will"; *Let Your Words Be Few: Symbolism of Speaking and Silence among Seventeenth-Century Quakers* (Cambridge: Cambridge University Press, 1983), 22. See also Phillip Cary, *Outward Signs: The Powerlessness of External Things in Augustine's Thought* (New York: Oxford University Press, 2008).

3. New Ulm Diocesan Review Board on Sexual Misconduct, Report to the Bishop, August 24, 1993, RF, A686.

4. Important ethnographies are organized around the life of one person, often working from the assumption that these individuals embody a story that is more than their own. Powerful examples include Ruth Behar, *Translated Woman: Crossing the Border with Esperanza's Story* (Boston: Beacon Press, 2003); João Biehl, *Vita: Life in a Zone of Social Abandonment* (Berkeley: University of California Press, 2005); Philippe Bourgois, *In Search of Respect: Selling Crack in El Barrio* (New York: Cambridge University Press, 1996); Karen McCarthy Brown, *Mama Lola: A Vodou Priestess in Brooklyn*, updated and expanded edition (Berkeley: University of California Press, 2001); Vincent Crapanzano, *Tuhami: Portrait of a Moroccan* (Chicago: University of Chicago Press, 1985); Robert R. Desjarlais, *Sensory Biographies: Lives and Deaths among Nepal's Yolmo Buddhists* (Berkeley: University of California Press, 2003); Angela Garcia, *The Pastoral Clinic: Addiction and Dispossession along the Rio Grande* (Berkeley: University of California Press, 2010); Neni Panourgiá, *Fragments of Death, Fables of Identity: An Athenian Anthropography* (Madison: University of Wisconsin Press, 1995).

5. These numbers have become public knowledge through the efforts of a nonprofit that tracks data on the legal, financial, and emotional fallout of clerical sexual abuse in the U.S. and elsewhere. For further context related to the numbers quoted here, see "Lists of Accused Priests Released by Dioceses and Religious Institutes," Bishop Accountability, accessed December 7, 2023; "Bankruptcy Protection in the Abuse Crisis: Documents and Articles [Milwaukee WI, Portland OR, San Diego CA, Tucson AZ, Davenport IA, Spokane WA, Fairbanks AK, Wilmington DE & MD, Oregon Province of the Jesuits]," Bishop Accountability, accessed December 7, 2023; "Major Sexual Abuse Settlements in the Catholic Church," Bishop Accountability, accessed December 7, 2023.

6. The literature on clerical sexual abuse is vast in terms of disciplines; for anthropology, see Nancy Scheper-Hughes, "Institutionalized Sex Abuse and the Catholic Church," in *Small Wars: The Cultural Politics of Childhood*, ed. Nancy Scheper-Hughes and Carolyn Sargent (Berkeley: University of California Press, 1998), 295–317; for sociolegal studies, see Timothy D. Lytton, *Holding Bishops Accountable: How Lawsuits Helped the Catholic Church Confront Clergy Sexual Abuse* (Cambridge Harvard University Press, 2008); for psychology, see A. W. Richard Sipe, *Sex, Priests, and Power: Anatomy of a Crisis* (New York: Brunner/Mazel, 1995); for theology, see Mark D. Jordan, *Telling Truths in Church: Scandal, Flesh, and Christian Speech* (Boston: Beacon Press, 2003); for history, see Kathleen Holscher, "The Trouble of an Indian Diocese: Catholic Priests and Sexual Abuse in Colonized Places," in *Religion and U.S. Empire: Critical New Histories*, ed. Tisa Wenger and Sylvester A. Johnson (New York: New York University Press, 2022), 231–52; for religious studies, see Anthony M. Petro, "Beyond Accountability," *Radical History Review*, no. 122 (2015): 160–76; and for the history of ideas, see Robert A. Orsi, "Events of Abundant Evil," in *History and Presence* (Cambridge: Harvard University Press, 2016), 215–48. The geographical range of these studies, however, is rather narrow, focusing almost exclusively on the continental United States.

7. The movement of sexually abusive priests from the United States to countries such as Guatemala calls to mind processes of "wastelanding." See Traci Brynne Voyles, *Wastelanding: Legacies of Uranium Mining in Navajo Country* (Minneapolis: University of Minnesota Press, 2015). Wastelands, in Voyles's account, are places "from which resources are increasingly extracted and where (often toxic) waste is increasingly dumped" (9).

8. See CEH, "Memoria del silencio. Guatemala: Comisión para el Esclarecimiento Histórico" (Guatemala: Comisión para el Esclarecimiento Histórico, 1999). The literature on Guatemala's civil war is dense. Some key points of references include Ricardo Falla, *Masacres de La Selva: Ixcán, Guatemala, 1975–1982* (Guatemala City: Editorial Universitaria, 1992); Linda Green, *Fear as a Way of Life: Mayan Widows in Rural Guatemala* (New York: Columbia University Press, 1999); Victoria Sanford, *Buried Secrets: Truth and Human Rights in Guatemala* (New York: Palgrave Macmillan, 2003). Regarding the U.S.-backed coup in 1954, see Greg Grandin, *The Last Colonial Massacre: Latin America in the Cold War* (Chicago: University of Chicago Press, 2011); Grandin argues that the United States promised to turn Guatemala into a model democracy but instead created a laboratory of repression. See also Jean Franco, *The Decline and Fall of the Lettered City: Latin America in the Cold War* (Cambridge: Harvard University Press, 2002); Stephen Schlesinger and Stephen Kinzer, *Bitter Fruit: The Story of the American Coup in Guatemala*, revised and expanded edition (Cambridge: Harvard University, David Rockefeller Center for Latin American Studies, 2005); Nick Cullather, *Secret History: The CIA's Classified Account of*

Its Operations in Guatemala, 1952–1954 (Stanford: Stanford University Press, 1999). It is important to note that Roney's cross-border maneuvers would have been impossible without U.S. imperialism, as would the great irony of his victims in Guatemala seeking justice from U.S. institutions.

9. The themes of legibility and governance are central to the work of James Scott, with the former determining the capacity of the latter. Two key examples include *The Art of Not Being Governed: An Anarchist History of Upland Southeast Asia* (New Haven: Yale University Press, 2009) and *Seeing Like a State: How Certain Schemes to Improve the Human Condition Have Failed* (New Haven: Yale University Press, 1998). The logic of the state, Scott insists, is to render populations legible so that they can be governed, while anarchist tactics center on evading projects of legibility. The story of David Roney, in far less romantic terms, attends to the costs or perils of illegibility, providing a counterbalance to Scott's embrace of illegibility's.

10. The claim that clerical sexual abuse does not exist in Guatemala fits within a larger conceptual tradition that pinpoints the historical emergence of ideas and their corresponding identities. In *Historical Ontology* (Cambridge: Harvard University Press, 2004), Ian Hacking reflects on "the possible ways to be a person" (2), noting the historical contingency of such ideas and identities as those of perverts (99), multiple personalities (101), homosexuals (103), and suicide (112). In *The Order of Things: An Archaeology of the Human Sciences* (New York: Vintage Books, 1994), Michel Foucault makes an even grander claim: "It is comforting, however, and a source of profound relief to think that man is only a recent invention, a figure not yet two centuries old, a new wrinkle in our knowledge, and that he will disappear again as soon as that knowledge has discovered a new form" (xxv). For a particularly deft execution of this approach, see Michelle Murphy, *Sick Building Syndrome and the Problem of Uncertainty: Environmental Politics, Technoscience, and Women Workers* (Durham: Duke University Press, 2006). See also Mary Poovey, *A History of the Modern Fact: Problems of Knowledge in the Sciences of Wealth and Society* (Chicago: University of Chicago Press, 1998); Arnold I. Davidson, *The Emergence of Sexuality: Historical Epistemology and the Formation of Concepts* (Cambridge: Harvard University Press, 2004).

11. The psychiatrists, anthropologists, hygienists, forensic scientists, sociologists, and phrenologists that emerged in the nineteenth century advanced theories about society that set the conditions not just of truth and falsity but also of existence itself. This is the argument that Michel Foucault makes in "The Subject and Power," *Critical Inquiry* 8, no. 4 (1982): 777–95. He also advances the point in *The Birth of the Clinic: An Archaeology of Medical Perception*, trans. Alan Sheridan (London: Routledge, 2003). He details the creation of expertises propelled not by charismatic thinkers but rather by systems of thought that support the existence of such ideas and identities as madness and deviance. Knowledge

becomes power when the diagnoses of experts gain the capacity to result in the very disciplinary regimes that Foucault details in *Discipline and Punish: The Birth of the Prison*, trans. Alan Sheridan (New York: Vintage Books, 1977).

12. My research for this book relies on archival materials both as sources of evidence to be assessed and as techniques of governance to be analyzed. In *Paper Cadavers: The Archives of Dictatorship in Guatemala* (Durham: Duke University Press, 2014), Kirsten Weld approaches the Historical Archives of the National Police in Guatemala City with a similar tack, via an approach that she calls "archival thinking." To this end, she helpfully draws on a cluster of key sources: Michel-Rolph Trouillot, *Silencing the Past: Power and the Production of History* (Boston: Beacon Press, 1995); Ann Laura Stoler, *Along the Archival Grain: Epistemic Anxieties and Colonial Common Sense* (Princeton: Princeton University Press, 2009); Jacques Derrida, *Archive Fever: A Freudian Impression*, trans. Eric Prenowitz (Chicago: University of Chicago Press, 2008). I draw on this body of thought as well, but I am also interested in the limits of the archive as a technique of evasion, especially when an entity such as the Roman Catholic Church, itself an archivally minded institution, transfers some of its most suspicious members to live beyond the archive's panoptic gaze. In this sense, my ethnographic fieldwork in rural Guatemala is in line with Louis Bickford's call for activists to preserve primary materials relating to human rights abuses. See Louis Bickford, "The Archival Imperative: Human Rights and Historical Memory in Latin America's Southern Cone," *Human Rights Quarterly* 21, no. 4 (1999): 1097–112.

13. Feminist historians have consistently emphasized how imperial mobilities both respond to and are generated through processes of making, unmaking, and remaking. See Ann Laura Stoler, *Carnal Knowledge and Imperial Power: Race and the Intimate in Colonial Rule* (Berkeley: University of California Press, 2010); Lisa Lowe, *The Intimacies of Four Continents* (Durham: Duke University Press, 2015); Amy Kaplan, "Manifest Domesticity," *American Literature* 70, no. 3 (1998): 581–606.

14. Ethnography often begins from the limits of historical knowledge. This is a major liability, but it is also, as Alpa Shah writes, an opportunity to produce "new knowledge and has the potential to transform ideology and action, challenge dominant theory, propose alternative theories, and take action that may potentially challenge the forces around us, change the course of history." See Shah, "Ethnography? Participant Observation, a Potentially Revolutionary Praxis," *HAU: Journal of Ethnographic Theory* 7, no. 1 (45–59): 50–51. See also Eric R. Wolf, *Europe and the People without History* (Berkeley: University of California Press, 1982).

15. Following standard anthropological conventions, I name such public figures as Bishop Raymond Lucker and Father Gregory Schaffer, but others whom I interviewed remain anonymous or are cited by pseudonym. Quotations are from recorded interviews or from detailed notes. All translations are my own.

16. The allegory of sacrifice reverberates across this book, with bishops in the United States moving sexually abusive priests to Guatemala and thus sacrificing the well-being of Guatemalan children for the safety of American children. Sacrifice can be understood as resolving a tension between excess and expenditure, as with Georges Bataille, *Theory of Religion*, trans. Robert Hurley (New York: Zone Books, 1989); between crisis and scapegoat, as with René Girard, *Violence and the Sacred*, trans. Patrick Gregory (Baltimore: Johns Hopkins University Press, 1979); and between secrecy and forgiveness, as with Jacques Derrida, *The Gift of Death*, trans. David Wills (Chicago: University of Chicago Press, 1996). Here, it might be more helpful to track the centrality of sacrifice to the Christian tradition. See Daniel Boyarin, *Dying for God: Martyrdom and the Making of Christianity and Judaism* (Stanford: Stanford University Press, 1999).

17. What would it mean to fail on pastoral terms? Pastoralism is a mode of power modeled after the Christian image of the shepherd, who cares for his flock and yet would risk the herd to save even one lost sheep. The image of the good shepherd is an image of one who governs with "constant kindness"—through what Michel Foucault has called the "art of conducting, directing, leading, guiding, taking in hand, and manipulating men"; see *Security, Territory, Population: Lectures at the College de France, 1977–78*, ed. Michel Senellart, trans. Graham Burchell (New York: Palgrave Macmillan, 2007), 165. The good shepherd's counterpart is the bad shepherd, who "disperses the flock, lets it die of thirst, [and] shears it solely for profit's sake"; see Michel Foucault, "'Omnes et Singulatim': Toward a Critique of Political Reason," in *Power*, vol. 3 of *Essential Works of Foucault*, ed. James D. Faubion (New York: New Press, 2001), 301. Lucker, Schaffer, and Roney are bad shepherds, complete failures at their jobs.

PART I. A PRIEST FOREVER, 1945–1987

1. Direct quote comes from Plaintiff Jane Doe 43 G's First Supplemental Answers to Defendant's Interrogatories, March 14, 2006, RF, A916–17. Jason Grabinger's *Willmar* (Charleston: Arcadia Publishing, 2018) proved insightful, as did Sinclair Lewis's *Main Street* (New York: Harcourt, Brace, 1920). Sociological companions to *Main Street* include Robert Wuthnow, *Small-Town America: Finding Community, Shaping the Future* (Princeton: Princeton University Press, 2013), and Kathleen Stewart, *A Space on the Side of the Road: Cultural Poetics in an "Other" America* (Princeton: Princeton University Press, 1996).

2. Direct quotes in this paragraph come from David Roney, Foundation House Personal History Sheet, April 12, 1987, RF, A8.

3. David Roney, Foundation House Personal History Sheet, April 12, 1987, RF, A9.

NOTES TO PAGES 5-8

4. Plaintiff Jane Doe 43 G's First Supplemental Answers to Defendant's Interrogatories, March 14, 2006, RF, A917.

5. *The Willmar 8*, directed by Lee Grant (GTY Productions, 1981). The documentary chronicles the eight women who organized the longest bank strike in American history.

6. Plaintiff Jane Doe 43 G's First Supplemental Answers to Defendant's Interrogatories, March 14, 2006, RF, A920.

7. Plaintiff Jane Doe 43 G's First Supplemental Answers to Defendant's Interrogatories, March 14, 2006, RF, A917.

8. In *Complaint!* (Durham: Duke University Press, 2021), Sara Ahmed emphasizes that while forms of domination often deprive people of their ability to refuse an act, this does not mean that they refrain altogether from refusing.

9. Direct quotes in this paragraph come from deposition of Father John Berger, December 18, 2014, RF, 27, 28.

10. Direct quotes in this paragraph come from David Roney, Foundation House Personal History Sheet, April 12, 1987, RF, A5–A8.

11. David Roney, Foundation House Personal History Sheet, April 12, 1987, RF, A8.

12. Deposition of Father John Berger, December 18, 2014, RF, 29.

13. Roney's loneliness does not warrant our sympathy, but the emotion does lend itself to philosophical reflection. Hannah Arendt, in *The Origins of Totalitarianism* (New York: Schocken Books, 2004), distinguishes loneliness from solitude (477), emphasizing how loneliness can wrench a person from the common world.

14. Plaintiff Jane Doe 43 G's First Supplemental Answers to Defendant's Interrogatories, March 14, 2006, RF, A917.

15. Roney's abuse was extensive. The legal record provides evidence that Roney abused children (mostly but not exclusively girls) between the ages of seven and fourteen, exposing himself, groping children, and coercing them into touching him. See Anonymous to Bishop Raymond Lucker, March 25, 1987, RF, A756; Anonymous to Bishop Raymond Lucker, April 7, 1987, RF, A758–60; New Ulm Diocesan Review Board on Sexual Misconduct, Report to the Bishop, August 24, 1993, RF, A686–9; Gene Burke, Memo to Files, Subject: Father David Roney, March 2, 1994, RF, A770–71; Anonymous to Gene Burke, July 10, 1996, RF, A779; Rev. Douglas L. Grams, Memo to the File of Rev. David Roney, August 21, 2002, RF, A788–89; Plaintiff Jane Doe 43G's First Supplemental Answers to Defendant's Interrogatories, March 14, 2006, RF, A915–35; Plaintiff Jane Doe 43 C's First Supplemental Answers to Defendant's Interrogatories, June 22, 2006, RF, A2–19; Affidavit of Sister Virginia McCall, August 8, 2007, RF, A748–50; Affidavit of Allen Iverson, August 8, 2007, RF, A751–52; Affidavit of Theresa Iverson, August 8, 2007, RF, A753–55; Memorandum of Law in Support of Defendants' Motion for Summary Judgment concerning the Claims of

Jane Doe 43G, August 24, 2007, RF, A235–58; Jane Doe 43C, Jane Doe 43D, Jane Doe 43E, Jane Doe 43F, and Jane Doe 43G vs. Diocese of New Ulm, St. Francis Parish, and St. Mary's Parish, Memorandum of Law, January 18, 2008, RF, A879–89; Jane Doe 43C, Jane Doe 43D, Jane Doe 43E, Jane Doe 43F, and Jane Doe 43G vs. Diocese of New Ulm, St. Francis Parish, and St. Mary's Parish, Appellants' Brief, March 25, 2010, RF, 1–38; Doe 6 and Doe 7 vs. Diocese of New Ulm, Complaint, July 10, 2013, RF, 1–15; Plaintiff Doe 18's Complaint against Diocese of New Ulm, September 12, 2013, RF, 1–11; Reed Anfinson, "Lawsuit Claims Children at St. Francis Were Abused by Priest in the 1960s," *Swift County Monitor News*, September 18, 2013, 1, 9; Plaintiff Doe 7's Opposition to Defendant Diocese of New Ulm's Motion for Summary Judgment, September 9, 2015, RF, 1–51; Plaintiffs Doe 6 and 7's Memorandum and Order on Motion for Summary Judgment, November 20, 2015, RF, 1–23; History of Father David A. Roney, n.d., RF, 1–2.

16. Here there seems to exist a very fine line between willful ignorance and a public secret. In *Summa Theologica* (Merrimack: Thomas More College Press, 1948), Thomas Aquinas writes that willful ignorance is a grave sin against faith. The public secret, however, is an "active not-knowing," at least for Michael Taussig in his *Defacement: Public Secrecy and the Labor of the Negative* (Stanford: Stanford University Press, 1999). See Georg Simmel, "The Sociology of Secrecy and of Secret Societies," *Journal of Sociology* 11, no. 4 (1906): 441–98. See also Kimberly Theidon, "The Mask and the Mirror: Facing Up to the Past in Postwar Peru," *Anthropologica* 48, no. 1 (2006): 87–100. In reference to Roney as magician, see Graham M. Jones, *Trade of the Tricks: Inside the Magician's Craft* (Berkeley: University of California Press, 2011).

17. Plaintiff Doe 7's Opposition to Defendant Diocese of New Ulm's Motion for Summary Judgment, September 9, 2015, RF, 2–3; Plaintiff Doe 18's Complaint against Diocese of New Ulm, September 12, 2013, RF, 2; Plaintiffs Doe 6 and 7's Memorandum and Order on Motion for Summary Judgment, November 20, 2015, RF, 6.

18. One subtle but significant advantage that Roney held over these children was architectural: the pulpit literally elevated him above the congregation. Michel Foucault's study of the modern prison, *Discipline and Punish: The Birth of the Prison*, trans. Alan Sheridan (New York: Vintage Books, 1977), famously opened a window onto a historical period defined by the disciplinary practice of surveillance. See also Emmanuel Levinas's "Transcendence and Height," in *Basic Philosophical Writings*, ed. Adriaan T. Peperzak, Simon Critchley, and Robert Bernasconi (Bloomington: Indiana University Press, 1996), 11–32.

19. In *Centuries of Childhood: A Social History of Family Life*, trans. Robert Baldick (New York: Vintage Books, 1962), Philippe Ariès makes the striking argument that "in medieval society the idea of childhood did not exist" (125). He means that the qualities and characteristics that make up the category of the

child vary considerably across time and cultures. For more on social reproduction, see Pierre Bourdieu and Jean-Claude Passeron's *Reproduction in Education, Society and Culture*, trans. Richard Nice (London: Sage Publications, 1977).

20. Plaintiff Jane Doe 43 G's First Supplemental Answers to Defendant's Interrogatories, March 14, 2006, RF, A917.

21. Free play is often a space through which children process trauma. Instances of this recur throughout the literature on police violence. See Alice Goffman, *On the Run: Fugitive Life in an American City* (Chicago: University of Chicago Press, 2014). On the politics of child's play, see also Nancy Scheper-Hughes and Carolyn Fishel Sargent, eds., *Small Wars: The Cultural Politics of Childhood* (Berkeley: University of California Press, 1998).

22. By taking such care in writing her letter to the bishop, this young girl intuited what Erving Goffman argues in *The Presentation of Self in Everyday Life* (New York: Anchor Books, 1959): our credibility is always at stake, and we must present ourselves to others with as much care as possible (66). For another powerful resource concerning the subtle importance of penmanship, see Pierre Bourdieu, *Distinction: A Social Critique of the Judgement of Taste*, trans. Richard Nice (Cambridge: Harvard University Press, 1984).

23. Affidavit of Sister Virginia McCall, August 8, 2007, RF, A749.

24. Direct quotes in this paragraph come from Deposition of Father Francis Garvey, April 19, 2007, RF, A711.

25. Deposition of Father Francis Garvey, April 19, 2007, RF, A711.

26. Deposition of Father Francis Garvey, April 19, 2007, RF, A709.

27. Affidavit of Sister Virginia McCall, August 8, 2007, RF, A749.

28. Affidavit of Sister Virginia McCall, August 8, 2007, RF, A749.

29. Affidavit of Sister Virginia McCall, August 8, 2007, RF, A749–50. There is something curious about Roney's piqued silence. In *Stone Age Economics* (Chicago: Aldine-Atherton, 1972), Marshall Sahlins calls such silence "negative reciprocity, the unsociable extreme" (177). Relatedly, David Graeber, in *Debt: The First 5,000 Years* (Brooklyn, NY: Melville House, 2012) writes: "The moment we recognize someone as a different sort of person, either above or below us, then ordinary rules of reciprocity become modified or are set aside" (111).

30. Deposition of Father Francis Garvey, April 19, 2007, RF, A713–14.

31. See Thomas Doyle, "Marital Fidelity in the Canonical Tradition of the Catholic Church" (JCD diss., Washington, DC, Catholic University of America, 1978).

32. For a complete history of the clerical sexual abuse scandal in Lafayette, Louisiana, see Jason Berry, *Lead Us Not into Temptation: Catholic Priests and the Sexual Abuse of Children* (Urbana: University of Illinois Press, 2000).

33. David Kohn, "The Church on Trial: Part 1," *60 Minutes*, aired June 11, 2002, on CBS. This lie was also a denial, though lies and denials are two very

different things. In *States of Denial: Knowing about Atrocities and Suffering* (Malden: Polity, 2001), Stanley Cohen describes what he calls the paradox of denial: "In order to use the term 'denial' to describe a person's statement 'I did not know,' one has to assume that she knew or knows about what it is that she claims not to know" (6).

34. Thomas Doyle and Ray Mouton, "The Problem of Sexual Molestation by Roman Catholic Clergy: Meeting the Problem in a Comprehensive and Responsible Manner," Bishop Accountability, June 9, 1985.

35. See Thomas Doyle, "Organized Religion in Marxist-Leninist Philosophy" (MA thesis, River Forest, IL, Aquinas Institute of Philosophy, 1968); "Liberation Theology in the Context of Social Needs in South America" (MA thesis, Dubuque, IA, Aquinas Institute of Theology, 1971); "Vladimir Lenin's Theory of Social Revolution" (MA thesis, Madison, WI, University of Wisconsin, 1971).

36. Direct quotes come from Doyle and Mouton, "Problem of Sexual Molestation," 3, 5, 6. It is also worth reflecting on Doyle's use of dollar amounts. Numbers are the language of risk, as one sees clearly in Ian Hacking's *The Taming of Chance* (New York: Cambridge University Press, 1990) and Peter Bernstein's *Against the Gods: The Remarkable Story of Risk* (New York: Wiley, 1998), but there is also something more fundamental at play with the invocation of dollar amounts. As Georg Simmel notes in *The Philosophy of Money*, trans. Tom Bottomore and George Frisby (New York: Routledge, 2011 [1900]), money is a structuring agent that helps people understand the totality of life.

37. Direct quotes in this paragraph come from Doyle and Mouton, "Problem of Sexual Molestation," 4, 39, 40.

38. Doyle's confidential report on clerical sexual abuse provides a compelling example of a *problematic*. For Michel Foucault, to problematize a term is an act that "constitutes it as an object for thought"; see "The Concern for Truth: An Interview by Francis Ewald," in *Politics, Philosophy, Culture: Interviews and Other Writings 1977–1984*, ed. Lawrence D. Kritzman, trans. Alan Sheridan (New York: Routledge, 1990), 257. See Michel Foucault, "Polemics, Politics, and Problematizations," in *Ethics: Subjectivity and Truth*, vol. 1 of *Essential Works of Foucault, 1954–1984*, ed. Paul Rabinow, trans. Robert Hurley et al. (New York: New Press, 1998), 111–19; Gilles Deleuze and Leopold Sacher-Masoch, *Masochism*, trans. Jean MacNeil (Cambridge: Zone Books, 1989), 14.

39. Doyle and Mouton, "Problem of Sexual Molestation," 16, 23, 24, 27, 28, 29.

40. Doyle and Mouton, "Problem of Sexual Molestation," 25.

41. Doyle and Mouton, "Problem of Sexual Molestation," 36.

42. Claire Taylor, "List of Accused Priests in Lafayette Diocese Grows to 42," *Lafayette Daily Advertiser*, January 16, 2019.

43. The Diocese of New Ulm and the law offices of Jeff Anderson & Associates released a joint statement on March 29, 2016. The statement discloses the names

of sixteen men they mutually identified as being credibly accused of sexual abuse of a minor while they were assigned as priests; see Roman Catholic Diocese of New Ulm, "Disclosures of Names of Priests Credibly Accused of Sexual Abuse of a Minor," Bishop Accountability, March 29, 2016. They are Cletus Altermatt, Dennis Becker, Gordon Buckley, Robert Clark, James Fitzgerald, John Gleason, Joseph Heitzer, Rudolph Henrich, Harry Majerus, Francis Markey, William Marks, John Murphy, David Roney, Douglas Schleisman, Michael Skoblik, and Charles Stark. For "in the parish rectory after bedtime," see Leah Buletti, "Diocese of New Ulm Faces 98 Sex Abuse Claims," *Mankato Free Press*, May 25, 2016. For "to prepare [them] for adult relationships," see Steve McGonigle, "Priest Abuse Inquiry Widens," *Dallas Morning News*, October 10, 2002. For "whiskers and hugs" and "through kissing, fondling, and finally, simulated intercourse," see Kitty McGarry, "Diocese Struggles with Fa [Full Title Unknown]," *The Journal*, May 22, 1994. Bernard Steiner, Richard Gross, and Edward Ardolf were publicly identified for the first time on April 15, 2016; see Elin Lindstrom, "News Release: Three Diocese of New Ulm Priests Identified as Child Abusers in New Lawsuits," Jeff Anderson & Associates, April 15, 2016. A 2003 memorandum from the Diocese of New Ulm acknowledges the abusive behavior of Germain Kunz; see Rev. Douglas L. Grams, "Memorandum," Bishop Accountability, June 20, 2003. Edward Graff, William Sprigler, Joseph Balent, John Cooney, Samuel Wagner, and James Devorak were publicly named by the Diocese of New Ulm as recently as June 2021; see Roman Catholic Diocese of New Ulm, "Disclosures," Protect and Heal, June 19, 2021. Michael Guetter was accused of "improper conduct . . ., including sexual misconduct" against minors under his care; see "Fr. Michael Guetter," Bishop Accountability, accessed November 24, 2022.

44. The literature on clerical sexual abuse in Latin America, Africa, parts of Asia, and much of Europe continues to expand. See Juan Pablo Barrientos, *Dejad que los niños vengan a mí* (Bogotá: Editorial Planeta Colombia, 2019); *Este es el cordero de Dios* (Bogotá: Editorial Planeta Colombia, 2021).

45. Doyle and Mouton, "Problem of Sexual Molestation," 73.

46. Anthropologists and historians tend to associate the regimentation of time with the rise of capitalism. E. P. Thompson, for one, famously demonstrates how clocks allowed capitalist societies to treat time as a currency: "[Time] is not passed but spent"; "Time, Work-Discipline, and Industrial Capitalism," *Past & Present* 38, no. 1 (1967): 60–61. However, Max Weber, in a footnote in *The Protestant Ethic and the "Spirit" of Capitalism*, argues that "we ought not, however, to forget that the first people to live (in the Middle Ages) with careful measurement of time were the monks, and that the church bells were meant above all to meet their needs"; *The Protestant Ethic and the "Spirit" of Capitalism and Other Writings*, ed. and trans. Peter Baehr and Gordon C. Wells (New York: Penguin Books, 2002), 231. In response, Giorgio Agamben, in *The Highest Poverty:*

Monastic Rules and Form-of-Life, trans. Adam Kotsko (Stanford: Stanford University Press, 2013), explores the incredible lengths and methods monastic communities employ to keep track of time in order to keep track of themselves (25).

47. David Roney, Foundation House Personal History Sheet, April 12, 1987, RF, A11.

48. These titles of student sermons come from the annual *St. Thomas Seminary Bulletin*, from vol. 45 in 1940 to vol. 54 in 1949. The listed titles about sin, it should be noted, represent just the tip of a rather anxious iceberg.

49. Quoted in Miles Hollingworth's "The Peace of Babylon (and What It Censors): St. Augustine of Hippo's City of God," in *Censorship Moments: Reading Texts in the History of Censorship and Freedom of Expression*, ed. Geoff Kemp (London: Bloomsbury Academic, 2015), 28.

50. Augustine, *Writings in Connection with the Donatist Controversy*, ed. Marcus Dods, trans. John Richard King (Project Gutenberg, 2014), https://www.gutenberg.org/files/45843/45843-h/45843-h.htm.

51. Augustine, *Confessions*, trans. F. J. Sheed (Indianapolis: Hackett, 1992), 170.

52. For a fuller understanding of this tension between Donatists and Augustine, see Brent D. Shaw, *Sacred Violence: African Christians and Sectarian Hatred in the Age of Augustine* (New York: Cambridge University Press, 2011); as well as Adam Ployd, *Augustine, the Trinity, and the Church: A Reading of the Anti-Donatist Sermons* (New York: Oxford University Press, 2015); and Maureen A. Tilley, ed., *Donatist Martyr Stories: The Church in Conflict in Roman North Africa* (Liverpool: Liverpool University Press, 1996).

53. The invocation of infrastructure here is analogical. There is no theological precedent for understanding priests within the Roman Catholic Church as infrastructural. Conceptually, AbdouMaliq Simone has developed the idea of "people as infrastructure" to emphasize the economic collaboration that happens among marginalized city dwellers; see "People as Infrastructure: Intersecting Fragments in Johannesburg," *Public Culture* 16, no. 3 (2004): 407–29.

54. Arnold van Gennep thought a great deal about the priesthood and its transformative qualities. He writes: "For a layman to enter the priesthood or for a priest to be unfrocked calls for ceremonies, acts of a special kind, derived from a particular feeling and a particular frame of mind"; *The Rites of Passage*, trans. Monika B. Vizedom and Gabrielle L. Caffee, 2nd ed. (Chicago: University of Chicago Press, 2019), 1.

55. Pius XII, *Encyclical Letter Mediator Dei on the Sacred Liturgy (20 Nov. 1947)*, trans. John A. O'Flynn (New York: America Press, 1961), 84.

56. See Mark O'Keefe, *In Persona Christi: Reflections on Priestly Identity and Holiness* (St. Meinrad: Abbey Press, 1998). The notion that Christ literally speaks through the priest invokes, at least for the anthropologist, a rather robust literature on spirit possession. Consider Aihwa Ong, "The Production of Posses-

sion: Spirits and the Multinational Corporation in Malaysia," *American Ethnologist* 15, no. 1 (1988): 28–42; Paul Stoller, *Fusion of the Worlds: An Ethnography of Possession among the Songhay of Niger* (Chicago: University of Chicago Press, 1989); and Janice Boddy, *Wombs and Alien Spirits: Women, Men, and the Zar Cult in Northern Sudan* (Madison: University of Wisconsin Press, 1989).

57. Ps. 110:4. The bishop's imposition of hands and its transformative powers is probably best described as a speech act; see J. L. Austin, *How to Do Things with Words: The William James Lectures Delivered at Harvard University in 1955* (Oxford: Clarendon Press, 1962). John Searle, in *Speech Acts: An Essay on the Philosophy of Language* (Cambridge: Cambridge University Press, 1969), and others developed different schemata.

58. The plurality of personhood is not unprecedented. Marcel Mauss draws on the etymology of "person" to understand the term as "the mask through which (*per*) resounds the voice"; see Marcel Mauss, "A Category of the Human Mind," trans. W. D. Halls, in *The Category of the Person: Anthropology, Philosophy, History*, ed. Michael Carrithers, Steven Collins, and Steven Lukes (Cambridge: Cambridge University Press, 1985), 14. Relatedly, Émile Durkheim argues that man is double: "There are two beings in him." See Émile Durkheim, *The Elementary Forms of the Religious Life*, trans. Joseph Ward Swain (Mineola: Dover Books, 2008 [1912]), 14.

59. Roney Class Photo at Saint Paul Seminary, n.d., RF.

60. "About Us," St. Francis of Assisi—Lake St. Croix Beach, MN, December 28, 2022.

61. "About Us."

62. "About Us."

63. David Roney, Foundation House Personal History Sheet, April 12, 1987, RF, A8.

64. David Roney, Foundation House Personal History Sheet, April 12, 1987, RF, A8.

65. David Roney, Foundation House Personal History Sheet, April 12, 1987, RF, A8.

PART II. BECOMING DEVIANT, 1987–1994

1. Anonymous to Bishop Raymond Lucker, April 7, 1987, RF, A758.
2. Anonymous to Bishop Raymond Lucker, March 25, 1987, RF, A756.
3. Anonymous to Bishop Raymond Lucker, April 7, 1987, RF, A759.
4. Anonymous to Bishop Raymond Lucker, March 25, 1987, RF, A756.
5. Anonymous to Bishop Raymond Lucker, March 25, 1987, RF, A756.
6. Anonymous to Bishop Raymond Lucker, April 23, 1987, RF, A761. It is worth noting that letters are a semi-private correspondence, given from writer to

recipient, but they also include the possibility for wider readership. Franz Kafka knew this well: "Writing letters is actually an intercourse with ghosts"; see *Letters to Milena*, trans. Philip Boehm (New York: Schocken Books, 2015), 223. In this capacity, feminist thinkers have argued that women's letters should be seen as "as spaces of intersubjective and relational engagement, as arenas of self-making and practicing, and thus more properly as sites for the negotiation of public and private meanings"; Clare Hemmings, *Considering Emma Goldman: Feminist Political Ambivalence and the Imaginative Archive* (Durham: Duke University Press, 2018), 31.

7. Anonymous to Bishop Raymond Lucker, April 7, 1987, RF, A758.

8. Bishop Raymond A. Lucker, *My Experience: Reflections on Pastoring* (Kansas City: Sheed & Ward, 1988), 122. See also Bishop Raymond A. Lucker, "Bishop's Message: Priests," *The Prairie Catholic*, April 1987.

9. Lucker, *My Experience*, 122. Lucker's insistence that Roney be treated with the same compassion as everyone else is similar to the genre of moral relativism that Nancy Scheper-Hughes calls "false neutrality"; "The Primacy of the Ethical: Propositions for a Militant Anthropology," *Current Anthropology* 36, no. 3 (1995): 411. In the face of a fairness that prevents the possibility of justice, a common strategy is refusal—a way of claiming rights. For more on the intricacies of this argument and the debates surrounding it, see Roy D'Andrade, "Moral Models in Anthropology," *Current Anthropology* 36, no. 3 (1995): 399–408; Emmanuel Levinas, *Totality and Infinity: An Essay on Exteriority*, trans. Alphonso Lingis (Pittsburgh: Duquesne University Press, 2011).

10. Anonymous to Bishop Raymond Lucker, April 7, 1987, RF, A758.

11. Anonymous to Bishop Raymond Lucker, April 7, 1987, RF, A759.

12. Anonymous to Bishop Raymond Lucker, April 7, 1987, RF, A759.

13. Anonymous to Bishop Raymond Lucker, March 25, 1987, RF, A756.

14. Anonymous to Bishop Raymond Lucker, April 7, 1987, RF, A759.

15. Anonymous to Bishop Raymond Lucker, April 7, 1987, RF, A759.

16. "Deposition of Father Thomas Paul Adamson," DocumentCloud, contributed by Madeleine Baran (Minnesota Public Radio), March 19, 1986, 162.

17. Jeff Anderson & Associates, "Deposition Clip of Thomas Adamson | May 16, 2014 (Never Consider Sexual Abuse of a Minor a Crime)," YouTube, June 11, 2014. Context and quotes from the Thomas Adamson case also come from a three-part story written by Bob Ehlert in the *Star Tribune*; see Bob Ehlert, "'Don't Tell Anybody . . . You'll Get in Trouble, and So Will I,'" *Star Tribune*, December 11–13, 1988, 1E, 4E–5E. Adamson's comments also raise the matter of jurisdiction, or as Justin Richland explains, the scope of a legal institution's power as understood in relationship to other institutions; see "Jurisdiction: Grounding Law in Language," *Annual Review of Anthropology* 42 (2013): 212. Émile Benveniste, possibly in simpler terms, understands jurisdiction as the

power to speak the law; see *Indo-European Language and Society*, trans. Elizabeth Palmer (London: Faber & Faber, 1973), 391–92.

18. For a summary of Thomas Adamson's record of clerical assignments and confirmed acts of sexual abuse, see "Assignment Record—Rev. Thomas Adamson," Bishop Accountability, September 30, 2014.

19. For a deeper engagement with clerical sexual abuse in Minnesota, see the four-part series "Betrayed by Silence: A Radio Documentary" (Minnesota Public Radio, July 14, 2014).

20. "Betrayed by Silence: A Radio Documentary."

21. "A St. Paul Park, Minn.," United Press International, February 3, 1987, Bishop Accountability.

22. Anonymous to Bishop Raymond Lucker, April 7, 1987, RF, A758.

23. Jane Doe 43C, Jane Doe 43D, Jane Doe 43E, Jane Doe 43F, and Jane Doe 43G vs. Diocese of New Ulm, St. Francis Parish, and St. Mary's Parish, Memorandum of Law, January 18, 2008, RF, A882.

24. Plaintiff Jane Doe 43G's First Supplemental Answers to Defendant's Interrogatories, March 14, 2006, RF, A916.

25. Anonymous to Bishop Raymond Lucker, April 7, 1987, RF, A758–59. What to make of candy? Sidney Mintz in *Sweetness and Power: The Place of Sugar in Modern History* (New York: Penguin Books, 1986) historicizes how people whom he understands as Western have made the Industrial Revolution tolerable with the consumption of sugar; see also Mintz, "The Changing Roles of Food in the Study of Consumption," in *Consumption and the World of Goods*, ed. John Brewer and Roy Porter (London: Routledge, 1996), 269. Marshall Sahlins considers these rather moral coordinates in an essay titled "The Sadness of Sweetness" and rightly connects this tension between virtue and sin not simply to Christianity but also its most fundamental authors, such as Augustine; see "The Sadness of Sweetness: The Native Anthropology of Western Cosmology," *Current Anthropology* 37, no. 3 (1996): 395–415.

26. Anonymous to Bishop Raymond Lucker, April 23, 1987, RF, A761.

27. Many of these letters carry a tone of discretion. They are efforts to delicately manage the boundaries of who knows a secret. Lilith Mahmud defines discretion in anthropological terms as "a set of embodied practices that conceal and reveal potentially significant information and that performatively establish a subject's positionality within a specific community of practice"; "'The World Is a Forest of Symbols': Italian Freemasonry and the Practice of Discretion," *American Ethnologist* 39, no. 2 (2012): 429. This kind of discretion is evident throughout the history of anthropological thought, with examples in Victor Turner's *The Forest of Symbols: Aspects of Ndembu Ritual* (Ithaca: Cornell University Press, 1967) and E. E. Evans-Pritchard's *Witchcraft, Oracles, and Magic among the Azande* (Oxford: Clarendon Press, 1976). Both understand the management of secrets as directly related to the management of community.

28. Lucker, *My Experience*, 89. See also Bishop Raymond A. Lucker, "A Word from the Bishop: Competition," *Diocese of New Ulm Newsletter*, January 1984.

29. Lucker, *My Experience*, 89. Bishop Raymond A. Lucker, "Word from the Bishop," *Diocese of New Ulm Newsletter*, February 1979.

30. Anonymous to Bishop Raymond Lucker, n.d., RF, A757.

31. Lucker, *My Experience*, 122. See also Lucker, "Bishop's Message: Priests."

32. Rev. Bill Sprigler to Anonymous, May 1, 1987, RF, A762.

33. Lucker, *My Experience*, 122. See also Lucker, "Bishop's Message: Priests."

34. Archdiocese of San Antonio, "Report on Child Sexual Abuse by Clergy in the Archdiocese of San Antonio," Bishop Accountability, January 31, 2019; Roman Catholic Diocese of New Ulm, "Fr. William Sprigler," Protect and Heal, February 27, 2019.

35. Father John B. Feit, "A Footnote from the Top," May 8, 1967, RF, 3.

36. Father John B. Feit, "A Footnote from the Top," May 8, 1967, RF, 12.

37. Susan Burritt, "Center to Explore New Directions," *Jemez Thunder*, March 1, 1995.

38. Thomas Doyle, "The Servants of the Paraclete and Their Work with Clerics Who Sexually Abuse Minors" (January 11, 2020), unpublished report in the author's possession.

39. David Roney, Foundation House Personal History Sheet, April 12, 1987, RF, A15.

40. Gerald Fitzgerald, "Report from Gerald Fitzgerald to Congregation of Holy Office," Bishop Accountability, April 11, 1962.

41. Gerald Fitzgerald, "Letter to Priest, Name Redacted," Bishop Accountability, September 27, 1948.

42. Gerald Fitzgerald, "Report to Congregation of Holy Office," Bishop Accountability, April 11, 1962.

43. Gerald Fitzgerald, "Letter to William J. Kenneally," Bishop Accountability, July 21, 1960.

44. Gerald Fitzgerald, "Letter to Edwin Byrne," Bishop Accountability, September 18, 1957.

45. Gerald Fitzgerald, "Letter to Edwin Byrne," Bishop Accountability, September 18, 1957.

46. Servants of the Paraclete, Treatment Plan for Sex Offenders, n.d., RF, 1–9.

47. David Roney, Foundation House Personal History Sheet, April 12, 1987, RF, A4.

48. David Roney, Foundation House Personal History Sheet, April 12, 1987, RF, A15.

49. David Roney, Foundation House Personal History Sheet, April 12, 1987, RF, A11.

50. Michel Foucault, *An Introduction*, vol. 1 of *The History of Sexuality*, trans. Robert J. Hurley (New York: Vintage Books, 1990), 31–32.

51. Foucault, *An Introduction*, 31.

52. Foucault, *An Introduction*, 31. It is important to note that Michel Foucault mentions the trial of Jouy somewhat sympathetically. There has been debate for decades as to whether Foucault was guilty of an irresponsible nostalgia for a premodern era of sexuality; Haythem Guesmi, "Reckoning with Foucault's Alleged Sexual Abuse of Boys in Tunisia," *Al Jazeera*, April 16, 2021.

53. Foucault, *An Introduction*, 31.

54. Foucault, *An Introduction*, 32.

55. David Roney, Foundation House Personal History Sheet, April 12, 1987, RF, A12.

56. Processes of discovery do not simply entail the addition of new or more sophisticated knowledge but rather a reorganization of the very conditions upon which knowledge emerges. Consider Georges Canguilhem's *The Normal and the Pathological*, trans. Carolyn R. Fawcett and Robert S. Cohen (New York: Zone Books, 1991), but more importantly the works of Michel Foucault, whose scholarship—be it on the history of prisons (*Discipline and Punish: The Birth of the Prison*, trans. Alan Sheridan [New York: Vintage Books, 1977]), sexuality (*History of Sexuality*), or psychiatry (*Psychiatric Power: Lectures at the Collège de France, 1973–74*, trans. Graham Burchell [New York: Picador, 2008])—routinely begins with a break.

57. David Roney, Foundation House Personal History Sheet, April 12, 1987, RF, A6–7.

58. Debates over classification have been one of the major concerns of social theory over the last century. Foucault both critiqued and built upon Lévi-Strauss's program of comparative classificatory structures to show that categories are entangled in power relations. More recently, historians and anthropologists have questioned whether classification is itself a product of the European colonial project. See Claude Lévi-Strauss, *Wild Thought: A New Translation of "La Pensée Sauvage,"* trans. Jeffrey Mehlman and John Leavitt (Chicago: University of Chicago Press, 2021); Michel Foucault, *The Order of Things: An Archaeology of the Human Sciences* (New York: Vintage Books, 1994); Harriet Ritvo, *The Platypus and the Mermaid, and Other Figments of the Classifying Imagination* (Cambridge: Harvard University Press, 1997).

59. In the words of the philosopher Ian Hacking, "a kind of person [comes] into being at the same time as the kind itself [is] being invented." Ian Hacking, "Making Up People," in *The Science Studies Reader*, ed. Mario Biagioli (New York: Routledge, 1999), 165.

60. David Roney, Foundation House Personal History Sheet, April 12, 1987, RF, A7.

61. Ian Hacking calls this process "making up people": a term that marks those moments when modes of description "create new ways for people to be"; "Making Up People," 161.

62. David Roney, Foundation House Personal History Sheet, April 12, 1987, RF, A7–8.

63. The psychological framework of Carl Jung—see *Modern Man in Search of a Soul*, trans. W. S. Dell and Cary F. Baynes (New York: Harcourt, Brace, 1933)—organizes most mid- to late-century personality tests, including the Myers-Briggs. While these kinds of self-management can be understood as technologies of freedom that allow individuals to assume greater responsibilities—see Nikolas Rose, *Governing the Soul: The Shaping of the Private Self*, 2nd ed. (London: Free Association Books, 1999)—they ultimately ensnare the subject in a web of disciplinary mechanisms; see Foucault, *Psychiatric Power*.

64. Therapeutic Programs Offered by the Servants of the Paraclete, n.d., RF, 7.

65. Ian Hacking argues that "numerous kinds of human beings and human acts come into being hand in hand with our invention of the categories labeling them"; "Making Up People," 171.

66. David Roney, Foundation House Personal History Sheet, April 12, 1987, RF, A10.

67. David Roney, Foundation House Personal History Sheet, April 12, 1987, RF, A15.

68. The internal exile of the Lourdes Retreat evokes the work of Michel Foucault in *Madness and Civilization: A History of Insanity in the Age of Reason*, trans. Richard Howard (New York: Vintage Books, 1988), when he references the allegory of the ship of fools from Plato's *Republic*. Foucault writes fictitiously about ships that would carry the mentally disturbed ("madmen" in his parlance) from the port of one European city to the port of another.

69. Rev. William D. Perri to Rev. David A. Roney, May 18, 1987, RF, A763.

70. Therapeutic Programs Offered by the Servants of the Paraclete, n.d., RF, 5–8.

71. The language of "guest-priest" is compelling. Andrew Shryock and Jatin Dua both make the point that hospitality can blend quickly into captivity, that the guest can quickly become a prisoner of the host; see Shryock, "Breaking Hospitality Apart: Bad Hosts, Bad Guests, and the Problem of Sovereignty," *Journal of the Royal Anthropological Institute* 18, no. 1 (2012): 20–33; Dua, *Captured at Sea: Piracy and Protection in the Indian Ocean* (Oakland: University of California Press, 2019).

72. Therapeutic Programs Offered by the Servants of the Paraclete, n.d., RF, 20. A full list of books that the Servants of the Paraclete recommended to guest-priests includes William A. Miller, *Make Friends with Your Shadow: How to Accept and Use Positively the Negative Side of Your Personality* (Minneapolis: Augsburg Publishing House, 1981); Morton Kelsey and Barbara Kelsey, *Sacrament of Sexuality: The Spirituality and Psychology of Sex* (Warwick: Amity House, 1986); David Keirsey and Marilyn Bates, *Please Understand Me: Char-*

acter and Temperament Types (Del Mar: Prometheus Nemesis Book Company, 1978); Morton Kelsey, *Adventure Inward: Christian Growth through Personal Journal Writing* (Minneapolis: Augsburg Publishing House, 1980); Desmond Morris, *Manwatching: A Field Guide to Human Behavior* (New York: Harry N. Abrams, 1977); Donald Symons, *The Evolution of Human Sexuality* (Oxford: Oxford University Press, 1979).

73. David Roney, Foundation House Personal History Sheet, April 12, 1987, RF, A11.

74. David Roney, Foundation House Personal History Sheet, April 12, 1987, RF, A11.

75. David Roney, Foundation House Personal History Sheet, April 12, 1987, RF, A11.

76. David Roney, Foundation House Personal History Sheet, April 12, 1987, RF, A15.

77. Therapeutic Programs Offered by the Servants of the Paraclete, n.d., RF, 9. It is worth noting that the state of New Mexico seems to attract secrecy. The Los Alamos National Laboratory in New Mexico has long been a harbinger of scientific secrets associated with the American nuclear complex, as several scholars have documented. See Joseph Masco, *The Theater of Operations: National Security Affect from the Cold War to the War on Terror* (Durham: Duke University Press, 2014), 282; Matthew Farish, *The Contours of America's Cold War* (Minneapolis: University of Minnesota Press, 2010); Hugh Gusterson, *Nuclear Rites: A Weapons Laboratory at the End of the Cold War* (Berkeley: University of California Press, 1998).

78. Anthropologists have consistently shown that what is considered moral is rarely dictated by religious codes. Instead, the ethnographic insight has been that people make morality through practices and actions such as what Matthew Hull calls the "materiality of bureaucracy"; see *Government of Paper: The Materiality of Bureaucracy in Urban Pakistan* (Berkeley: University of California Press, 2012). According to the work of Veena Das and Joel Robbins, ethical norms develop out of routine; moral failures emerge "not by orienting oneself to transcendental, agreed-upon values but rather through the cultivation of sensibilities *within* the everyday"; see Veena Das, "Ordinary Ethics," in *A Companion to Moral Anthropology*, ed. Didier Fassin (Hoboken: Wiley-Blackwell, 2012), 134; quoted in Joel Robbins, "What Is the Matter with Transcendence? On the Place of Religion in the New Anthropology of Ethics," *Journal of the Royal Anthropological Institute* 22, no. 4 (2016): 770.

79. Rev. William D. Perri to Rev. David A. Roney, May 18, 1987, RF, A763.

80. The Servants of the Paraclete promised its guest-priests a break with the past. Constantin Fasolt describes the break between past and present as "the founding principle of history," claiming that "whatever else may be said about the past (and there is an infinite number of possibilities, on which historians never

can agree), this much seems certain: all aspects of the past are gone, and none of them can be changed"; *The Limits of History* (Chicago: University of Chicago Press, 2004), 5–6. See also Charles Hirschkind, *The Feeling of History: Islam, Romanticism, and Andalusia* (Chicago: University of Chicago Press, 2021), 18–19.

81. The Paraclete Program at Via Coeli, January 25, 1967, RF, 1.

82. David Roney, Foundation House Personal History Sheet, April 12, 1987, RF, A8.

83. Kenneth J. Pierre, Report of Psychological Evaluation, September 4, 1990, RF, A767.

84. Kenneth J. Pierre, Report of Psychological Evaluation, September 4, 1990, RF, A767.

85. Kenneth J. Pierre, Report of Psychological Evaluation, September 4, 1990, RF, A767.

86. Father David Roney to Anonymous, July 20, 1993, RF, 1.

87. Austin maintains that sincerity is a condition for felicity; see J. L. Austin, *How to Do Things with Words: The William James Lectures Delivered at Harvard University in 1955* (Oxford: Clarendon Press, 1962). For more on sincerity and illocutionary acts, see Hent de Vries, "Must We (Not) Mean What We Say," in *The Rhetoric of Sincerity*, ed. Mieke Bal, Ernst van Alphen, and Carel E. Smith (Stanford: Stanford University Press, 2009), 90–120. See also Webb Keane, "Sincerity, 'Modernity,' and the Protestants," *Cultural Anthropology* 17, no. 1 (2002): 66.

88. Kenneth J. Pierre, Report of Psychological Evaluation, September 4, 1990, RF, A766.

89. Kenneth J. Pierre, Report of Psychological Evaluation, September 4, 1990, RF, A766.

90. Roney's letter felt shallow to Susan. Social theorists such as Erving Goffman have long argued that the apology is a process through which a person symbolically splits into two parts: "the part that is guilty of an offense and the part that dissociates itself from the delict and affirms a belief in the offended rule"; *Relations in Public: Microstudies of the Public Order* (New York: Basic Books, 1971), 113. Roney here never seems to disassociate. And see Paul De Man, *Allegories of Reading: Figural Language in Rousseau, Nietzsche, Rilke, and Proust* (New Haven: Yale University Press, 1979) for a distinction between the structure of a confession and the structure of an excuse.

91. While the secular state relies heavily on bureaucracy, studies in global history have also emphasized how the Catholic Church developed expansive archival practices. Ignatius of Loyola, for example, instructed his missionaries in 1554 to detail as many of their observations as possible: "Finally if there are other things that may seem extraordinary, let them be noted, for instance, details

about animals and plants that either are not known at all, or not of such a size, etc. And this news . . . may come in the same letters or in other letters separately." Cited in Paula Findlen, "How Information Travels: Jesuit Networks, Scientific Knowledge, and the Early Modern Republic of Letters, 1540–1640," in *Empires of Knowledge: Scientific Networks in the Early Modern World*, ed. Paula Findlen (Abingdon: Routledge, 2019), 57–105. See also Luke Clossey, *Salvation and Globalization in the Early Jesuit Missions* (New York: Cambridge University Press, 2008).

92. Father David Roney, "In Love with a Beautiful Girl," *Diocese of New Ulm Newsletter*, August 1982.

93. Father David Roney, "Loving the Flaws," *Diocese of New Ulm Newsletter*, April 1982.

94. Father David Roney, "The Guatemalan Child," *Diocese of New Ulm Newsletter*, December 1982.

95. Roney, "Loving the Flaws."

96. Father David Roney, "Random Impressions of a Quick Visit," *Diocese of New Ulm Newsletter*, February 1983.

97. Kenneth J. Pierre, Report of Psychological Evaluation, September 4, 1990, RF, A767.

98. Kenneth J. Pierre, Report of Psychological Evaluation, September 4, 1990, RF, A767.

99. New Ulm Diocesan Review Board on Sexual Misconduct, Report to the Bishop, August 24, 1993, RF, A686.

100. Gene Burke, Memo to Files, Subject: Fr. David Roney, July 21, 1993, RF, A768.

101. New Ulm Diocesan Review Board on Sexual Misconduct, Report to the Bishop, August 24, 1993, RF, A688.

102. New Ulm Diocesan Review Board on Sexual Misconduct, Report to the Bishop, August 24, 1993, RF, A688-9.

103. New Ulm Diocesan Review Board on Sexual Misconduct, Report to the Bishop, August 24, 1993, RF, A686.

104. Gene Burke, Memo to Files, Subject: Fr. David Roney, July 21, 1993, RF, A768.

105. Gene Burke, Memo to Files, Subject: Fr. David Roney, October 27, 1993, RF, A769.

106. Gene Burke, Memo to Files, Subject: Fr. David Roney, October 27, 1993, RF, A769.

107. Gene Burke, Memo to Files, Subject: Fr. David Roney, October 27, 1993, RF, A769.

108. Sexual Misconduct Cases Pertaining to Minors that Did Not Go Public, n.d., RF, 1-2.

PART III. A TOWN WITHOUT PEDOPHILIA,
1994–2003

1. U.S. Department of State, "Guatemala—Travel Warning," March 30, 1994. It is interesting to note that this travel warning inverted a longstanding set of associations about country and city in Guatemala, with the countryside suddenly the site of danger and the city a refuge. Raymond Williams explored this classic division in *The Country and the City* (New York: Oxford University Press, 1973).

2. After the signing of the 1996 Peace Accords, the number of lynchings (*linchamantos*) in Guatemala accelerated, with approximately 500 lynchings or intents to lynch occurring in the immediate years of the postwar context. There are no exact figures because many of these acts of violence occurred in distant communities. Regardless, the literature on lynching in postwar Guatemala is expansive. Key insights come from Jim Handy, "Chicken Thieves, Witches, and Judges: Vigilante Justice and Customary Law in Guatemala," *Journal of Latin American Studies* 36, no. 3 (2004): 533–61; Angelina Snodgrass Godoy, "Lynchings and the Democratization of Terror in Postwar Guatemala: Implications for Human Rights," *Human Rights Quarterly* 24, no. 3 (2002): 640–61; Carlos Mendoza and Edelberto Torres-Rivas, eds., *Linchamientos: ¿Barbarie o justicia popular?* (Guatemala: Colección Cultura de Paz, 2003).

3. Daniel Rothenberg, "The Panic of Robaniños: Gringo Organ Stealers, Narratives of Mistrust, and the Guatemalan Political Imagination" (PhD diss., University of Chicago, 2018), 167. Rothenberg synthetizes nearly every possible piece of documentation to provide stunning insights about trauma and moral panic in wartime Guatemala. Other analyses of this panic include Diane M. Nelson, *A Finger in the Wound: Body Politics in Quincentennial Guatemala* (Berkeley: University of California Press, 1999); Abigail Adams, "Gringas, Ghouls and Guatemala: The 1994 Attacks on North American Women Accused of Body Organ Trafficking," *Journal of Latin American Anthropology* 4, no. 1 (1999): 112–33; Anne Collinson, "The Littlest Immigrants: Cross-Border Adoption in the Americas, Policy, and Women's History," *Journal of Women's History* 19, no. 1 (2007): 132–41.

4. "Trasplante de órganos es un proceso muy complejo," *Prensa Libre*, April 8, 1994. Lest there is any question as to whether the global traffic in humans for their organs is complete rumor, see the multisited ethnographic work of Nancy Scheper-Hughes, especially "Theft of Life: The Globalization of Organ Stealing Rumours," *Anthropology Today* 12, no. 3 (1996): 3–11; as well as "The New Cannibalism," *The New Internationalist*, April 1998; and "The Global Traffic in Human Organs," *Current Anthropology* 41, no. 2 (2000): 191–224.

5. "Florece el mercado negro de organos humanos," *Prensa Libre*, March 13, 1994. Other examples of irresponsible journalism here include "Se venden niños, bonitos y baratos," *Prensa Libre*, October 25, 1992; "Se ha hecho frecuente la

compra de niños para mutilarlos," *Prensa Libre*, March 13, 1994; "Niños y segu-ridad," *La Hora*, April 14, 1994; "Crece robo de recién nacidos," *El Grafico*, October 13, 1993; "Policía descubrió un nuevo caso de tráfico de niños," *Prensa Libre*, August 25, 1992; "La venta de niños, un negocio de adultos," *Siglo XXI*, September 20, 1993; "Robo de niños se ha vuelto gran negocio," *La República*, August 16, 1993; "Rumores de robo de órgano," *Diario de Centro America*, April 14, 1994. Note that Guatemala's civil war famously involved sophisticated prop-aganda and the manipulation of print media by well-heeled public relations firms. See Stephen Schlesinger and Stephen Kinzer, *Bitter Fruit: The Story of the American Coup in Guatemala*, revised and expanded edition (Cambridge: Har-vard University, David Rockefeller Center for Latin American Studies, 2005).

6. William Booth, "Witch Hunt," *Washington Post*, May 17, 1994.

7. Booth, "Witch Hunt."

8. From the work of Émile Durkheim and Sigmund Freud to that of José Ortega y Gasset and Elias Canetti, theorists have painted the emergent energy of groups with a decidedly primitive hue: as ids without egos. The general consen-sus is that crowds are easily roused, with individuals losing their cognitive facul-ties to the whim of shared emotions. "In crowds," Gustave Le Bon writes, "it is stupidity and not mother-wit that is accumulated"; *The Crowd: A Study of the Popular Mind* (London: T. F. Unwin, 1897), 9. See also Walter Benjamin, *One Way Street and Other Writings*, trans. Edmund Jephcott and Kingsley Shorter (London: Verso, 1997); Elias Canetti, *Crowds and Power*, trans. Carol Stewart (New York: Farrar, Straus and Giroux, 1984); Émile Durkheim, *The Elementary Forms of the Religious Life*, trans. Joseph Ward Swain (Mineola: Dover Books, 2008 [1912]); Sigmund Freud, *Group Psychology and the Analysis of the Ego*, trans. James Strachey (New York: W. W. Norton, 1975); José Ortega y Gasset, *The Revolt of the Masses* (New York: W. W. Norton, 1932).

9. Booth, "Witch Hunt."

10. Victor Perera, "Behind the Kidnaping of Children for Their Organs," *Los Angeles Times*, May 1, 1994; Edward Orlebar, "Child Kidnaping Rumors Fuel Attacks on Americans," *Los Angeles Times*, April 2, 1994; Booth, "Witch Hunt"; "Foreigners Attacked in Guatemala," *New York Times*, April 5, 1994.

11. "'94 Beating Victim Still in Nursing Home," *Fairbanks Daily News-Miner*, June 13, 2004.

12. Rothenberg, "Panic of Robaniños," 186.

13. Booth, "Witch Hunt." Francisco Goldman is the author of *The Long Night of White Chickens* (New York: Grove Press, 1992), a novel in part about Guate-mala's confused and often sordid international adoption industry.

14. Karen Dubinsky synthesizes statistics on adoption in Guatemala at the time of the peace accords in *Babies without Borders: Adoption and the Symbolic Child in a Globalizing World* (Toronto: University of Toronto Press, 2010): "Gua-temala's documented participation in transnational adoption systems almost

doubled, from 731 children in 1996 to 1,278 in 1997, and climbed steadily every year thereafter. By 2006, 4,918 children were adopted internationally, making Guatemala the country with the highest per capita transnational adoption rate in the world. One hundred and sixty adoption agencies have ties to Guatemalan adoption programs; in 2005 adoption was the fourth-highest earner of foreign currency" (108).

15. Rachel Nolan, "Children for Export: A History of International Adoption from Guatemala" (PhD diss., New York, New York University, 2019).

16. Booth, "Witch Hunt."

17. "El 'floreciente' negocio del tráfico de niños," *La República*, February 13, 1994. Translated by Daniel Rothenberg in "Panic of Robaniños," 115.

18. See CEH, "Memoria del silencio. Guatemala: Comisión para el Esclarecimiento Histórico" (Guatemala: Comisión para el Esclarecimiento Histórico, 1999); Ricardo Falla, *Masacres de La Selva: Ixcán, Guatemala, 1975-1982* (Guatemala City: Editorial Universitaria, 1992); Greg Grandin, *The Last Colonial Massacre: Latin America in the Cold War* (Chicago: University of Chicago Press, 2011); Linda Green, *Fear as a Way of Life: Mayan Widows in Rural Guatemala* (New York: Columbia University Press, 1999); Victoria Sanford, *Buried Secrets: Truth and Human Rights in Guatemala* (New York: Palgrave Macmillan, 2003).

19. Father David Roney, "From San Lucas: From Peace to Danger," *The Prairie Catholic*, October 1991.

20. See Green, *Fear as a Way of Life.*

21. See REMHI, *Guatemala, nunca más: Proyecto interdiocesano de recuperación de la memoria histórica, volúmenes I, II, III, IV* (Guatemala: Oficina de Derechos Humanos Arzobispado de Guatemala, 1998); CEH, "Memoria del silencio."

22. Aldous Huxley, *Beyond the Mexique Bay: A Traveller's Journal* (London: Chatto & Windus, 1950), 139.

23. Alternatively, groups of well-wishers would sing *adios* to those leaving the Mission to the same tune. Roney, "From San Lucas: From Peace to Danger."

24. Roney often quoted Huxley when describing his proximity to young Guatemalan children. In one published article about a child at the Mission whom he sponsored, Roney writes, "I believe in prayer. Nevertheless, this may be on occasion too much of a good thing." Father David Roney, "San Lucas Mission," *The Prairie Catholic*, October 1987.

25. Bonar L. Hernández Sandoval, *Guatemala's Catholic Revolution: A History of Religious and Social Reform, 1920-1968* (Notre Dame: University of Notre Dame Press, 2018). One of Hernández's central observations is that anticlerical policies in the late nineteenth century accompanied efforts at liberalization in ways that made the Roman Catholic Church in Guatemala "a ghost of its former self" (9).

26. The study of Guatemala's liberal era includes important insights on the country's violent transition towards modernity and church-state relationships, each emphasizing the intense struggle over land and power between these two stalwart institutions and the role that the Church played in consolidating power in a time of stark changes. See Jim Handy, *Gift of the Devil: A History of Guatemala* (Boston: South End Press, 1984); Carol A. Smith, ed., *Guatemalan Indians and the State, 1540 to 1988* (Austin: University of Texas Press, 1990), especially the chapter by Arturo Arias, "Changing Indian Identity: Guatemala's Violent Transition to Modernity," 230–57; David McCreery, *Rural Guatemala, 1760-1940* (Stanford: Stanford University Press, 1994); Hubert J. Miller, *La iglesia y el estado en tiempo de Justo Rufino Barrios*, trans. Jorge Luján Muñoz (Guatemala City: Editorial Universitaria, 1976).

27. Virginia Garrard-Burnett, "Liberalism, Protestantism, and Indigenous Resistance in Guatemala, 1870-1920," *Latin American Perspectives* 24, no. 2 (1997): 35–55.

28. Edward M. Haymaker, "A Study in Latin American Futures" (mimeographed, 1917), quoted in Garrard-Burnett, "Liberalism, Protestantism, and Indigenous Resistance," 40–41.

29. The point to stress here is the diminishing power of the Church as a sacramental institution and its waning abilities to perform its most fundamental liturgical acts for Guatemala. This clerical weakening appears throughout the literature, with the number of priests often used to illustrate the Church's broader challenges in this era. See Hernández Sandoval, *Guatemala's Catholic Revolution*, 65. See also Ricardo Bendaña Perdomo, *La iglesia en Guatemala: Síntesis histórica del Catolicismo Guatemalteco, 1524-1951*, 2nd ed. (Guatemala City: Artemis Edinter, 2001); Bruce Johnson Calder, *Crecimiento y cambio de la Iglesia Católica Guatemalteca, 1944-1966* (Guatemala City: Editorial José de Pineda Ibarra, 1970); Miller, *La iglesia y el estado.*

30. Miller, *La iglesia y el estado.*

31. Bonar L. Hernández, "Reforming Catholicism: Papal Power in Guatemala during the 1920s and 1930s," *The Americas* 71, no. 2 (2014): 255.

32. Luis Samandú, Hans Siebers, and Oscar Sierra, *Guatemala: Retos de la Iglesia Catolicá en una sociedad en crisis* (San José, Costa Rica: Editorial DEI, 1990), 9.

33. Agustín Estrada Monroy, *Datos para la historia de la iglesia en Guatemala*, vol. 3 (Guatemala City: Sociedad de Geografía e Historia de Guatemala, 1973), 363–64, quoted in Hernández, "Reforming Catholicism," 262.

34. Hernández Sandoval, *Guatemala's Catholic Revolution*, 23.

35. For histories of the Roman Catholic Church's transnational capacity, especially how the Church in the United States participated as a relatively new outpost for the Vatican, see Stephen J. C. Andes, *The Vatican and Catholic Activism in Mexico and Chile: The Politics of Transnational Catholicism, 1920-1940*

(Oxford: Oxford University Press, 2014); Peter R. D'Agostino, *Rome in America: Transnational Catholic Ideology from the Risorgimento to Fascism* (Chapel Hill: University of North Carolina Press, 2004). The scholarship of Bonar Hernández has proven especially important for my work on transnational clerical sexual abuse in Guatemala; see Hernández Sandoval, *Guatemala's Catholic Revolution*.

36. Edward T. Brett, *The U.S. Catholic Press on Central America: From Cold War Anticommunism to Social Justice* (South Bend: University of Notre Dame Press, 2003); Gerald M. Costello, *Mission to Latin America: The Successes and Failures of a Twentieth-Century Crusade* (Maryknoll: Orbis Books, 1979). See also Richard Newbold Adams, *Crucifixion by Power: Essays on Guatemalan National Social Structure, 1944-1966* (Austin: University of Texas Press, 1970).

37. Adams, *Crucifixion by Power*, 321.

38. The idea of pagan babies could seem out of step with today's seemingly more progressive politics, but North American Christian programs have long been intervening in the lives of poor children in Africa, Asia, and Latin America. See Erica Bornstein, "Child Sponsorship, Evangelism, and Belonging in the Work of World Vision Zimbabwe," *American Ethnologist* 28, no. 3 (2001): 595-622; Kevin Lewis O'Neill, "Left Behind: Security, Salvation, and the Subject of Prevention," *Cultural Anthropology* 28, no. 2 (2013): 204-26.

39. Clint Burton, "Resurrection Elementary: Adopt A Pagan Baby—1959," The Brookline Connection, accessed January 3, 2023.

40. Clerical transfers from the United States did allow the Roman Catholic Church to cultivate a pronounced political voice during Guatemala's civil war. One young man from Oklahoma named Stanley Rother settled only a few kilometers from where Roney would eventually retire, ultimately dying at the hands of the military in 1981 for his solidarity with Guatemala's indigenous communities. See Stanley Rother, *The Shepherd Cannot Run: Letters of Stanley Rother, Missionary and Martyr* (Oklahoma City: Archdiocese of Oklahoma City, 1984).

41. Theologically, atonement is the process by which sinners reconcile with God. In the Christian tradition, especially within Roman Catholicism, sacraments, or ritual sacrifices, remove obstacles to this reconciliation. See for example Caroline Walker Bynum, "The Power in the Blood: Sacrifice, Satisfaction, and Substitution in Late Medieval Soteriology," in *The Redemption: An Interdisciplinary Symposium on Christ as Redeemer*, ed. Stephen T. Davis, Daniel Kendall, and Gerald O'Collins (Oxford: Oxford University Press, 2004), 177-204; Avery Dulles, "The Eucharist as Sacrifice," in *Rediscovering the Eucharist: Ecumenical Conversations*, ed. Roch A. Kereszty (Mahwah: Paulist Press, 2003), 175-87; John Milbank, *Being Reconciled: Ontology and Pardon* (London: Routledge, 2003).

42. Papal concerns about the vitality of the Roman Catholic Church in Latin America set the institutional conditions for the movement of U.S. priests to Cen-

tral America. Throughout the second half of the twentieth century, young celibates from across the United States—from Oklahoma, Minnesota, and Wisconsin, for example—moved to the highlands of Guatemala to minister to historically disenfranchised Indigenous communities. See Hernández Sandoval, *Guatemala's Catholic Revolution*; and Garrard-Burnett, "Liberalism, Protestantism, and Indigenous Resistance," 35–55.

43. Hernández Sandoval, *Guatemala's Catholic Revolution*, 84.

44. David Roney, Foundation House Personal History Sheet, April 12, 1987, RF, A9.

45. David Roney, Foundation House Personal History Sheet, April 12, 1987, RF, A10.

46. Father David Roney, "The Storyteller," *The Prairie Catholic*, October 1986.

47. Roney's care for Justina presents a case study for the history of transracial adoption. See Diana Marre and Laura Briggs, eds., *International Adoption: Global Inequalities and the Circulation of Children* (New York: New York University Press, 2009); Kathryn A. Mariner, *Contingent Kinship: The Flows and Futures of Adoption in the United States* (Oakland: University of California Press, 2019).

48. This moment accentuates the racial hierarchies within the Roman Catholic Church, with the lives of Indigenous men, women, and children essentially sacrificed for the sake of a white, middle-class cleric from the United States.

49. Affidavit, August 8, 2007, RF, A753.

50. Affidavit, August 8, 2007, RF, A754.

51. Bishop Raymond Lucker, Handwritten Memo, n.d., RF, A784.

52. Ian Hacking, "Making Up People," in *The Science Studies Reader*, ed. Mario Biagioli (New York: Routledge, 1999), 161–71.

53. Michel Foucault, *An Introduction*, vol. 1 of *The History of Sexuality*, trans. Robert J. Hurley, (New York: Vintage Books, 1990), 32.

54. Foucault, *An Introduction*, 32.

55. "Código penal de Guatemala," Decreto no. 17–73 (2009).

56. Many people of privilege enjoyed widespread impunity during the civil war of 1960–96 in Guatemala. Since the war, this impunity has persisted in Guatemalan society. See Raúl Molina Mejía, "The Struggle Against Impunity in Guatemala," *Social Justice* 26, no. 4 (1999): 55–83; Helen Mack Chang, "Impunity in Guatemala: A Never-Ending Battle," in *Human and Environmental Justice in Guatemala*, ed. Stephen Henighan and Candace Johnson (Toronto: University of Toronto Press, 2018), 118–29.

57. Hacking, "Making Up People," 165. Hacking, to be clear, does not believe that there is "a general story to be told about making up people. Each category has its own history" (168). The same can be said about unmaking people. The only amendment is the expectation that unmaking not only marks the end of one way of being but also the start of another. People can be made into different

kinds of subjects again and again and again. See also Ian Hacking, "The Making and Molding of Child Abuse," *Critical Inquiry* 17, no. 2 (1991): 253–88.

58. The unmaking of people tends to be a far more deliberate effort than the making up of people. Unmaking people tends to be agentive, calculating, and conniving, characteristics that appear to set the process apart from making up people. It is this scheming, calculating, and conspiring that ultimately make possible not just new insights into clerical sex abuse, but also the possibility of a new literature on the unmaking of people, centered on dramatic and sometimes desperate attempts to evade the kinds of people that people have become.

59. Foucault, *An Introduction*, 32.

60. Foucault, *An Introduction*, 31.

61. Haythem Guesmi, "Reckoning with Foucault's Alleged Sexual Abuse of Boys in Tunisia," *Al Jazeera*, April 16, 2021.

62. Michel Foucault and Duccio Trombadori, *Remarks on Marx: Conversations with Duccio Trombadori*, trans. R. James Goldstein and James Cascaito (New York: Semiotext(e), 1991), 136.

63. Foucault, *An Introduction*, 31–32.

64. It is worth noting the military's use of sexual violence as a weapon against Guatemala's Indigenous communities during the war and the eerie overlay this created with David Roney's abuse of this Indigenous orphan. See Victoria Sanford, Sofia Duyos Álvarez-Arenas, and Kathleen Dill, "Sexual Violence as a Weapon during the Guatemalan Genocide," in *Women and Genocide: Survivors, Victims, Perpetrators*, ed. Elissa Bemporad and Joyce W. Warren (Bloomington: Indiana University Press, 2018), 207–22.

65. Gene Burke, Memo to Files, Subject: Fr. David Roney, October 27, 1993, RF, A769.

66. Father David Roney, "From San Lucas: The Nutrition Center," *The Prairie Catholic*, March 1991.

67. Father David Roney, "The Problem with Pictures," *The Prairie Catholic*, May 1989.

68. Thomas Merton's photography tends to be direct and straight as well as black and white. He never staged or posed his subjects. He sought a kind of transcendent realism with the camera. See Paul M. Pearson, *A Hidden Wholeness: The Zen Photography of Thomas Merton* (Louisville: Thomas Merton Center, 2004); Paul M. Pearson, ed., *Beholding Paradise: The Photographs of Thomas Merton* (Mahwah: Paulist Press, 2015).

69. David Roney, Foundation House Personal History Sheet, April 12, 1987, RF, A10.

70. David Roney, Foundation House Personal History Sheet, April 12, 1987, RF, A7, A8.

71. Ariella Azoulay argues that a photograph is the product of an encounter of several protagonists, mainly photographer and photographed, camera and spec-

tator; it is this emphasis on encounter that helps to contextualize Roney's use of the camera as a prop. See Azoulay, *The Civil Contract of Photography*, trans. Rela Mazali and Ruvik Danieli (Brooklyn: Zone Books, 2008).

72. The veil and white gloves that Justina wore for her First Holy Communion are not without theological precedent. Pope Benedict XVI notes in his post-synodal apostolic exhortation "Sacramentum Caritatis" (2007) that "the Eucharist, as the sacrament of charity, has a particular relationship with the love of man and woman united in marriage." Both sacraments—marriage and the eucharist—strive toward the communion of two distinct realms. Marriage unites one man and one woman, and they become one flesh. First Holy Communion is the union of the believer and Christ. See "Sacramentum Caritatis: Post-Synodal Apostolic Exhortation on the Eucharist as the Source and Summit of the Church's Life and Mission," The Holy See, February 22, 2007.

73. Memory is an uneven terrain and one that seems to parallel the literature on photography. Ulrich Baer, in *Spectral Evidence: The Photography of Trauma* (Cambridge: MIT Press, 2002), relies on Sigmund Freud's understanding of the photographic process as a metaphor for the unconscious. Sarah Kofman, in *Camera Obscura: On Ideology*, trans. Will Straw (Ithaca: Cornell University Press, 1999), explains that "Freud's use of the model of the photographic apparatus is intended to show that all psychic phenomena necessarily pass first through an unconscious phase, through darkness and the negative, before acceding to consciousness" (75).

74. Kevin Coleman describes a sort of "self-forging" through photography, a way that subalterns (in his work, banana plantation workers) could make visual demands and self-author even when they were totally outmatched by foreign capital and a murderous state. In these terms, Roney was using the camera as a technology of (perverted) self-making; see Coleman, *A Camera in the Garden of Eden: The Self-Forging of a Banana Republic* (Austin: University of Texas Press, 2016).

75. Here attention should be paid to the tactile nature of photographs and their relationship to intimacy. Photographs, in other words, are things in the world that can be traded within an economy of trust and dependency. See Christian Metz, "Photography and Fetish," *October*, no. 34 (1985): 81–90; Elspeth H. Brown and Thy Phu, eds., *Feeling Photography* (Durham: Duke University Press, 2014).

76. Consistent across the literature on photography and violence is the idea that photographs are primarily a form of visual representation. See, for example, Susan Sontag, *On Photography* (New York: Farrar, Straus and Giroux, 1977); Judith Butler, *Frames of War: When Is Life Grievable?* (New York: Verso, 2009); Azoulay, *Civil Contract*; see also Sarah Sentilles, "How We Should Respond to Photographs of Suffering," *The New Yorker*, August 3, 2017. And yet this assumption obscures an ethnographic fact that Roney understood all too well. It is that

photographs are not just meant to be seen but also touched, held, and gifted, and it is their haptics rather than their optics that allowed this prolifically abusive priest from Minnesota to perpetrate violence in the highlands of Guatemala. For an appreciation of photographs as material objects, see Elizabeth Edwards, "Objects of Affect: Photography beyond the Image," *Annual Review of Anthropology* 41 (2012): 221–34; Tina M. Campt, *Listening to Images* (Durham: Duke University Press, 2017).

77. Azoulay writes in *Civil Contract* that everyone who engages with photographs, especially anyone who produces, poses, or even looks at photographs, is a citizen of photography. The citizenry of photography includes anyone who addresses others through images or who takes the position of a photo's addressee. Roney's photographs, in this sense, allowed the mother of these young girls to become a citizen—to be seen.

78. Father David Roney, "My Family in Guatemala," *Diocese of New Ulm Newsletter*, March 1986.

79. Leah Dickerman compares the use of monuments by the Soviet Union and those in the American South; see "Monumental Propaganda," *October*, no. 165 (2018): 178–91. Her interest is in the construction of alternative commemorative landscapes, and it is this question of commemorative landscapes that this statue of Justina raises. Unlike Roney's novelty t-shirt with Justina's image on it, this statue did not travel about town for a time and then disappear but instead remained for decades, marking territory all the while.

80. Amendment to David A. Roney Revocable Trust Agreement, August 1, 2001, RF, A780–81.

81. Bishop John C. Nienstedt to David A. Roney, April 18, 2002, RF, A785.

82. Bishop John C. Nienstedt, Memo to Rev. Douglas L. Grams, Subject: Fr. David Roney, June 20, 2002, RF, A787.

PART IV. AT THE MARGINS OF VICTIMHOOD, 2003–2017

1. "Rev. David Arthur Roney," *Star Tribune*, January 30, 2003, sec. Obituaries.

2. Report or Affidavit of Susan Phipps-Yonas, PhD, October 21, 2004, RF, 1.

3. The Investigative Staff of the *Boston Globe*, *Betrayal: The Crisis in the Catholic Church* (New York: Little, Brown, 2002); see also Office of the Attorney General, *The Sexual Abuse of Children in the Roman Catholic Archdiocese of Boston* (Boston: Office of the Attorney General, 2003); John Jay College, *The Nature and Scope of Sexual Abuse of Minors by Catholic Priests and Deacons in the United States, 1950–2002* (Washington, DC: United States Conference of Catholic Bishops, 2004).

4. Associated Press, "Statement by President of the U.S. Catholic Bishops on Sexual Abuse," *New York Times*, June 14, 2002, sec. U.S.

5. The Church is not new either to public relations or to the parallel pursuit of propaganda, arguably inaugurating both in the seventeenth century. Founded by Pope Gregory XV in 1622, the Propagation of the Faith, or the Propaganda Fide, arranged missionary work and related activities. Its central task was to evangelize with a centralized, controlled message. Peter Guilday, "The Sacred Congregation de Propaganda Fide (1622–1922)," *Catholic Historical Review* 6, no. 4 (1921): 478–94.

6. Laurie Goodstein, "Abuse Victims Lay Blame at Feet of Catholic Bishops," *New York Times*, June 14, 2002, sec. U.S.

7. Michael Bland, "Impact Statement of Michael Bland," Bishop Accountability, June 13, 2002.

8. Goodstein, "Abuse Victims."

9. "Bishop: 'We Did Not Go Far Enough,'" *CNN*, June 13, 2002.

10. Apologies are often framed as speech acts, but they are also performative—hence the invocation of a theater of contrition. See John Borneman, "Public Apologies as Performative Redress," *SAIS Review of International Affairs* 25, no. 2 (2005): 53–66; Alice MacLachlan, "'Trust Me, I'm Sorry': The Paradox of Public Apology," *The Monist* 98, no. 4 (2015): 441–56.

11. United States Conference of Catholic Bishops (USCCB), *Charter for the Protection of Children and Young People* (Washington, DC: United States Conference of Catholic Bishops, 2002).

12. The National Catholic Risk Retention Group, Inc. (National Catholic) opened June 30, 1988, in response to a commercial insurance market instability. Its intention is to prevent sexual abuse within religious organizations. National Catholic licenses VIRTUS programs, including Protecting God's Children® for Adults; Empowering God's Children®; VIRTUS® Online Training / Tracking Platform; VIRTUS® Online; Keeping the Promise Alive™ Refresher Program; Technology and Virtual Boundaries Awareness: Online Communication with Youth; Children's Programs Lesson Leader Orientation and Certification Training [for the Empowering God's Children Programming]; Vulnerable Adult Training™; Sexual Harassment Online Training Module™ 1.0; Anti-Harassment Training Module™ 2.0; The International Priests™ Program.

13. "TIME Magazine Cover: Insurance—Mar. 24, 1986," TIME.com.

14. François Ewald's *The Birth of Solidarity* provides a history of the welfare state in France. The book details the rise of social insurance and how this discourse came to undergird the twentieth-century welfare state. As National Catholic framed abuse with the logic of social insurance and its technique of prevention, clerical sexual abuse became something of an eventuality for which the Church could plan. François Ewald, *The Birth of Solidarity: The History of the French Welfare State*, ed. Melinda Cooper, trans. Timothy Scott Johnson

(Durham: Duke University Press, 2020). See also François Ewald, "Insurance and Risk," in *The Foucault Effect: Studies in Governmentality*, ed. Graham Burchell, Colin Gordon, and Peter Miller (Chicago: University of Chicago Press, 1991), 197–210.

15. Michel Foucault describes a similar phenomenon in *An Introduction*, vol. 1 of *The History of Sexuality*, trans. Robert J. Hurley, (New York: Vintage Books, 1990). The growing discourse on sex, particularly in the nineteenth century, not only turned sex into a problem of truth but also something that people discussed incessantly: "What is peculiar to modern societies, in fact, is not that they confined sex to a shadow existence, but that they dedicated themselves to speaking of it *ad infinitum*, while exploiting it as *the* secret" (35).

16. The metaphors of voice and language have long been used to describe the interior thoughts and desires of political consciousness. A new language of clerical sexual abuse empowered Jane Doe 43C. It gave her a voice. The capacity for people to articulate their agency and selfhood through contemporary democratic publics has thus become a point of reference in philosophical and anthropological literatures. See Judith Butler, *Notes toward a Performative Theory of Assembly* (Cambridge: Harvard University Press, 2015); Webb Keane, "Voice," *Journal of Linguistic Anthropology* 9, no. 1 (1999): 271–73; William Mazzarella, "The Myth of the Multitude, or Who's Afraid of the Crowd?," *Critical Inquiry* 36, no. 4 (2010): 697–727.

17. Plaintiff Jane Doe 43C's First Supplemental Answer to Defendant's Interrogatories, June 22, 2006, RF, A5.

18. Plaintiff Jane Doe 43C's First Supplemental Answer to Defendant's Interrogatories, June 22, 2006, RF, A5.

19. David Schimke, "True Believer," Bishop Accountability, April 16, 2003.

20. Jane Doe 43C, Jane Doe 43D, Jane Doe 43E, Jane Doe 43F, and Jane Doe 43G vs. Diocese of New Ulm, St. Francis Parish, and St. Mary's Parish, Memorandum of Law, January 18, 2008, RF, A879–89. "Social change," Ian Hacking writes, "creates new categories of people, but the counting is no mere report of developments. It elaborately, often philanthropically, creates new ways for people to be." "Making Up People," in *The Science Studies Reader*, ed. Mario Biagioli (New York: Routledge, 1999), 161–62.

21. Associated Press State & Local Wire, "Women Sue New Ulm Catholic Diocese for Decades-Old Abuse," Bishop Accountability, September 17, 2003.

22. Jeff Anderson & Associates, "Press Conference: Two Women Speak Publicly about Sexual Abuse at Willmar by Father David A. Roney," YouTube, September 16, 2013. On the use of photographs during public protest, a curious overlap in aesthetic forms could be noted between the survivors of clerical sexual abuse in the United States, who routinely pose publicly with photographs of their younger selves, and those throughout Latin America who deploy similar images of the disappeared. For the cultural work of photographs in Argentina, see Ana

Longoni, "Photographs and Silhouettes: Visual Politics in the Human Rights Movement of Argentina," *Afterall: A Journal of Art, Context and Enquiry*, no. 25 (2010): 5-17; Diana Taylor, *Disappearing Acts: Spectacles of Gender and Nationalism in Argentina's "Dirty War"* (Durham: Duke University Press, 1997).

23. Jean Hopfensperger, "More than 800 Sex Abuse Claims Filed under Minnesota Law," *Star Tribune*, May 23, 2016.

24. Foucault, *An Introduction*, 32.

25. It is important to flag the amazement that Justina experienced while traveling in an airplane for the first time. In *Strange Wonder: The Closure of Metaphysics and the Opening of Awe* (New York: Columbia University Press, 2011), Mary-Jane Rubenstein considers awe more than a mere stimulus for thinking. Drawing on Emmanuel Levinas's *Totality and Infinity: An Essay on Exteriority*, trans. Alphonso Lingis (Pittsburgh: Duquesne University Press, 2011), Rubenstein insists that thought thrives within a raw experience of amazement. Awe is a constitutive dimension of awakening. See also Søren Kierkegaard, *Fear and Trembling / Repetition*, ed. and trans. Howard V. Hong and Edna H. Hong (Princeton: Princeton University Press, 1983).

26. Justina's shift in perspective calls to mind the experience of Michel de Certeau at the top of the World Trade Center. He writes, "To be lifted to the summit of the World Trade Center is to be lifted out of the city's grasp. . . . When one goes up there, he leaves behind the mass that carries off and mixes up in itself any identity of authors or spectators." De Certeau also has something of an ominous experience once he returns to earth, which he likens to an "Icarian fall"; *The Practice of Everyday Life*, trans. Steven Rendall (Berkeley: University of California Press, 1984), 92.

27. Diane Nelson's *A Finger in the Wound: Body Politics in Quincentennial Guatemala* (Berkeley: University of California Press, 1999) notes that Maya women tend to ground the Maya movement, in large part because of an impression that they are bearers of traditional culture. This is a conservative, deeply racist vision of Maya women as rural, non-Spanish-speaking subjects who find it difficult to navigate the so-called modern world. Nelson is right to spot those moments when Indigenous women from Guatemala perform so-called traditional culture in the form of pan-Mayan ideology to placate and/or manipulate international audiences. See also Kay B. Warren, *Indigenous Movements and Their Critics: Pan-Maya Activism in Guatemala* (Princeton: Princeton University Press, 1998).

28. Amendment to David A. Roney Revocable Trust Agreement, August 1, 2001, RF, A780-81.

29. Anonymous to Bishop Raymond Lucker, n.d., RF, A757.

30. Kenneth J. Pierre, Report of Psychological Evaluation, September 4, 1990, RF, A767.

31. Gene Burke, Memo to Files, Subject: Fr. David Roney, July 21, 1993, RF, A768.

32. Bishop Raymond Lucker, Handwritten Memo, n.d., RF, A784.

33. Mark Reffner to Eugene A. Burke, January 20, 1997, RF, A776-78.

34. Bishop John C. Nienstedt to David A. Roney, April 18, 2002, RF, A785.

35. Jeffrey R. Anderson to Bishop John C. Nienstedt, August 22, 2002, RF, A790.

36. Affidavit of Theresa Iverson, August 8, 2007, RF, A754.

37. Jane Doe 43C, Jane Doe 43D, Jane Doe 43E, Jane Doe 43F, and Jane Doe 43G vs. Diocese of New Ulm, St. Francis Parish, and St. Mary's Parish, Memorandum of Law, January 18, 2008, RF, A879-89.

38. See Laurie Goodstein, "Archdiocese of Louisville Reaches Abuse Settlement," *New York Times*, June 11, 2003, sec. U.S.; Fox Butterfield, "Church in Boston to Pay $85 Million in Abuse Lawsuits," *New York Times*, September 10, 2003, sec. U.S.; Nick Madigan, "California Diocese Settles Sexual Abuse Case for $100 Million," *New York Times*, January 5, 2005, sec. U.S.; Associated Press, "Spokane Diocese OKs $48 Million Settlement," NBC News, January 4, 2007; Reuters Staff, "Oregon Archdiocese Ends Bankruptcy with Abuse Deal," Reuters, April 13, 2007, sec. U.S. News; Laurie Goodstein, "Payout Is Bittersweet for Victims of Abuse," *New York Times*, July 17, 2007, sec. U.S.; Randal C. Archibold, "San Diego Diocese Settles Lawsuit for $200 Million," *New York Times*, September 8, 2007, sec. U.S.; Laurie Goodstein, "Delaware Diocese Settles with Victims of Abuse," *New York Times*, February 4, 2011, sec. U.S.

39. See James Ferguson, *Give a Man a Fish: Reflections on the New Politics of Distribution* (Durham: Duke University Press, 2015). Ferguson examines social welfare programs in southern Africa that make cash payments to low-income citizens. These are programs in contradistinction to models of development that incite the poor and downtrodden to "work on oneself" (162), as Anand Pandian writes in *Crooked Stalks: Cultivating Virtue in South India* (Durham: Duke University Press, 2009). Schaffer's concern with a settlement is in part about his legacy, but it can also be interpreted as the very anxiety that Ferguson considers when institutions give the needy money. See also James Ferguson, *Presence and Social Obligation: An Essay on the Share* (Chicago: Prickly Paradigm Press, 2021).

40. The observation is not new, but it is enduring: Arjun Appadurai notes that certain people can be confined to certain places at an almost metaphysical level, such that someone like Justina could be considered inherently out of place not just in Minnesota but also within the context of clerical sexual abuse. See Arjun Appadurai, "Putting Hierarchy in Its Place," *Cultural Anthropology* 3, no. 1 (1988): 36-49; see also Liisa Malkki, "National Geographic: The Rooting of Peoples and the Territorialization of National Identity among Scholars and Refugees," *Cultural Anthropology* 7, no. 1 (1992): 24-44.

41. Kenneth J. Pierre, Report of Psychological Evaluation, September 4, 1990, RF, A767.

42. To use the logic and language of Ian Hacking, Justina did not find herself in the right time, the right place, or the right social setting to be made up into the kind of person that she had every right to become: a victim. Hacking, "Making Up People," 167.

43. Schaffer's gift to Justina of a few hundred dollars fits squarely within what anthropologists understand as micro development projects. These are not acts of charity but instead microloans or small-scale infusions of capital meant to support a sustainable enterprise. Anthropologists have been right to spot the morality of these interventions, either when advanced by those espousing explicitly moral statements or those working within the supposedly objective framework of economics. See Rebecca C. Bartel, *Card-Carrying Christians: Debt and the Making of Free Market Spirituality in Colombia* (Oakland: University of California Press, 2021); Julia Elyachar, *Markets of Dispossession: NGOs, Economic Development, and the State in Cairo* (Durham: Duke University Press, 2005); Tania Li, *The Will to Improve: Governmentality, Development, and the Practice of Politics* (Durham: Duke University Press, 2007).

44. CNA Daily News, "Minnesota Diocese, Facing Abuse Lawsuits, Files for Bankruptcy," *Catholic World Report*, March 7, 2017.

45. Bankruptcy also allowed Church leadership to limit its liability for sexual abuse in much the same way as it has allowed other major corporations to limit their liability. In *Corporate Sovereignty: Law and Government under Capitalism* (Minneapolis: University of Minnesota Press, 2013), Joshua Barkan argues that corporations have attained a level of political sovereignty in the contemporary world. With an interest in U.S., British, and international corporate law, Barkan writes, "The problems corporate-led globalization presents for democratic politics do not result from regulatory failures as much as from an Anglo-American conception of corporate immunity that has been increasingly exported across the globe" (13). See also Joshua Barkan, "Law and the Geographic Analysis of Economic Globalization," *Progress in Human Geography*, no. 5 (2011): 589–607.

46. Josh Saul, "Catholic Church Shields $2 Billion in Assets to Limit Abuse Payouts," *Bloomberg Businessweek*, January 8, 2020, sec. Businessweek.

47. Sam Patet, "Newly Formed Nonprofit to Carry on Msgr. Schaffer's Committment, Vision," *The Prairie Catholic*, April 2013.

48. Carol, Sexual Abuse Proof of Claim Form, June 9, 2017, RF, 6–7.

49. Carol, Sexual Abuse Proof of Claim Form, June 9, 2017, RF, 13.

50. Carol, Sexual Abuse Proof of Claim Form, June 9, 2017, RF, 15.

51. Carol, Sexual Abuse Proof of Claim Form, June 9, 2017, RF, 15.

52. Carol, Sexual Abuse Proof of Claim Form, June 9, 2017, RF, 12.

53. Carol, Sexual Abuse Proof of Claim Form, June 9, 2017, RF, 12–13.

54. Carol, Sexual Abuse Proof of Claim Form, June 9, 2017, RF, 14.

55. Carol, Sexual Abuse Proof of Claim Form, June 9, 2017, RF, 15.

56. Carol, Sexual Abuse Proof of Claim Form, June 9, 2017, RF, 14.

57. Here, we might consider Carol's community of fellow survivors as "imagined." In *Imagined Communities: Reflections on the Origin and Spread of Nationalism* (New York: Verso, 2016), Benedict Anderson writes about the formation of the modern nation-state, not as a political entity but rather as a cultural artifact. His interest is in the affects of association. He writes, "It is imagined because the members of even the smallest nation will never know most of their fellow-members, meet them, or even hear of them, yet in the minds of each lives the image of their communion" (6). See also Manu Goswami, "Benedict Anderson, Imagined Communities (1983)," *Public Culture* 32, no. 2 (2020): 441-48.

58. Hannah Yang, "Judge Approves $34M Clergy Abuse Settlement with New Ulm Diocese," MPR News, March 10, 2020.

59. Father David A. Roney (Assignments Map by Jeff Anderson & Associates), n.d., RF.

60. *Ligne de fuite* translates from the French as either "line of flight" or "line of escape." It is a concept that Gilles Deleuze and Félix Guattari develop in *A Thousand Plateaus: Capitalism and Schizophrenia*, trans. Brian Massumi (Minneapolis: University of Minnesota Press, 1987). See also Brian Massumi, *A User's Guide to Capitalism and Schizophrenia: Deviations from Deleuze and Guattari* (Cambridge: MIT Press, 1992). Massumi writes that "according to Deleuze and Guattari, all social formations are defined by what escapes them— the 'lines of escape' or becomings running through them" (204).

61. The work of John Brian Harley is important here, especially his critical interest in the silences and secrecies that maps create; see J. B. Harley, "Silences and Secrecy: The Hidden Agenda of Cartography in Early Modern Europe," *Imago Mundi* 40 (1988): 57-76. The imperative is to read maps critically—to deconstruct them as one would any other text. See also Harley's "Deconstructing the Map," *Cartographica: The International Journal for Geographic Information and Geovisualization* 26, no. 2 (1989): 3.

62. Akhil Gupta and James Ferguson remind us that cultures and peoples "cease to be plausibly identifiable as spots on the map"; "Beyond 'Culture': Space, Identity, and the Politics of Difference," *Cultural Anthropology* 7, no. 1 (1992): 10. See also Michel Foucault, "Questions on Geography," in *Power/Knowledge: Selected Interviews and Other Writings 1972-1977*, ed. Colin Gordon, trans. Colin Gordon et al. (New York: Pantheon Books, 1980), 63-77; Michel Foucault, "Space, Knowledge, and Power," in *The Foucault Reader*, ed. Paul Rabinow (New York: Pantheon Books, 1984), 239-56.

63. See Julie Cidell, "Challenging the Contours: Critical Cartography, Local Knowledge, and the Public," *Environment and Planning A: Economy and Space* 40, no. 5 (2008): 1202-18; Jeremy W. Crampton, "Cartography: Performative, Participatory, Political," *Progress in Human Geography* 33, no. 6 (2009):

840–48; Nancy Lee Peluso, "Whose Woods Are These? Counter-Mapping Forest Territories in Kalimantan, Indonesia," *Antipode* 27, no. 4 (1995): 383–406.

PART V. THE WILL TO SURVIVE, 2017–2023

1. The boat is an ethnographic trope. Bronisław Malinowski is best known for his dinghy and its role in the making of ethnographic alterity. "Imagine yourself," he famously writes, "suddenly set down surrounded by all your gear, alone on a tropical beach close to a native village, while the launch or dinghy which has brought you sails away out of sight"; *Argonauts of the Western Pacific: An Account of Native Enterprise and Adventure in the Archipelagoes of Melanesian New Guinea* (London: George Routledge and Sons, 1922), 4. For a more menacing take on boats and alterity, see Joseph Conrad, *Heart of Darkness* (New York: Dover, 1990).

2. The ghost of Roney could be said to haunt the town. Jacques Derrida, in *Specters of Marx: The State of Debt, the Work of Mourning, and the New International*, trans. Peggy Kamuf (New York and London: Routledge, 1994), writes that "haunting belongs to the structure of every hegemony" (37). The subtle evidence that marks Roney's history in town is uncanny, in the language of Sigmund Freud; see *The Uncanny*, trans. David McLintock (New York: Penguin Books, 2003). Freud writes, "There is no doubt that this belongs to the realm of the frightening, of what evokes fear and dread" (123). The spectral nature of Roney ultimately structures this history of his abuse: "To articulate the past historically," writes Walter Benjamin, "means to seize hold of a memory as it flashes up at a moment of danger"; "On the Concept of History," in *Selected Writings*, vol. 4, *1938–1940*, ed. Howard Eiland and Michael W. Jennings (Cambridge: Harvard University Press, 2006), 391. See also Avery Gordon, *Ghostly Matters: Haunting and the Sociological Imagination* (Minneapolis: University of Minnesota Press, 2008).

3. Father David Roney, "Guatemala Revisited Is Still Challenging, Rewarding," *Diocese of New Ulm Newsletter*, February 1975.

4. Father David Roney, "Willmar People Plan Third Trip to Guatemala," *Diocese of New Ulm Newsletter*, December 1974.

5. "Diocese of New Ulm News Release #355," Bishop Accountability, August 1, 2003.

6. Father Greg Schaffer, "Fr. Roney Celebrates Jubilee in Guatemala," *The Prairie Catholic*, October 1995.

7. Schaffer's statue is one of many testaments to morally dubious figures. David Freedberg's *Iconoclasm* (Chicago: University of Chicago Press, 2021) provides a summary of the debate: "Either acknowledge the ambivalence and polyinterpretability of images, and let them stand, or emphasize what they unambiguously

stand for (or might be taken to stand for)—and take them down" (215). See also Leah Dickerman, "Monumental Propaganda," *October*, no. 165 (2018): 178–91.

8. Care can be predatory. See Kevin Lewis O'Neill, *Hunted: Predation and Pentecostalism in Guatemala* (Chicago: University of Chicago Press, 2019). The point here is to illuminate the predatory terrain upon which care operates. These are moments when the intent to do good functions through calculated levels of force and coercion. See also Clara Han, *Life in Debt: Care and Violence in Neoliberal Chile* (Berkeley: University of California Press, 2012); Annemarie Mol, *The Logic of Care: Health and the Problem of Patient Choice* (London: Routledge, 2008); Miriam Ticktin, *Casualties of Care: Immigration and the Politics of Humanitarianism in France* (Berkeley: University of California Press, 2011).

9. Taking an indirect approach to the study of clerical sexual abuse often reminded me of Talal Asad's work on the secular and secularism. See Asad, *Formations of the Secular: Christianity, Islam, Modernity* (Stanford: Stanford University Press, 2003). Asad notes that the secular is so much a part of modern life that he could not pursue it directly but only through its "shadows." For him, this meant addressing the secular's entangled relationship with human rights and nationalism, for example. For me, this often meant discussing the history of the Mission and Justina's life history.

10. Much of this fieldwork recalled Clifford Geertz's famous line about the distinction between a blink and a wink: that is, a matter of interpretative anthropology. See *The Interpretation of Cultures: Selected Essays* (New York: Basic Books, 1973). A blink is involuntary and is a matter of mere eye movement. A wink, on the other hand, is a signal. While the two are identical as movements, each has a distinct meaning "as anyone unfortunate enough to have had the first taken for the second knows" (6). It is ultimately an appreciation for what Victor Turner understands as a "forest of symbols." See Turner, *The Forest of Symbols: Aspects of Ndembu Ritual* (Ithaca: Cornell University Press, 1967).

11. The interviews or open conversation within the fieldwork setting could be seen, in something of a Foucauldian sense, as a mode of knowledge production like the confession in the Middle Ages. I found the time with Justina online to be clearly less sacramental than the confession but still a space set apart—literally boxed off—from life, a space in which we could talk. For a thought-provoking engagement of the interview itself, see Charles Briggs, "Anthropology, Interviewing, and Communicability in Contemporary Society," *Current Anthropology* 48, no. 4 (2007): 551–80. For a more instructive approach, see Charles L. Briggs, *Learning How to Ask: A Sociolinguistic Appraisal of the Role of the Interview in Social Science Research* (Cambridge: Cambridge University Press, 1986). See also Paul Rabinow, *Reflections on Fieldwork in Morocco* (Berkeley: University of California Press, 1977).

12. Nancy Scheper-Hughes shows how in contexts of institutional violence, parents may choose to abandon a child. Kinship, in these contexts, can be seen as

bricolage—a process of connecting "good-enough" children with "good-enough" parents. See *Death without Weeping: The Violence of Everyday Life in Brazil* (Berkeley: University of California Press, 1992).

13. For the politics of burial practices in Guatemala, see Kevin Lewis O'Neill, "There Is No More Room: Cemeteries, Personhood, and Bare Death," *Ethnography* 13, no. 4 (2012): 510–30. According to cemetery rules, relatives pay a fixed amount for the initial burial. Six years later, they must pay another amount to renew permission for another four years. They can then pay another amount for another four years. Once payment has ceased, however, Guatemala's Ministry of Public Health tries to contact the family with a letter. Sometimes an announcement is placed in a local newspaper. After a grace period of at least three months, and sometimes much longer, the body is disinterred and the remains slid into the cemetery's mass grave. For a broader conversation on death and burial, see Philippe Ariès, *Western Attitudes toward Death: From the Middle Ages to the Present*, trans. Patricia M. Ranum (Baltimore: Johns Hopkins University Press, 1975); Claudio Lomnitz, *Death and the Idea of Mexico* (New York: Zone Books, 2008).

14. The term "willful unknowing" here is meant to distinguish Justina's hesitancy about having a full conversation about clerical sexual abuse from what other anthropologists and philosophers might call skepticism, error, or even stupidity. See Veena Das, *Life and Words: Violence and the Descent into the Ordinary* (Berkeley: University of California Press, 2007); Georges Canguilhem, *The Normal and the Pathological*, trans. Carolyn R. Fawcett and Robert S. Cohen (New York: Zone Books, 1991); David Graeber, "Beyond Power/Knowledge: An Exploration of the Relation of Power, Ignorance and Stupidity" (Annual Malinowksi Memorial Lecture, London School of Economics and Political Science, May 25, 2006). I had long appreciated Justina's tactic of avoidance, never thinking that it marked a complete absence of knowledge.

15. The country's ethnographic record is awash with unease and rumour. From Linda Green's *Fear as a Way of Life: Mayan Widows in Rural Guatemala* (New York: Columbia University Press, 1999) to Anthony Fontes's *Mortal Doubt: Transnational Gangs and Social Order in Guatemala City* (Oakland: University of California Press, 2018), the social-scientific consensus is that Guatemala can provoke a profound sense of uncertainty. Diane M. Nelson's *Reckoning: The Ends of War in Guatemala* (Durham: Duke University Press, 2009) offers an extended reflection on the experience of feeling duped by postwar Guatemala, asking, "How do you trust others, yourself, what you know (or thought you did) for sure?" (xv). See also Deborah Levenson, *Adiós Niño: The Gangs of Guatemala City and the Politics of Death* (Durham: Duke University Press, 2013).

16. Few survivors report their sexual assault to authorities. This reticence appears throughout the ethnographic archive. See Begoña Aretxaga, *Shattering Silence: Women, Nationalism, and Political Subjectivity in Northern Ireland*

(Princeton: Princeton University Press, 1997); Pratiksha Baxi, *Public Secrets of Law: Rape Trials in India* (New Delhi: Oxford University Press, 2014); Kristin Bumiller, *In an Abusive State: How Neoliberalism Appropriated the Feminist Movement against Sexual Violence* (Durham: Duke University Press, 2008).

17. The work of Victoria Sanford on wartime rape and postwar violence has been exemplary. See Victoria Sanford, Katerina Stefatos, and Cecilia M. Salvi, eds., *Gender Violence in Peace and War: States of Complicity* (New Brunswick: Rutgers University Press, 2016), as well as Victoria Sanford, *Violencia y genocidio en Guatemala* (Guatemala: F&G Editores, 2012). And yet, given that Roney's rapprochement with Justina took place during Guatemala's civil war, it is important to consider her abuse as yet another episode of wartime sexual abuse and to attend to the role of the Roman Catholic Church amid the civil wars of Central America. See Nancy Scheper-Hughes, "Institutionalized Sex Abuse and the Catholic Church," in *Small Wars: The Cultural Politics of Childhood*, ed. Nancy Scheper-Hughes and Carolyn Sargent (Berkeley: University of California Press, 1998), 295–317; Carolyn Nordstrom, "Rape: Politics and Theory in War and Peace," *Australian Feminist Studies* 11, no. 23 (1996): 147–62.

18. Justina here makes a vague reference to the recovery of repressed memories through hypnosis. Of interest is how memory can often come to exist independent of a person, captured by the subconscious. In *The Resonance of Unseen Things: Poetics, Power, Captivity, and UFOs in the American Uncanny* (Ann Arbor: University of Michigan Press, 2016), Susan Lepselter writes, "Memory itself became the subject of a secondary captivity story: memory was taken away, converted in captivity with false images or 'screen memories,' then through the help of professionals, released" (65). See also Sigmund Freud, "Repression," in *Collected Papers*, vol. 4, trans. Joan Riviere (London: Hogarth Press, 1956).

19. Anonymous to Bishop Raymond Lucker, April 7, 1987, RF, A758.

20. Sigmund Freud wrote about the possibility of something called dissociation. This is when the mind splits when confronted with danger. See Sigmund Freud, "An Outline of Psycho-Analysis and Splitting of the Ego in the Process of Defence," in *The Standard Edition of the Complete Works of Sigmund Freud*, vol. XXIII, *1937–39*, ed. James Strachey (London: Hogarth Press, 1938), 139–208. Justina endured a rift in her ego as she navigated two worlds at the same time, continuing to exist in her town as she apparently always had while also existing as a survivor in the state of Minnesota.

21. Lauren Berlant defines cruel optimism "as a kind of relation in which one depends on objects that block the very thriving that motivates our attachment in the first place"; *Cruel Optimism* (Durham: Duke University Press, 2011). Augustine, it is said, first coined the term. During his debates with Pelagius on the importance of grace and salvation, Pelagius insisted to Augustine that one could will oneself back into God's proximity. Augustine suggested that this heroic

asceticism was a kind of cruel optimism. No one can do it on his own, Augustine suggested; *Confessions*, trans. F. J. Sheed (Indianapolis: Hackett, 1992).

22. Elizabeth F. Cohen's *The Political Value of Time: Citizenship, Duration and Democratic Justice* (Cambridge: Cambridge University Press, 2018) explores the way that borders and sovereignty are not just spatial but also temporal claims. She writes, "The existence of temporal boundaries reminds us that rights derive not just from who we are and where we are but also from when we are" (5–6). Contemporary political framings of children as subjects awaiting rights is a potent example of this. Systematically excluding children from the "substantive aspects of citizenship" makes them vulnerable to everything from "abusive clergy members at whose hands children have suffered to developmental damage resulting from exposure to chemicals not safe for developing bodies" (222). See Elizabeth F. Cohen, "Neither Seen Nor Heard: Children's Citizenship in Contemporary Democracies," *Citizenship Studies* 9, no. 2 (2005): 221–40.

23. Ian Hacking, "Making Up People," in *The Science Studies Reader*, ed. Mario Biagioli (New York: Routledge, 1999), 167.

24. Maybe sometimes the subaltern does speak. In Gayatri Chakravorty Spivak's famed historiographical essay, she questions the capacity to understand the voices of the most marginalized. See "Can the Subaltern Speak?," in *Marxism and the Interpretation of Culture*, ed. Cary Nelson and Lawrence Grossberg (London: Macmillan, 1988), 271–313. As a result, ethnographers have turned to an analytical minimalism in order to push against the "familiar authority of the expert's voice," which always threatens to subsume valuable narrative, as Lila Abu-Lughod argued in *Writing Women's Worlds: Bedouin Stories* (Berkeley: University of California Press, 1993), xvii–xviii.

25. Max Gluckman writes that "Gossip and even scandal unite a group within a larger society, or against another"; see "Gossip and Scandal," *Cultural Anthropology* 4, no. 3 (1963): 313. Cultural anthropologists have not, for the most part, approached gossip as an object of study. For one of the few examples of gossip from the region, see John Haviland, *Gossip, Reputation, and Knowledge in Zinacantan* (Chicago: University of Chicago Press, 1977). The general approach is to understand gossip as what Erving Goffman calls a "form of talk"; see *Forms of Talk* (Philadelphia: University of Pennsylvania Press, 1981).

26. The obstacles to Justina providing a signature raised for us philosophical questions about the signature. Jacques Derrida notes that there is a tension with every signature. It must be verifiably repeatable and yet a singular event. He writes, "In order to function, that is, in order to be legible, a signature must have a repeatable, iterable, imitable form, it must be able to detach itself from the present and singular intention of its production" (328). Jacques Derrida, *Margins of Philosophy*, trans. Alan Bass (Chicago: University of Chicago Press, 1982). See also Giorgio Agamben, *The Signature of All Things: On Method*, trans. Luca D'Isanto and Kevin Attell (New York: Zone Books, 2009).

27. Mary Douglas describes it as "the tyranny of the home"; see "The Idea of a Home: A Kind of Space," *Social Research* 58, no. 1 (1991): 287. "The very regularity of home's processes," Douglas adds, "is both inexorable and absurd. It is this regularity that needs focus and explaining. How does it go on being what it is? And what is it?" See also Irene Cieraad, ed., *At Home: An Anthropology of Domestic Space* (Syracuse: Syracuse University Press, 1999); Gwendolyn Wright, "Prescribing the Model Home," *Social Research* 58, no. 1 (1991): 213–25.

28. The most iconic example of *testimonio* from Guatemala is Rigoberta Menchú's *I, Rigoberta Menchú: An Indian Woman in Guatemala*, trans. Elisabeth Burgos-Debray (New York: Verso, 2009). This is an account of Guatemala's civil war as told by an Indigenous woman. Its opening lines crystalize the intentions of the entire genre: "My Name is Rigoberta Menchú. I am 23 years old. This is my testimony. I didn't learn it from a book and I didn't learn it alone. I'd like to stress that it's not only *my* life, it's also the testimony of my people. . . . My story is the story of all poor Guatemalans. My personal experience is the reality of a whole people" (1). See Terry Eagleton, "Self-Undoing Subjects," in *Rewriting the Self: Histories from the Renaissance to the Present*, ed. Roy Porter (New York: Routledge, 1997).

29. Justina, Sexual Abuse Proof of Claim Form, 2022, RF, 4.

30. Important here is the anthropological point that "proper" parenting varies according to context, with labor and stability hallmarks of North American parenthood. The ethnographic record, however, is quite clear that mobility, or what is known as child circulation, is common throughout Latin America and a rather strong kin-building practice. See Jessaca B. Leinaweaver, "On Moving Children: The Social Implications of Andean Child Circulation," *American Ethnologist* 34, no. 1 (2007): 163–80; Claudia Fonseca, "Orphanages, Foundlings, and Foster Mothers: The System of Child Circulation in a Brazilian Squatter Settlement," *Anthropological Quarterly* 59, no. 1 (1986): 15–27.

31. Justina, Sexual Abuse Proof of Claim Form, 2022, RF, 4.

32. Justina, Sexual Abuse Proof of Claim Form, 2022, RF, 5.

33. Justina, Sexual Abuse Proof of Claim Form, 2022, RF, 5.

34. "Fr. Paul Madden," Bishop Accountability, accessed December 9, 2023. See also Will Carless, "South America Has Become a Safe Haven for the Catholic Church's Alleged Child Molesters," GlobalPost Investigations, September 16, 2015; Brendan Case, Brooks Egerton, and Reese Dunklin, "Too Much Tolerance?," *Dallas Morning News*, March 16, 2005.

35. "Fr. Jeffrey David Newell," Bishop Accountability, accessed December 9, 2023. See also "Injusticia divina en la Iglesia Católica de Tijuana," *En Linea BC*, December 10, 2020, sec. Inicio; Katie Zavadski et al., "Dozens of Catholic Priests Credibly Accused of Abuse Found Work Abroad, Some with the Church's Blessing," ProPublica, March 6, 2020; David Agren, "Mexico Archdiocese Suspends Seven Priests for Abuse," *National Catholic Reporter*, accessed December 9, 2023.

36. "Fr. Jose Luis Urbina," Bishop Accountability, accessed December 9, 2023. See also Zavadski et al., "Dozens of Catholic Priests Credibly Accused of Abuse Found Work Abroad, Some With the Church's Blessing"; David Eads et al., "Fugitives from Justice: Roman Catholic Priests," *Chicago Tribune*, March 11, 2012.

37. "Fr. Thomas A. Kane," Bishop Accountability, accessed December 9, 2023. See also Kathleen A. Shaw and Richard Nangle, "Accused Priest in Mexico—Rev. Kane Settled Early '90s Sex Suit," *Worcester Telegram and Gazette*, February 7, 2002; Jason Berry, "Institutional Lying at Heart of the Crisis," *National Catholic Reporter*, February 20, 2019; "Thomas Kane, su historia en México," *El Universal*, April 16, 2002.

38. "Fr. Eric Ensey," Bishop Accountability, accessed December 9, 2023. See also Tom Kane, "Suppressed Society of Priests Surfaces in South America," *River Reporter*, March 9, 2006; Mark Guydish, "Latest Case Shows Change in Church," *Times Leader*, April 7, 2014; Gordon Hoekstra, "Priest Apologizes to Parishioners," *Vancouver Sun*, December 19, 2011.

39. "Fr. Carlos Urrutigoity," Bishop Accountability, accessed December 9, 2023. See also "Suspenden ordenaciones sacerdotales en Ciudad Del Este, Paraguay," *El Nuevo Herald*, July 26, 2014; "Paraguay: Obispos se enfrentan por cura acusado de pedofilia," *El Universal*, June 7, 2014; Will Carless, "EXCLUSIVE: After U.S. Sex Abuse Scandals, an Accused Priest Rises Again in Paraguay," *GlobalPost*, December 17, 2014.

40. "Fr. Austin Peter Keegan," Bishop Accountability, accessed December 9, 2023. See also "Expulsan a sacerdote de México," *El Siglo de Torreón*, March 4, 2003; "Exsacerdote pederasta estadunidense fue expulsado de México," *Proceso*, March 3, 2003; Don Lattin, "3 Priests Sued—Molestation of Boys Alleged: 9 Men Say They Were Abused and That Church Covered," *San Francisco Chronicle*, May 24, 1994. "To the best of our knowledge," Lattin quotes a spokesman for the San Francisco Archdiocese as having said, "[Keegan] is in Mexico."

41. "Fr. Jose Antonio Pinal," Bishop Accountability, accessed December 10, 2023. See also Eads et al., "Fugitives from Justice"; Terry Vau Dell, "Sex Charges against Ex–Gridley Priest Void under Ruling," *Chico Enterprise-Record*, June 28, 2003; Katie Zavadski, Topher Sanders, and Nicole Hensley, "Diocese of Sacramento Priest, Dozens of Others Found Work Abroad despite Abuse Allegations," *Sacramento Bee*, March 8, 2020.

42. "Fr. Carl D. Tresler," Bishop Accountability, accessed December 10, 2023. See also Case, Egerton, and Dunklin, "Too Much Tolerance?"; Glenn F. Bunting, Ralph Frammolino, and Richard Winton, "Sex Abuse Allegations against Los Angeles Archdiocese Priests," *Los Angeles Times*, August 18, 2002; "The Accused," *USA Today*, November 11, 2002.

43. "Rev. Siegfried F. Widera—Assignment Record," Bishop Accountability, accessed December 10, 2023. See also David Haldane, "Fugitive Ex-Priest Falls

to His Death," *Los Angeles Times*, May 27, 2003, sec. World & Nation; Isaac Guzman, "Ex cura prófugo de EEUU se suicida en hotel de México," *LMT Español*, May 25, 2003; "Fugitive Ex-Priest Leaps to Death in Mexico," *New York Times*, May 27, 2003.

44. "Fr. Arthur C. Mertens," Bishop Accountability, accessed December 10, 2023. See also Nina Culver, "A Look at the Six Priests Accused of Child Abuse," *Spokesman Review*, October 24, 2002; Virginia De Leon, "Man Files Sexual Abuse Lawsuit against Diocese," *Spokesman Review*, July 16, 2004: "In 1989, the diocese learned from the Bishop of Sololá in Guatemala—where Mertens had worked as a missionary from 1961 to 1977—that the priest was suspected to have sexually abused adolescent males there, as well, according to the diocese."

45. "Fr. Ronald J. Voss," Bishop Accountability, accessed December 10, 2023. See also Brooks Egerton and Brendan M. Case, "2 Priests, 1 Former Cleric Leave Jobs Abroad after News Report," *Dallas Morning News*, April 14, 2005; Robert King, "Haitian Police Question Ex-Priest from Indiana," *Indianapolis Star*, February 25, 2005; Jane Regan, "Ex-Priest Questioned in Jail Break," *Miami Herald*, February 24, 2005.

46. "Fr. Carlos Enrique Peralta," Bishop Accountability, accessed December 10, 2023. See also Cathleen Falsani and Frank Main, "Suits Say Archdiocese Aided Molester Priests," *Chicago Sun-Times*, April 4, 2002; "The Long Arm of Abuse: Problem Priests Cross Not Just States but Oceans as Well," *U.S. News & World Report*, May 3, 2002; "Runaway Priests Hiding in Plain Sight," *Dallas Morning News*, December 5, 2004.

47. "Fr. Donald J. Bowen," Bishop Accountability, accessed December 10, 2023. See also Tom Mashberg, "Bristol DA Rips Bishop for Late List of Alleged Abusers," *Boston Herald*, September 27, 2002; Daniel Barbarisi, "Massachusetts Prosecutor Lists Names of 21 Alleged Abusive Priests," *Providence Journal*, September 27, 2002; Ralph Ranalli, "Ex-Norton Priest Pleads Guilty to Indecent Assault," *Boston Globe*, July 16, 2005.

48. "Theatine Fathers—CR," Bishop Accountability, accessed December 10, 2023. See also Kirk Mitchell, "Two Abusive Priests Continued Work," *Denver Post*, April 29, 2002; Jo Tuckman, "Abuser Priests Go to Mexico for Sanctuary," *The Guardian*, May 12, 2002, sec. World News; Associated Press, "Snapshots of Catholic Priests Accused of Abuse," *San Diego Union-Tribune*, April 14, 2010.

49. "Rev. Kevin F. Hederman—Assignment Record," Bishop Accountability, accessed December 10, 2023. See also Kevin Killeen, "Civil Suit Accuses Former St. Louis Area Priest," *KMOX*, May 26, 2009; Tim Townsend, "St. Louis Priest Who Lives in Belize Accused of Abuse," *St. Louis Post-Dispatch*, May 27, 2009; "Catholic Priest Accused of Sexual Assault," *News 7 Belize*, May 29, 2009.

50. "Fr. Laurence F. X. Brett," Bishop Accountability, accessed December 10, 2023. See also Gerald Renner, "Diocese Disavows Actions of Priest," *Hartford Courant*, August 12, 1997; "Egan Resources," Bishop Accountability,

accessed December 10, 2023; Rodolphe Lamy and Associated Press, "US Priest Accused of Pedophilia Dies in Martinique," *San Diego Union-Tribune*, January 7, 2011.

51. "Fr. Francisco Montero," Bishop Accountability, accessed December 10, 2023. See also Madeleine Baran, "Cover-Up Unravels from the Inside," MPR News, July 14, 2014; Carless, "South America Has Become a Safe Haven"; Eads et al., "Fugitives from Justice."

52. "Rev. John Jairo Velez, S.M.—Assignment Record," Bishop Accountability, accessed December 10, 2023. See also Alex Friedrich, "Man Sues Diocese over Alleged Abuse in Salinas, Arizona," *Monterey Herald*, June 6, 2003; Virginia Hennessey, "Civil Suit Charts History of Church Abuse in County," *Monterey Herald*, May 17, 2009; Virginia Hennessey, "Path to Abuse: Monterey Diocese Turned Blind Eye to Priests' Victims," *Monterey Herald*, July 19, 2009.

53. "Fr. Robert J. Reiss," Bishop Accountability, accessed December 10, 2023. See also Pat Kinney, "Ex-Priest May Have Been Murdered," *Waterloo-Cedar Falls Courier*, March 2, 2005; Mary Nevans-Pederson, "Sins and Silence: Victims Recall Abuse: Men Recount How Priests Befriended, Abused Them," *Dubuque Telegraph Herald*, March 6, 2006.

54. "Fr. Joseph Cervantes Briceno," Bishop Accountability, accessed February 25, 2024. See also Eads et al., "Fugitives from Justice"; "Pedirá EU a México extraditar a presunto sacerdote pederasta," *El Universal*, June 10, 2003; Joseph A. Reaves, "Lawsuit Accuses Bishop of Continued Cover-Up," *Arizona Republic*, June 11, 2003.

55. "Fr. Augusto Cortez," Bishop Accountability, accessed February 25, 2024. See also Kirk Semple, "Long Island Family Sues Catholic Order and Diocese in Molestation Case," *New York Times*, November 16, 2015; Alex Ginsberg, "Pervert Priest Nabbed," *New York Post*, June 5, 2008; "Fugitive Former Priest Accused of Sexually Abusing a Six-Year-Old Girl Is Extradited to the U.S. to Face Charges," *Daily Mail*, April 25, 2017.

56. "Fr. Stanley F. Banaszek," Bishop Accountability, accessed February 25, 2024. See also Daniel Tepfer, "Lori Moving to Oust Priest in Sex Case," *Connecticut Post*, October 20, 2002; Andrew Adkins, "Former Catholic Priest Who Served in Blacksburg Among 6 More Clergy Linked to Child Sex Abuse," *Richmond Times Dispatch*, June 27, 2019.

57. "Bro. Fidelis DeBerardinis," Bishop Accountability, accessed February 25, 2024. See also Robin Washington, "Catholic Brother Arrested in Lowell; Charges Include Rape of Hub Altar Boys," *Boston Herald*, August 15, 2002; Robin Washington, "Friar Guilty of Molesting Altar Boys 30 Years Ago," *Boston Herald*, May 27, 2004.

58. "Fr. Mario Pezzotti," Bishop Accountability, accessed February 25, 2024. See also "Sex Abuse Victims Call for Online Registry of Abuser Priests," *Boston Herald*, April 15, 2010; "The Long Arm of Abuse."

Selected Bibliography

Abu-Lughod, Lila. *Writing Women's Worlds: Bedouin Stories*. Berkeley: University of California Press, 1993.

Adams, Abigail. "Gringas, Ghouls and Guatemala: The 1994 Attacks on North American Women Accused of Body Organ Trafficking." *Journal of Latin American Anthropology* 4, no. 1 (1999): 112–33.

Adams, Richard Newbold. *Crucifixion by Power: Essays on Guatemalan National Social Structure, 1944–1966*. Austin: University of Texas Press, 1970.

Agamben, Giorgio. *The Highest Poverty: Monastic Rules and Form-of-Life*. Trans. Adam Kotsko. Stanford: Stanford University Press, 2013.

Ahmed, Sara. *Complaint!* Durham: Duke University Press, 2021.

Ahrendt, Hannah. *The Origins of Totalitarianism*. New York: Schocken Books, 2004.

Anderson, Benedict. *Imagined Communities: Reflections on the Origin and Spread of Nationalism*. New York: Verso, 2016.

Appadurai, Arjun. "Putting Hierarchy in Its Place." *Cultural Anthropology* 3, no. 1 (1988): 36–49.

Aquinas, Thomas. *Summa Theologica*. Merrimack: Thomas More College Press, 1948.

Aretxaga, Begoña. *Shattering Silence: Women, Nationalism, and Political Subjectivity in Northern Ireland*. Princeton: Princeton University Press, 1997.

Ariès, Philippe. *Centuries of Childhood: A Social History of Family Life*. Trans. Robert Baldick. New York: Vintage Books, 1962.

Asad, Talal. *Formations of the Secular: Christianity, Islam, Modernity*. Stanford: Stanford University Press, 2003.

Augustine. *Confessions*. Trans. F. J. Sheed. Indianapolis: Hackett, 1992.

Austin, J. L. *How to Do Things with Words: The William James Lectures Delivered at Harvard University in 1955*. Oxford: Clarendon Press, 1962.

Azoulay, Ariella. *The Civil Contract of Photography*. Trans. Rela Mazali and Ruvik Danieli. Brooklyn: Zone Books, 2008.

Baer, Ulrich. *Spectral Evidence: The Photography of Trauma*. Cambridge: MIT Press, 2002.

Baran, Madeleine, et al. *Betrayed by Silence*. Minnesota Public Radio, 2014.

Barkan, Joshua. *Corporate Sovereignty: Law and Government under Capitalism*. Minneapolis: University of Minnesota Press, 2013.

Barrientos, Juan Pablo. *Dejad que los niños vengan a mí*. Bogotá: Editorial Planeta Colombia, 2019.

Bartel, Rebecca C. *Card-Carrying Christians: Debt and the Making of Free Market Spirituality in Colombia*. Berkeley: University of California Press, 2021.

Barthes, Roland. *How to Live Together: Novelistic Simulations of Some Everyday Spaces*. Trans. Kate Briggs. New York: Columbia University Press, 2013.

Bataille, Georges. *Theory of Religion*. Trans. Robert Hurley. New York: Zone Books, 1989.

Bauman, Richard. *Let Your Words Be Few: Symbolism of Speaking and Silence Among Seventeenth-Century Quakers*. Cambridge: Cambridge University Press, 1983.

Baxi, Pratiksha. *Public Secrets of Law: Rape Trials in India*. New Delhi: Oxford University Press, 2014.

Behar, Ruth. *Translated Woman: Crossing the Border with Esperanza's Story*. Boston: Beacon Press, 2003.

Bendaña Perdomo, Ricardo. *La iglesia en Guatemala: Síntesis histórica del Catolicismo Guatemalteco, 1524–1951*. 2nd ed. Guatemala City: Artemis Edinter, 2001.

Benjamin, Walter. "On the Concept of History." In *Selected Writings*, vol. 4, *1938–1940*, ed. Howard Eiland and Michael W. Jennings. Cambridge: Harvard University Press, 2006.

Berlant, Lauren. *Cruel Optimism*. Durham: Duke University Press, 2011.

Bernstein, Peter L. *Against the Gods: The Remarkable Story of Risk*. New York: Wiley, 1998.

Berry, Jason. *Lead Us Not into Temptation: Catholic Priests and the Sexual Abuse of Children*. Urbana: University of Illinois Press, 2000.

Bickford, Louis. "The Archival Imperative: Human Rights and Historical Memory in Latin America's Southern Cone." *Human Rights Quarterly* 21, no. 4 (1999): 1097–1112.

Biehl, João. *Vita: Life in a Zone of Social Abandonment*. Berkeley: University of California Press, 2005.

Boddy, Janice. *Wombs and Alien Spirits: Women, Men, and the Zar Cult in Northern Sudan*. Madison: University of Wisconsin Press, 1989.

Borneman, John. "Public Apologies as Performative Redress." *The SAIS Review of International Affairs* 25, no. 2 (2005): 53–66.

Bornstein, Erica. "Child Sponsorship, Evangelism, and Belonging in the Work of World Vision Zimbabwe." *American Ethnologist* 28, no. 3 (2001): 595–622.

Bourdieu, Pierre. *Distinction: A Social Critique of the Judgement of Taste*. Trans. Richard Nice. Cambridge: Harvard University Press, 1984.

Bourgois, Philippe. *In Search of Respect: Selling Crack in El Barrio*. New York: Cambridge University Press, 1996.

Boyarin, Daniel. *Dying for God: Martyrdom and the Making of Christianity and Judaism*. Stanford: Stanford University Press, 1999.

Briggs, Charles L. *Learning How to Ask: A Sociolinguistic Appraisal of the Role of the Interview in Social Science Research*. Cambridge: Cambridge University Press, 1986.

Brown, Elspeth H., and Thy Phu, eds. *Feeling Photography*. Durham: Duke University Press, 2014.

Brown, Karen McCarthy. *Mama Lola: A Vodou Priestess in Brooklyn*. Updated and expanded ed. Berkeley: University of California Press, 2001.

Bumiller, Kristin. *In an Abusive State: How Neoliberalism Appropriated the Feminist Movement against Sexual Violence*. Durham: Duke University Press, 2008.

Butler, Judith. *Frames of War: When Is Life Grievable?* New York: Verso, 2009.

Campt, Tina M. *Listening to Images*. Durham: Duke University Press, 2017.

Canetti, Elias. *Crowds and Power*. Trans. Carol Stewart. New York: Farrar, Straus and Giroux, 1984.

Canguilhem, Georges. *The Normal and the Pathological*. Trans. Carolyn R. Fawcett and Robert S. Cohen. New York: Zone Books, 1991.

Cary, Phillip. *Outward Signs: The Powerlessness of External Things in Augustine's Thought*. New York: Oxford University Press, 2008.

CEH. "Memoria del silencio. Guatemala: Comisión para el Esclarecimiento Histórico." Guatemala: Comisión para el Esclarecimiento Histórico, 1999.

Certeau, Michel de. *The Practice of Everyday Life*. Trans. Steven Rendall. Berkeley: University of California Press, 1984.

Clossey, Luke. *Salvation and Globalization in the Early Jesuit Missions*. New York: Cambridge University Press, 2008.

Cohen, Elizabeth F. *The Political Value of Time: Citizenship, Duration and Democratic Justice*. Cambridge: Cambridge University Press, 2018.

Cohen, Stanley. *States of Denial: Knowing about Atrocities and Suffering*. Malden: Polity, 2001.

Coleman, Kevin. *A Camera in the Garden of Eden: The Self-Forging of a Banana Republic*. Austin: University of Texas Press, 2016.

Conrad, Joseph. *Heart of Darkness*. New York: Dover, 1990.

Costello, Gerald M. *Mission to Latin America: The Successes and Failures of a Twentieth-Century Crusade*. Maryknoll: Orbis Books, 1979.

Crampton, Jeremy W. "Cartography: Performative, Participatory, Political." *Progress in Human Geography* 33, no. 6 (2009): 840–48.

Crapanzano, Vincent. *Tuhami: Portrait of a Moroccan*. Chicago: University of Chicago Press, 1985.

Cullather, Nick. *Secret History: The CIA's Classified Account of Its Operations in Guatemala, 1952–1954*. Stanford: Stanford University Press, 1999.

D'Andrade, Roy. "Moral Models in Anthropology." *Current Anthropology* 36, no. 3 (1995): 399–408.

Das, Veena. *Life and Words: Violence and the Descent into the Ordinary*. Berkeley: University of California Press, 2007.

Davidson, Arnold I. *The Emergence of Sexuality: Historical Epistemology and the Formation of Concepts*. Cambridge: Harvard University Press, 2004.

De Man, Paul. *Allegories of Reading: Figural Language in Rousseau, Nietzsche, Rilke, and Proust*. New Haven: Yale University Press, 1979.

Deleuze, Gilles, and Félix Guattari. *A Thousand Plateaus: Capitalism and Schizophrenia*. Trans. Brian Massumi. Minneapolis: University of Minnesota Press, 1987.

Derrida, Jacques. *Archive Fever: A Freudian Impression*. Trans. Eric Prenowitz. Chicago: University of Chicago Press, 2008.

Desjarlais, Robert R. *Sensory Biographies: Lives and Deaths among Nepal's Yolmo Buddhists*. Berkeley: University of California Press, 2003.

Dickerman, Leah. "Monumental Propaganda." *October*, no. 165 (Summer 2018): 178–91.

Douglas, Mary. "The Idea of a Home: A Kind of Space." *Social Research* 58, no. 1 (1991): 287–307.

Doyle, Thomas, Richard Sipe, and Patrick Wall. *Sex, Priests, and Secret Codes: The Catholic Church's 2,000 Year Paper Trail of Sexual Abuse*. Los Angeles: Volt Press, 2006.

Dua, Jatin. *Captured at Sea: Piracy and Protection in the Indian Ocean*. Berkeley: University of California Press, 2019.

Dubinsky, Karen. *Babies without Borders: Adoption and the Symbolic Child in a Globalizing World*. Toronto: University of Toronto Press, 2010.

Durkheim, Émile. *The Elementary Forms of the Religious Life.* Trans. Joseph Ward Swain. Mineola: Dover Books, 2008 [1912].

Eagleton, Terry. "Self-Undoing Subjects." In *Rewriting the Self: Histories from the Renaissance to the Present,* ed. Roy Porter. New York: Routledge, 1997.

Edwards, Elizabeth. "Objects of Affect: Photography beyond the Image." *Annual Review of Anthropology* 41 (2012): 221–34.

Elyachar, Julia. *Markets of Dispossession: NGOs, Economic Development, and the State in Cairo.* Durham: Duke University Press, 2005.

Evans-Pritchard, E. E. *Witchcraft, Oracles, and Magic among the Azande.* Oxford: Clarendon Press, 1976.

Ewald, François. *The Birth of Solidarity: The History of the French Welfare State.* Ed Melinda Cooper, trans. Timothy Scott Johnson. Durham: Duke University Press, 2020.

Falla, Ricardo. *Masacres de La Selva: Ixcán, Guatemala, 1975–1982.* Guatemala City: Editorial Universitaria, 1992.

Farish, Matthew. *The Contours of America's Cold War.* Minneapolis: University of Minnesota Press, 2010.

Fasolt, Constantin. *The Limits of History.* Chicago: University of Chicago Press, 2004.

Ferguson, James. *Presence and Social Obligation: An Essay on the Share.* Chicago: Prickly Paradigm Press, 2021.

Fontes, Anthony W. *Mortal Doubt: Transnational Gangs and Social Order in Guatemala City.* Oakland: University of California Press, 2018.

Foucault, Michel. *Discipline and Punish: The Birth of the Prison.* Trans. Alan Sheridan. New York: Vintage Books, 1977.

———. *An Introduction.* Vol. 1 of *The History of Sexuality.* Trans. Robert J. Hurley. New York: Vintage Books, 1990.

———. *The Order of Things: An Archaeology of the Human Sciences.* New York: Vintage Books, 1994.

Franco, Jean. *The Decline and Fall of the Lettered City: Latin America in the Cold War.* Cambridge: Harvard University Press, 2002.

Freedberg, David. *Iconoclasm.* Chicago: University of Chicago Press, 2021.

Freud, Sigmund. *The Uncanny.* Trans. David McLintock. New York: Penguin Books, 2003.

Garcia, Angela. *The Pastoral Clinic: Addiction and Dispossession along the Rio Grande.* Berkeley: University of California Press, 2010.

Garrard-Burnett, Virginia. "Liberalism, Protestantism, and Indigenous Resistance in Guatemala, 1870–1920." *Latin American Perspectives* 24, no. 2 (1997): 35–55.

Geertz, Clifford. *The Interpretation of Cultures: Selected Essays.* New York: Basic Books, 1973.

Girard, René. *Violence and the Sacred.* Trans. Patrick Gregory. Baltimore: Johns Hopkins University Press, 1979.

Gluckman, Max. "Gossip and Scandal." *Cultural Anthropology* 4, no. 3 (1963): 307–16.

Goffman, Erving. *The Presentation of Self in Everyday Life.* New York: Anchor Books, 1959.

Goldman, Francisco. *The Long Night of White Chickens.* New York: Grove Press, 1992.

Gordon, Avery. *Ghostly Matters: Haunting and the Sociological Imagination.* Minneapolis: University of Minnesota Press, 2008.

Graeber, David. *Debt: The First 5,000 Years.* Brooklyn: Melville House, 2012.

Grandin, Greg. *The Last Colonial Massacre: Latin America in the Cold War.* Chicago: University of Chicago Press, 2011.

Green, Linda. *Fear as a Way of Life: Mayan Widows in Rural Guatemala.* New York: Columbia University Press, 1999.

Gupta, Akhil, and James Ferguson. "Beyond 'Culture': Space, Identity, and the Politics of Difference." *Cultural Anthropology* 7, no. 1 (1992): 6–23.

Gusterson, Hugh. *Nuclear Rites: A Weapons Laboratory at the End of the Cold War.* Berkeley: University of California Press, 1998.

Hacking, Ian. *Historical Ontology.* Cambridge: Harvard University Press, 2004.

———. "Making Up People." In *The Science Studies Reader,* ed. Mario Biagioli. New York: Routledge, 1999.

Han, Clara. *Life in Debt: Care and Violence in Neoliberal Chile.* Berkeley: University of California Press, 2012.

Haviland, John. *Gossip, Reputation, and Knowledge in Zinacantan.* Chicago: University of Chicago Press, 1977.

Hernández, Bonar L. "Reforming Catholicism: Papal Power in Guatemala during the 1920s and 1930s." *The Americas* 71, no. 2 (October 2014): 255–80.

Hernández Sandoval, Bonar L. *Guatemala's Catholic Revolution: A History of Religious and Social Reform, 1920–1968.* Notre Dame: University of Notre Dame Press, 2018.

Hirschkind, Charles. *The Feeling of History: Islam, Romanticism, and Andalusia.* Chicago: University of Chicago Press, 2021.

Holscher, Kathleen. "The Trouble of an Indian Diocese: Catholic Priests and Sexual Abuse in Colonized Places." In *Religion and U.S. Empire: Critical New Histories,* ed. Tisa Wenger and Sylvester A. Johnson, 231–52. New York: New York University Press, 2022.

Hull, Matthew S. *Government of Paper: The Materiality of Bureaucracy in Urban Pakistan.* Berkeley: University of California Press, 2012.

Huxley, Aldous. *Beyond the Mexique Bay: A Traveller's Journal.* London: Chatto & Windus, 1950.

Investigative Staff of the *Boston Globe*. *Betrayal: The Crisis in the Catholic Church*. New York: Little, Brown, 2002.

Jones, Graham M. *Trade of the Tricks: Inside the Magician's Craft*. Berkeley: University of California Press, 2011.

Jordan, Mark D. *Telling Truths in Church: Scandal, Flesh, and Christian Speech*. Boston: Beacon Press, 2003.

Jung, C. G. *Modern Man in Search of a Soul*. Trans. W. S. Dell and Cary F. Baynes. New York: Harcourt, Brace, 1933.

Kafka, Franz. *Letters to Milena*. Trans. Philip Boehm. New York: Schocken Books, 2015.

Kaplan, Amy. "Manifest Domesticity." *American Literature* 70, no. 3 (1998): 581–606.

Keane, Webb. "Sincerity, 'Modernity,' and the Protestants." *Cultural Anthropology* 17, no. 1 (2002): 65–92.

Kierkegaard, Søren. *Fear and Trembling / Repetition*. Ed. and trans. Howard V. Hong and Edna H. Hong. Princeton: Princeton University Press, 1983.

Kofman, Sarah. *Camera Obscura: On Ideology*. Trans. Will Straw. Ithaca: Cornell University Press, 1999.

Le Bon, Gustave. *The Crowd: A Study of the Popular Mind*. London: T. F. Unwin, 1897.

Leinaweaver, Jessaca B. "On Moving Children: The Social Implications of Andean Child Circulation." *American Ethnologist* 34, no. 1 (2007): 163–80.

Lepselter, Susan Claudia. *The Resonance of Unseen Things: Poetics, Power, Captivity, and UFOs in the American Uncanny*. Ann Arbor: University of Michigan Press, 2016.

Levenson, Deborah. *Adiós Niño: The Gangs of Guatemala City and the Politics of Death*. Durham: Duke University Press, 2013.

Levinas, Emmanuel. *Totality and Infinity: An Essay on Exteriority*. Trans. Alphonso Lingis. Pittsburgh: Duquesne University Press, 2011.

Lévi-Strauss, Claude. *Wild Thought: A New Translation of "La Pensée Sauvage."* Trans. Jeffrey Mehlman and John Leavitt. Chicago: University of Chicago Press, 2021.

Lewis, Sinclair. *Main Street*. New York: Harcourt, Brace, 1920.

Li, Tania. *The Will to Improve: Governmentality, Development, and the Practice of Politics*. Durham: Duke University Press, 2007.

Lomnitz, Claudio. *Death and the Idea of Mexico*. New York: Zone Books, 2008.

Lowe, Lisa. *The Intimacies of Four Continents*. Durham: Duke University Press, 2015.

Lytton, Timothy D. *Holding Bishops Accountable: How Lawsuits Helped the Catholic Church Confront Clergy Sexual Abuse*. Cambridge: Harvard University Press, 2008.

MacLachlan, Alice. "'Trust Me, I'm Sorry': The Paradox of Public Apology." *The Monist* 98, no. 4 (2015): 441–56.

Mahmud, Lilith. "'The World Is a Forest of Symbols': Italian Freemasonry and the Practice of Discretion." *American Ethnologist* 39, no. 2 (May 2012): 425–38.

Malinowski, Bronisław. *Argonauts of the Western Pacific: An Account of Native Enterprise and Adventure in the Archipelagoes of Melanesian New Guinea.* London: George Routledge and Sons, 1922.

Malkki, Liisa. "National Geographic: The Rooting of Peoples and the Territorialization of National Identity among Scholars and Refugees." *Cultural Anthropology* 7, no. 1 (1992): 24–44.

Mariner, Kathryn A. *Contingent Kinship: The Flows and Futures of Adoption in the United States.* Oakland: University of California Press, 2019.

Marre, Diana, and Laura Briggs, eds. *International Adoption: Global Inequalities and the Circulation of Children.* New York: New York University Press, 2009.

Masco, Joseph. *The Theater of Operations: National Security Affect from the Cold War to the War on Terror.* Durham: Duke University Press, 2014.

Mauss, Marcel. "A Category of the Human Mind." Trans. W. D. Halls. In *The Category of the Person: Anthropology, Philosophy, History,* ed. Michael Carrithers, Steven Collins, and Steven Lukes. Cambridge: Cambridge University Press, 1985.

Mazzarella, William. "The Myth of the Multitude, or Who's Afraid of the Crowd?" *Critical Inquiry* 36, no. 4 (2010): 2010.

McCreery, David. *Rural Guatemala, 1760–1940.* Stanford: Stanford University Press, 1994.

Menchú, Rigoberta. *I, Rigoberta Menchú: An Indian Woman in Guatemala.* Trans. Elisabeth Burgos-Debray. New York: Verso, 2009.

Metz, Christian. "Photography and Fetish." *October,* no. 34 (Autumn 1985): 81–90.

Milbank, John. *Being Reconciled: Ontology and Pardon.* London: Routledge, 2003.

Miller, Hubert J. *La iglesia y el estado en tiempo de Justo Rufino Barrios.* Trans. Jorge Luján Muñoz. Guatemala City: Editorial Universitaria, 1976.

Mintz, Sidney W. *Sweetness and Power: The Place of Sugar in Modern History.* New York: Penguin Books, 1986.

Mol, Annemarie. *The Logic of Care: Health and the Problem of Patient Choice.* London: Routledge, 2008.

Murphy, Michelle. *Sick Building Syndrome and the Problem of Uncertainty: Environmental Politics, Technoscience, and Women Workers.* Durham: Duke University Press, 2006.

Nelson, Diane M. *A Finger in the Wound: Body Politics in Quincentennial Guatemala.* Berkeley: University of California Press, 1999.

————. *Reckoning: The Ends of War in Guatemala*. Durham: Duke University Press, 2009.

Nolan, Rachel. "Children for Export: A History of International Adoption from Guatemala." PhD diss., New York, New York University, 2019.

Nordstrom, Carolyn. "Rape: Politics and Theory in War and Peace." *Australian Feminist Studies* 11, no. 23 (1996): 147–62.

O'Neill, Kevin Lewis. *Hunted: Predation and Pentecostalism in Guatemala*. Chicago: University of Chicago Press, 2019.

Ong, Aihwa. "The Production of Possession: Spirits and the Multinational Corporation in Malaysia." *American Ethnologist* 15, no. 1 (1988): 28–42.

Orsi, Robert A. "Events of Abundant Evil." In *History and Presence*, 215–48. Cambridge: Harvard University Press, 2016.

Ortega y Gasset, José. *The Revolt of the Masses*. New York: W. W. Norton, 1932.

Pandian, Anand. *Crooked Stalks: Cultivating Virtue in South India*. Durham: Duke University Press, 2009.

Panourgiá, Neni. *Fragments of Death, Fables of Identity: An Athenian Anthropography*. Madison: University of Wisconsin Press, 1995.

Pearson, Paul M. *A Hidden Wholeness: The Zen Photography of Thomas Merton*. Louisville: Thomas Merton Center, 2004.

Petro, Anthony M. "Beyond Accountability." *Radical History Review*, no. 122 (2015): 160–76.

Poovey, Mary. *A History of the Modern Fact: Problems of Knowledge in the Sciences of Wealth and Society*. Chicago: University of Chicago Press, 1998.

Rabinow, Paul. *Reflections on Fieldwork in Morocco*. Berkeley: University of California Press, 1977.

REMHI. *Guatemala, nunca más: Proyecto interdiocesano de recuperación de la memoria histórica, volúmenes I, II, III, IV*. Guatemala: Oficina de Derechos Humanos Arzobispado de Guatemala, 1998.

Richland, Justin. "Jurisdiction: Grounding Law in Language." *Annual Review of Anthropology* 42 (2013): 209–26.

Ritvo, Harriet. *The Platypus and the Mermaid, and Other Figments of the Classifying Imagination*. Cambridge: Harvard University Press, 1997.

Robbins, Joel. "What Is the Matter with Transcendence? On the Place of Religion in the New Anthropology of Ethics." *Journal of the Royal Anthropological Institute* 22, no. 4 (2016): 767–81.

Rose, Nikolas. *Governing the Soul: The Shaping of the Private Self*. London: Free Association Books, 1999.

Rothenberg, Daniel. "The Panic of Robaniños: Gringo Organ Stealers, Narratives of Mistrust, and the Guatemalan Political Imagination." PhD diss., University of Chicago, 2018.

Rubenstein, Mary-Jane. *Strange Wonder: The Closure of Metaphysics and the Opening of Awe*. New York: Columbia University Press, 2011.

Sahlins, Marshall. *Stone Age Economics*. Chicago: Aldine-Atherton, 1972.

Sanford, Victoria. *Buried Secrets: Truth and Human Rights in Guatemala*. New York: Palgrave Macmillan, 2003.

Scheper-Hughes, Nancy. *Death without Weeping: The Violence of Everyday Life in Brazil*. Berkeley: University of California Press, 1992.

Scheper-Hughes, Nancy, and Carolyn Fishel Sargent, eds. *Small Wars: The Cultural Politics of Childhood*. Berkeley: University of California Press, 1998.

Schirmer, Jennifer G. *The Guatemalan Military Project: A Violence Called Democracy*. Philadelphia: University of Pennsylvania Press, 1998.

Schlesinger, Stephen C., and Stephen Kinzer. *Bitter Fruit: The Story of the American Coup in Guatemala*. Rev. and expanded ed. Cambridge: Harvard University David Rockefeller Center for Latin American Studies, 2005.

Scott, James C. *Seeing Like a State: How Certain Schemes to Improve the Human Condition Have Failed*. New Haven: Yale University Press, 1998.

———. *The Art of Not Being Governed: An Anarchist History of Upland Southeast Asia*. New Haven: Yale University Press, 2009.

Searle, John R. *Speech Acts: An Essay on the Philosophy of Language*. Cambridge: Cambridge University Press, 1969.

Seitz, John. *No Closure: Catholic Practice and Boston Parish Shutdowns*. Cambridge: Harvard University Press, 2011.

Shaw, Brent D. *Sacred Violence: African Christians and Sectarian Hatred in the Age of Augustine*. New York: Cambridge University Press, 2011.

Shryock, Andrew. "Breaking Hospitality Apart: Bad Hosts, Bad Guests, and the Problem of Sovereignty." *Journal of the Royal Anthropological Institute* 18, no. 1 (2012): 20–33.

Simmel, Georg. *The Philosophy of Money*. Trans. Tom Bottomore and George Frisby. New York: Routledge, 2011 [1900].

———. "The Sociology of Secrecy and of Secret Societies." *Journal of Sociology* 11, no. 4 (1906): 441–98.

Simone, AbdouMaliq. "People as Infrastructure: Intersecting Fragments in Johannesburg." *Public Culture* 16, no. 3 (2004): 407–29.

Smith, Carol A., ed. *Guatemalan Indians and the State, 1540 to 1988*. Austin: University of Texas Press, 1990.

Sontag, Susan. *On Photography*. New York: Farrar, Straus and Giroux, 1977.

Stewart, Kathleen. *A Space on the Side of the Road: Cultural Poetics in an "Other" America*. Princeton: Princeton University Press, 1996.

Stoler, Ann Laura. *Along the Archival Grain: Epistemic Anxieties and Colonial Common Sense*. Princeton: Princeton University Press, 2009.

Stoller, Paul. *Fusion of the Worlds: An Ethnography of Possession among the Songhay of Niger*. Chicago: University of Chicago Press, 1989.

Taussig, Michael. *Defacement: Public Secrecy and the Labor of the Negative*. Stanford: Stanford University Press, 1999.

Taylor, Diana. *Disappearing Acts: Spectacles of Gender and Nationalism in Argentina's "Dirty War."* Durham: Duke University Press, 1997.

Theidon, Kimberly. "The Mask and the Mirror: Facing Up to the Past in Postwar Peru." *Anthropologica* 48, no. 1 (2006): 87–100.

Thompson, E. P. "Time, Work-Discipline, and Industrial Capitalism." *Past & Present* 38, no. 1 (1967): 56–97.

Ticktin, Miriam. *Casualties of Care: Immigration and the Politics of Humanitarianism in France.* Berkeley: University of California Press, 2011.

Trouillot, Michel-Rolph. *Silencing the Past: Power and the Production of History.* Boston: Beacon Press, 1995.

Turner, Victor. *The Forest of Symbols: Aspects of Ndembu Ritual.* Ithaca: Cornell University Press, 1967.

Voyles, Traci Brynne. *Wastelanding: Legacies of Uranium Mining in Navajo Country.* Minneapolis: University of Minnesota Press, 2015.

Vries, Hent de. "Must We (Not) Mean What We Say." In *The Rhetoric of Sincerity,* ed. Mieke Bal, Ernst van Alphen, and Carel E. Smith, 90–120. Stanford: Stanford University Press, 2009.

Warren, Kay B. *Indigenous Movements and Their Critics: Pan-Maya Activism in Guatemala.* Princeton: Princeton University Press, 1998.

Weber, Max. *The Protestant Ethic and the "Spirit" of Capitalism and Other Writings.* Ed. and trans. Peter Baehr and Gordon C. Wells. New York: Penguin Books, 2002.

Weld, Kirsten. *Paper Cadavers: The Archives of Dictatorship in Guatemala.* Durham: Duke University Press, 2014.

Williams, Raymond. *The Country and the City.* New York: Oxford University Press, 1973.

Wolf, Eric R. *Europe and the People without History.* Berkeley: University of California Press, 1982.

Index

abuser (notion of), xiii, 139–40, 171, 177. *See also* survivor, victim
Adamson, Father Thomas, 40–41, 44–45, 112, 208n17, 209n18
Agamben, Giorgio, 205n46
Ahmed, Sara, 201n8
Anderson, Jeff, xvi, 119, 130; and Father Roney, 124; fee of, 136–37; Greg Riedel case, 40–41; law firm of, 112, 115–16, 118, 127, 131–36, 157, 204n43; Minnesota statute of limitations, 116–17, 125; settlements by, 137. *See also* Justina: as litigant
April (survivor of abuse): letter to Bishop Lucker, 13–14, 37–39, 41, 42, 43, 45, 131, 155, 170
Aquinas, Thomas, 10, 57, 202n16,
Archdiocese of Boston, 112, 125, 130
Archdiocese of Milwaukee, 130
Archdiocese of Saint Paul and Minneapolis: assets of, 130; as defendant, 40–41, 159, 160–61, 162, 163, 174–75
Archdiocese of Santa Fe, 130
archives, 52, 71; archival thinking, 199n12; Catholic Church and, 20, 214n91. *See also* Roney, Father David: archive of
Arendt, Hannah, 201n13
Ariès, Philippe, 202n19

Asad, Talal, 232n9
Augustine of Hippo, Saint, 28–29, 38, 186, 234n21

Banaszek, Stanley, 183
Barthes, Roland, 195n1
Basilica of Saint Mary (Minneapolis), 69–70
Bauman, Richard, 196n2
Benedict XVI (pope), 223n72
Berger, Father John, 6, 7
Bickford, Louis, 199n12
Boston Globe, 112
Bowen, Donald, 182
Brett, Lawrence, 182
Briceno, Joseph Cervantez, 182–83

candy, 209n25
capitalism: time and, 204n46
Carol (survivor of abuse), xvi, 8, 12–13, 41–42, 84, 85, 170, 172–73, 176, 177, 189–90; becoming victim of, 118, 127; as claimant, 116, 118, 131–37, 166, 169, 170, 230n57
casas-cuna. See Guatemala: kidnapping in
Catholic Church: archives and, 199n12, 214n91; atonement in, 220n41; bankruptcy in, 22, 40, 118, 129–31, 145, 147, 159, 163, 174–75, 229n45;

Founded in 1893,
UNIVERSITY OF CALIFORNIA PRESS
publishes bold, progressive books and journals
on topics in the arts, humanities, social sciences,
and natural sciences—with a focus on social
justice issues—that inspire thought and action
among readers worldwide.

The UC PRESS FOUNDATION
raises funds to uphold the press's vital role
as an independent, nonprofit publisher, and
receives philanthropic support from a wide
range of individuals and institutions—and from
committed readers like you. To learn more, visit
ucpress.edu/supportus.